In the land of the Marq...

In the land of the Marquis

◆

An English family in northern Spain

Kenneth McKenney

iUniverse, Inc.
New York Lincoln Shanghai

In the land of the Marquis
An English family in northern Spain

Copyright © 2005 by Kenneth McKenney

All rights reserved. No part of this book may be used or reproduced by any means, graphic, electronic, or mechanical, including photocopying, recording, taping or by any information storage retrieval system without the written permission of the publisher except in the case of brief quotations embodied in critical articles and reviews.

iUniverse books may be ordered through booksellers or by contacting:

iUniverse
2021 Pine Lake Road, Suite 100
Lincoln, NE 68512
www.iuniverse.com
1-800-Authors (1-800-288-4677)

Cover photo: Gaudí's *Capricho* by Vicente Rozas

ISBN-13: 978-0-595-36218-9 (pbk)
ISBN-13: 978-0-595-80662-1 (ebk)
ISBN-10: 0-595-36218-4 (pbk)
ISBN-10: 0-595-80662-7 (ebk)

Printed in the United States of America

For all the good people in Comillas who shared their town with us

Oh, do not ask, 'What is it?'
Let us go and make our visit.

T.S. Eliot

Contents

To makes things clear xi
CHAPTER 1   Getting there 1
CHAPTER 2   Settling in 13
CHAPTER 3   The Master Builder 24
CHAPTER 4   Fantasies and other Things 36
CHAPTER 5   Going to the Flowers 49
CHAPTER 6   The old Republican 61
CHAPTER 7   The Church's embracing arms 73
CHAPTER 8   Outside looking In 85
CHAPTER 9   A Sport of Kings 98
CHAPTER 10   The Builder's Follies 110
CHAPTER 11   New York, New York 123
CHAPTER 12   Beauty within Crumbling Walls 134
CHAPTER 13   Fiestas, Fiestas, Fiestas 146
CHAPTER 14   The Yellow Bird 157
CHAPTER 15   Magic Castles 166
CHAPTER 16   Good Times and Bad 176
CHAPTER 17   Descubriendo Comillas 185
CHAPTER 18   Acts of Faith 193

To makes things clear

Apart from anything else, this is a book about writing a book. Before this one-*In the land of the Marquis*-I wrote, and published locally, a simple guide to Comillas. However, while working on it, other events in other parts of the world kept raising their determined heads. So, when the first book-*Descubriendo Comillas*-was put to bed my clever wife, Virginia, suggested I start again, right at the beginning, and allow everything free rein. Here it is.

1

Getting there

"Up there," I said, my finger on the map. "In the north of Spain. On the other side of the mountains."

"On the coast?" asked Virginia.

"That's right, where it's green."

"Just go and what? Find somewhere to live?"

"Why not?"

"I'm game if you are."

With that, the search began.

For four years we'd lived in Majorca, where each summer there was no escape from a relentless sun. A lovely sun that tourists relied on for perfect holiday weather, but one we were beginning to tire of. We felt the need for somewhere cool, somewhere that was more part of Spain, where they spoke Spanish, a language we'd come to terms with in Mexico, and not Mallorquin, a sub-dialect of Catalan. What's more, we'd welcome a place where British expatriates didn't descend on newcomers like gatherers in a distant Raj, eager for new bridge partners, someone fresh to share drinks with, exchange the latest gossip. So, one bright day we moved off to explore the north, to see if there was a house awaiting us.

We began with a long curving journey through Andorra, where we looked at a few solid-stone houses, set in valleys with splendid hillsides, but where the foreign tongue of Catalan still filled the mountain air. We spent hours climbing twisted tracks among wildflower bursting through the summer grasses, with Kitty, who was three that June, riding our shoulders beneath a pollen-coloured sun. It was all beautiful. But we weren't tempted, it was too similar to what we had.

We drove on to France and stayed with friends in the Bas Pyrenees, a mother and daughter who owned a small hotel, where we swam in rushing waters, icy as they came down from the mountains, bursting over rocks. We had picnics amid pines, admired a ruined castle clinging to a cliff, and discussed our plans with our friends who showed us a range of houses, found some we liked, some we didn't.

"It's possible, I suppose," I told Virginia. "But I'd have to learn French."

"I speak it," she replied.

"I know, but, Kitty's doing well with both Spanish and English. Seems a shame to complicate things now."

"*You'd* learn." She smiled, aware of my incompetence with foreign tongues. "Madam Sartou said she'd put you behind the bar."

"Let's think about it."

We did, and moved on, following the tug of the unknown. We drove back to Spain, traversed the deep wooded valleys of the Basque Country, curled along the steep-cliffed coast, with its curving sandy beaches, toward Cantabria, where green winding hills roll down to the sea and the black snow-capped Picos de Europa lie to the south.

"This looks promising," I said.

"They speak Castellano here," she reassured me, referring to the language sometimes known as *Cristiano*, the only pure tongue. "You're not too bad with that."

"It went into retreat in Majorca."

"If you opened your mouth when you spoke it might help. We were together three months before I understood a word you said."

"Maybe that's why you stayed."

"Maybe," she murmured, her eye on the outline of a red-bricked building high on an approaching hill. "Look at that. It's lovely."

"Comillas," I said, catching a sign. "Another town on the coast."

"Let's take a closer look."

So we came to Comillas, nestled in its hollow by the sea, and were immediately captured by the twisted streets, the cobbled squares, the sandstone buildings with their brown wooden balconies. We were impressed by the noble houses standing on selected hills, the ruined church, now the cemetery, with its white marble angel, sword raised above the town, and a sense of something inviting in the air.

"I like it," said Virginia, glancing at Kitty, restless in the back of the car. "Anyway, it's about time we stopped. Let's give it a try."

We rented a flat for a week in a long rectangle between the church the townsfolk built with their own determined hands, and cafes spilling over the sidewalks; a rectangle known as El Corro, the social centre of the town.

"What do we do now?" Virginia asked, after we'd searched the narrow streets to discover there was no estate agent in Comillas. "Knock on doors?"

"Right. Let's begin."

For the best part of a week we did, stopping people in the street, talking to cafe owners and barmen, looking at just about every available house in the town. They ran from a mansion with a splendid view of the sea to a cramped cottage, once owned by a fishermen. None seemed to be what we wanted, none was a house awaiting us.

Then one bright morning, while staring at a hilltop-ruin, a ferret-faced man tinkering with a car, which we later discovered wasn't his, asked us what we wanted.

A house, we said. Somewhere to live.

"For vacations?"

"We want to move here permanently."

"I know of such a house. I'll talk to the owner, if you like."

"We'd like that."

"Meet me tonight. At ten o'clock. In the Samovy. In the Corro." His eyes went from Virginia to me. "You know the place?"

"We are living above it, at the moment."

"Good. At ten, then."

The ferret-faced man was Alejandro, ex-driver, ex-customs avoider, who once raced the town's ambulance at high speed to Andorra, filled it with duty-free TVs radios, video-recorders, anything he could sell, and returned at the same break-neck pace to markets all over Cantabria. That was until he was caught and spent time in jail. Now he was moving into real estate.

"He's a *fooking*," our neighbour, Antonio, said much later, slipping the worst English word he knew into his Spanish. "He's a real *fooking*."

"We found him to be a perfect gentleman."

"You had luck. Ask anybody. He's a *fooking*."

Whatever his reputation, Alejandro was brimming with confidence the night we met him in the Samovy. After taking a swig from a large brandy, he told us he'd found the house we were looking for. "It's perfect," he said. "Do you want to see it?"

"Is it in the town?"

"Five minutes from here. Walking."

"Does it have a garden?" asked Virginia, thinking of the cats.

"A big garden. And many beds."

"Can we see it?"

"Ah." Alejandro sipped more brandy. "From the outside, yes."

"What's wrong with the inside?"

"Nothing. But I have to speak to the owner again."

"When?"

"In the morning. At eleven, I'll meet you here. For coffee." He smiled. "Or hot chocolate and churros, if you prefer."

"What are churros?"

"They're very good." Alejandro moved his hands eloquently. "They're made from dough and are fried. You put sugar on them. With hot chocolate they're delicious."

"Right." I shook his hand. "Until morning, then."

He nodded, glanced over his shoulder and left.

As soon as we saw the house we knew it was what we wanted. It was double-storied with thick stone walls, and stood at one end of a terrace on a quiet street. Along the front ran a heavy wooden balcony; on the free side was a triangular garden with flower beds and tiny lawns. It had a large accommodating garage.

"It's perfect," said Virginia.

"Can we look inside?" I asked Alejandro.

"*Bueno*, I'll have to talk to the owner again."

"You've not spoken to him?"

"To his wife, yes. But that's different."

"What's different about it?" Virginia asked. "Can't *she* show us the house?"

"Perhaps, but you know what women are like."

"Yes," replied Virginia, an edge to her voice. "I know all too well."

Our years in Majorca, as well as time spent in Mexico, where a man was unlikely to touch anything that suggested housework and a woman's word carried little weight in the world of business, had opened Virginia's English eyes. Often, she resorted to muttering, "*You* talk to him, he'll take no notice of me. I'm only a bloody woman. By God, they cook and scrub, spend all day looking after the children, and none of these machos listens to a word they say."

"When could you speak to the man?" I asked Alejandro.

"This afternoon, for certain."

"In that case…?"

"Meet me tonight. At the Samovy."

"At ten?"

Alejandro nodded, gave a sharp little smile, and hurried away.

After he left, we walked around the house. It seemed exactly right. The ridged roof, a roof of two waters as it is known in Spain, was covered with heavy red tiles, two chimney pots protruded. Like many in the north the dwelling had once been hearth and stable, a shelter shared by the farmer and his flock. Above, a hayloft had insulated against the weather. Below, man and beast lived side by side. There are still a few houses around Comillas that have remained unaltered, where the tools stacked inside the doorway are the same forks, rakes and scythes that have been used by many hands, where the scent of cow-breath filters through the rooms.

In the house Alejandro showed us the stable had been converted into a sitting room, the hayloft to several bedrooms. Even though the couple we finally bought it from lived as earlier dwellers had done, spending three quarters of the year in the kitchen, using the bathroom downstairs and only one of the fourteen beds. During the summer they moved out, let the house to tourists. This was commonplace we discovered, one of the ways Comillas survived, how it lived off the fat accumulated in July and August, made what it could in the months of plenty.

For most of the year the town has a population of three thousand, in summer this leaps to twenty-five or more. Bars and hotels, that have remained semi-dormant for the long damp winter, open with the coming of spring. The camping ground fills to bursting, and every house with any room takes in those looking for a bed. Children are doubled up to make space, grandma is confined to the sitting room, and much of the money that might go to hotel chains passes directly to the citizens. The weather and the beaches bring tourists by the thousand, mostly Spanish, but increasingly more from the rest of Europe. And, thanks to a trend set by the first Marquis of Comillas, it is said that in August there are more Spanish aristocrats per square kilometre in Comillas than in any other part of Spain.

"Think we're really going to get it?" Virginia asked that night, as we sat outside the Samovy waiting for Alejandro. "It all seems very dodgy to me."

"We'll know in a minute," I replied. "Here he comes."

"I hope so. I'm beginning to like it here."

As it happened everything turned out fine. The following morning the owner was waiting at the house. He showed us inside, and we were delighted. There were many rooms, many beds, and enough space for us and any who cared to visit. There was a long open sitting room with a dining table at one end and a wide fireplace at the other. Two bathrooms, a good-sized kitchen and all the furniture we cared to purchase. Wardrobes, sideboards, chests of drawers, some hand-crafted, were ours for the asking.

"Wrap it up," I said to the owner. "We'll take it as it is."

He looked at Virginia for clarification.

"Why not go to a bar," she suggested. "And talk about the details."

Later, when all was agreed and the price settled with a handshake, the owner told us that when Alejandro approached him he wasn't sure whether he wanted to sell or not. For some time he'd been thinking of getting rid of the property, but nothing had been decided. However, when Alejandro persuaded him that his *old English friends*, who in truth he'd known a full twenty-four hours, had fallen in love with the place, the owner agreed to let us take a look. After that our enthusiasm convinced him and the deal was done.

All that remained was a visit to a notary public in a town along the coast to sign the appropriate papers. It was as simple as that. He agreed to sell, I to buy, at a price we both confirmed. There were no surveys or contracts to be exchanged. It all happened on one bright sunny morning in a fishing port that smelled of the sea. I can't speak for the owner but it is a deal we've never regretted. The house worked. We've altered it a little, but it seemed like home from the day we arrived.

There was another small but warming incident that convinced us we were right to choose Comillas. When we told the landlady of the flat we'd rented that we'd like it for a few days more to conclude the purchase of the house, she waved away any extra rent.

"I appreciate people I can trust," she told us with a smile. "Forget it. After all, we're almost neighbours now."

All that remained was to go back to Majorca, sell our cottage and move to our new home in the north. That took longer than expected. There was no Alejandro to expedite the deal.

"Alejandro is a *fooking*," our neighbour, Antonio, grunted when we finally returned to Comillas. "He's back in jail again."

"That's a pity. If it weren't for him we wouldn't be here."

"Perhaps," replied Antonio, tall and dark-haired, a retired merchant seaman who wore an English cap. "He's a *fooking*, but he showed you a good house. And you've come to a good place." He indicated a neo-gothic building on the far side of the town with rows of arched windows and slender filigreed columns, which looked like a beige confection in the morning sun. "Do you know anything about the *palacio*? It was built by the Marquis of Comillas."

"I know very little about Comillas," I confessed. "We've only just got here."

"You were a long time coming."

"We had trouble selling the house in Majorca. The owner must have told you. In fact he was getting a bit impatient towards the end. Some of the letters..."

"I know," Antonio said quietly. "I wrote them for him. Otherwise, they would have been much worse."

"Thank you. We *have* come to a good place."

"This town was made by one man, you know. Everything that's important here is due to the first marquis. He made Comillas what it is. That palace was designed by an architect from Barcelona. One of the most famous of his time."

"The marquis have been pretty rich."

"The richest man in Spain. But, you know, when he began he had nothing. His mother sold fish beside the church wall. He went away to Cuba and made his fortune. When he returned he made Comillas what it is. Before, it was only a fishing village. Later, the king and his family came to spend the summer. Without the marquis we wouldn't be living with all these treasures." Antonio straightened his back. "I sailed on his ships for thirty-three years. I was a tiller man. I steered his boats. He steered my life. He gave a lot of work to the people here. We're proud of him."

I soon learnt that the first Marquis of Comillas was a feudal lord of the nineteenth century, a baron who refurbished his birthplace, made it befitting what he'd become; who turned Comillas into a small treasury of architecture, a town that is quite unique.

Antonio smiled quietly as I admired the palace, then asked, "Do you like fishing?"

"Well, yes," I replied, surprised by the change of subject. "I love fishing."

"Octopus? Ever caught an octopus?"

"Never."

"Then, I must take you. There are many here."

All my life I have fished. It was one of the things I shared with my father, whose clever hands could tickle a trout. He'd lie on a river bank, move his fingers through the rippling weed until they encountered a fish facing the current. Then, gently as the weed itself, he'd tickle his way up to the gills and with a little luck, a rapid snatch, he'd land it. That, I never accomplished, but I learned by watching him how to bait a hook, untangle a line, wait quietly for something to take the lure. I'd caught trout in New Zealand, knee-deep in streams, allowing a wet fly to run with the water, palming it slowly back, hoping for the electric tug that meant something had struck. Then the excitement of playing it, never knowing if you'd succeed or not, whether the fish, with a leap and shake of its head, would run free once again.

I have spearfished everywhere that had water I could get into. On one occasion, staying with my father in a dream house on an island in Pago Pago, I tried to spear a shark. The house was beautiful. It covered a knoll in a reef in the steep-hilled, green-clad harbour. On three sides you could lean out a window and watch tiny fish, in their rainbow colours, nibble amongst the coral.

By then my father, in his late seventies, had developed a taste for crème de menthe, and after supper would sit with a small glass sipping the sweet green liquid. Often he fell asleep in his chair, to awake much later to find a pale brown lizard, one of the geckos that appeared nightly on his walls, curled in the bottom of the glass, having licked up the dregs to join him in his slumbers.

"Bugger off," the old man would say, gently emptying the gecko onto the floor. "Time we both went to bed."

As for the shark, I caught its shape in blue water along the edge of a reef, gliding slowly with a lordly grace. In a moment of recklessness I fired. The spear hit the shark's back at an angle, left a white mark and glanced away. Instead of fleeing, the creature wheeled, no longer tranquil. I remained very still in a coral niche as it went past, its eye rolling with an anger that made me regret having disturbed its morning, and very glad I'd missed.

On another brilliant morning I swam among a group of tame groupers that a man, off the coast of Fiji, was to become famous for. He lived with his wife on a tiny island, in a native hut amidst a scattering of coconut trees, with a garden scratched out of sandy soil and a tank of rainwater. The garden, the tank and what he harvested from the sea, kept them alive. I'd sailed northward from Suva, returning to the gold mines where I worked as a geologist, on a fourteen-foot open launch owned by a fellow miner, a friend of the man who tamed groupers.

We arrived at nightfall, were invited to a turtle supper, dark flesh rich and fragrant, served with blue taro, and a dish made from taro leaves cooked in coconut milk. A colourful meal with all the hues of the sea, as delicious as the depths.

Early the following morning, I saw the grouper-man go to a kerosene-operated refrigerator and take out a small bag of mullet. "Want to come? Feed the fish?" he asked.

"What fish?"

"Rock cod," he replied, using the local name for grouper. "Coming?"

"Sure," I said, falling in with his taciturn ways. "Be good."

We walked past the tidy garden, down over the damp early-morning sand to where the water lay in a still line along a curve of the bay. There, their snouts almost on the beach, were four large grouper waiting for breakfast. They seemed enormous so close to shore.

"Where're they from?" I asked.

"From around." The man opened the bag. "Come every morning for a feed."

"All of them?"

"Sometimes there's more." He took a mullet by the tail, lowered it to the closest fish. There was a swirl and the mullet was gone. The big grouper edged closer, wanting more. Slowly, the man moved along the line, giving each of his guests a share. "Want a go?"

"Love one."

"Watch your fingers. They'll have them too."

It was a curious sensation feeding the groupers. The big fish didn't bite, just opened their mouths, drew in water, the mullet with it.

"They suck," I said.

"Suck or nibble. Depends how hungry they are." The sunburnt man grinned. "In the old days. When they caught a diver. You know, the ones with the heavy gear. They'd nibble his arm off before he could get away."

"How'd you begin to tame them?"

"That big feller." He pointed at a shadow cruising past. "Came along when I was gutting the catch one day. Threw him a bit and he stayed."

"And told his friends."

"Something like that."

"They always show up for breakfast?"

"Mostly. Big chap went away for a while. Came back with a hook in his jaw." He smiled fondly at the passing shadow. "Got rid of it somehow. Regular customer, now."

"Be all right if I got in with them?"

"Without your spear."

"Of course."

I spent a long time in that clear water with the creatures. At first they were timid and swam away, to return cautiously, eyeing me warily. After a while they became bolder and circled like friendly dogs. I could almost pat them as we shared the sea.

So when Antonio asked me if I liked fishing my response was positive.

"But you've not caught an octopus? *Bueno*, then I'll show you how." He looked at the sky, the high thin cloud, the touch of pink along the horizon. "Tomorrow will be good. Perhaps, we'll catch some *pulpo*."

"What do I need?"

"Nothing. I'll bring it."

At seven-thirty the following morning Antonio was ready and waiting, showing unusual promptness for a part of the world where *tomorrow* may mean *some day soon*, and *this evening* can extend past midnight.

"Here." He handed me a pair of canes. "These are for you."

As we walked toward the rocky coastline I examined what he'd given me. The first cane was about four feet long with a fishhook at one end. The other, twice the length, had a short piece of line on the tip. Both were beautifully crafted, the bindings neatly knotted by his mariner's hands.

"It's a good morning." Antonio sniffed the air. It was April, still chilly at that time of day. "They'll be coming in now. In the winter there are few. But now it's spring, and everything is renewed in the spring. Even the sea, so the *pulpo*'ll be coming in."

We arrived at the cliff-top, some two hundred metres from our door. Around the bay layers of bedded sandstone ran in folded bands, split by faults, snapped like biscuits on a plate. Below, low tide had left pools to be explored. Already figures were bent over them, their canes at work.

"We're not the first," observed Antonio, pointing to a cove not yet cornered. "But we might have some luck down there."

We trudged down through bracken, came out on flat barnacled rocks. "Now, we need bait," he added. "Something tough. If I have a *pulpo* I use his insides. If not, limpets are best."

"What do they usually eat?"

"Crabs. But they don't last. One touch and they're gone." He took a knife from his pocket and began lifting limpets from the rocks. I did the same. When we each had a dozen or so he cut one from its shell, then used its shell to scoop out the rest. From inside his jacket he produced one of his wife's hairpins. "This is best. Watch."

Taking up his long cane he fed its string through the eye of the hairpin and, using it as a needle, threaded limpets onto the cord. He passed me the hairpin and I did the same then, as he'd done, bound the limpets in a solid mass on the end.

"*Bueno.*" He nodded approvingly, moved to the water's edge, stared down to where dark fronds of weed floated in shadowy holes. "You have to look for the signs. They'll tell you where the octopus is hiding. When the water's high he comes in for crabs. When the water goes down, we try to find him." He glanced at me from beneath the brim of his English cap, pulled a little more firmly over his eyes. "Do you understand?"

"Yes," I replied, aware of the shortcomings of my Spanish. "I think so."

"Good. Sometimes you can tell where he's been by what he leaves behind. Bits of crab shell. Other shells. And when he hides he pulls stones in over him. Or digs up black sand. That's what you look for. The *rastros* he leaves."

"Okay." I held up the canes. "This, with the bait, is to find him."

"The other to catch him with. But, patiently. Look." Antonio slid his bait into a hole, moved it gently, took it out. "Nobody at home. If he's there, you'll feel nothing until you take the bait away. Then he pulls and you must be *very* patient."

"Not to frighten him?"

"To encourage him. To get the hook in behind him, to pull him out."

"I'll try."

"If you get one, bash him down on a rock to kill him. Later you must bash him more, to soften him. If not he'll be like a truck-tyre, not so good to eat. Now, try over there." Antonio pointed to a shelf of rock running into the sea. "In the clean holes. Not the ones with seaweed. He doesn't like to be where he can't see. Good luck."

We began. I became immediately absorbed, searched hollow after hollow in the rock. I saw small fish darting about in clear water, watched crabs scuttle, claws raised, into crevices to hide, but only once made contact with the eight-armed creature we'd come to hunt. As I began to remove the bait from what I took to be another unoccupied crevice I felt something elastic draw it back. I pulled. It returned the tug with surprising strength.

"I've got one," I shouted to Antonio.

"Then get him out," he called back. "Patiently."

But all my patience disappeared at first sight of the mottled pastel-brown body oozing from its hiding place. Eager to make a catch, I slashed with my hook and missed. The octopus released the bait. I stumbled back and almost fell in.

"Not like that," Antonio said gently, as if speaking to a child. "Slowly, next time."

But there wasn't a next time for me that day. Antonio caught two and gave me one. We threw them onto rocks until their delicate shades of brown, pink and green faded to pale grey. As we cleaned up other fishermen, *pulpos* dangling from their fingers, filling plastic bags, came by complaining how few octopus there were this year, how much better it had been in the past.

"The English, he likes to fish?" one asked.

"Very much," I replied, getting used to being called the English. As we were the only English family in the town it was an easy identification. "But I'm not much good."

"With practice it'll come."

"He'll be all right," Antonio said with a grin. "In time."

As we walked home on that lovely April morning, the sun up, the scent of wildflower in the air, I felt a sense of moving closer to the town. Antonio had introduced me to a part of Comillas few passing through might touch. And I wondered, as I looked toward the elegance of the marquis's palace, what else there was to discover here, what more lay hidden in the hollows all around me, what other *rastros* were to follow in this place of many turnings.

◆ ◆ ◆

"How'd you get on?" Virginia asked later. "Didn't say anything about Christmas underpants, by any chance?" She was referring to one of my more bizarre errors where, confusing *underpants* for *carols*, *calzoncillos* for *villancicos*, I had unwisely boasted of the children's abilities, saying they sang knickers well. "Anyway, I see you got something."

"Antonio caught two. He gave me one."

"They're nice people here."

Later, over the octopus Virginia had simmered in olive oil and red wine with onions and green peppers, I said. "Did you know this place was practically created by one man? A feudal lord of the nineteenth century. He went away, made a fortune, brought it back and rebuilt the town."

"So I've heard. They call him an *emigrante golondrino*. A swallow immigrant. He returned and spent his money on his nest. Isn't that a nice way of looking at it?"

I nodded, wondering what had led us here, what turn or casual chance had brought us to this particular place in the Cantabrian hills. Until we came here we'd moved so often we called Kitty *Moss* when she was in the womb. As a pair of rolling stones, she seemed something we'd gathered along the way. But, right from the start, Comillas reached out to us, suggesting there was much to be discovered in its sea-laden air, that we should stay a while.

2

Settling in

As things turned out, it took longer to sell the house in Majorca than we'd imagined and, by the time the deal was done, Michael had joined us in the world. We'd been married for ten years before Kitty was born. Travelling, working together on the margins of the film business, making commercials for television in England, much of Europe, once in Venezuela and for some years in Mexico, had kept us moving along. Although, we might have spent more time in Mexico had it not been for Virginia's father.

Wanting to be closer his daughter, he phoned to say he'd discovered a cottage he was sure would suit us, that it was such a bargain he'd buy it himself if we weren't interested. So, we returned to Europe as, by then, I was writing with enough success to keep Majorcan wolves from the door. We left the world of advertising and Mexico City, which we'd come to love. The food, the piles of fresh vegetables in the marketplace, the colourful clothing and the smiling faces helped compensate for the city's pollution. Some mornings the smog was so thick you could barely see the far side of the street.

"You've a good life here," Virginia's father said to her, soon after we'd settled into our Majorcan house. "There's only one thing that's missing."

"What?"

"I'd love to see a child of yours."

His comment was to change our lives. Funny, how a casual remark can have such a long-term effect. We thought about it, and decided that if we were ever going to have a family there could be no better time. The local gods seem to have agreed because along came Kitty, although not without a struggle. After twelve hours of labour Virginia was given a general anaesthetic to remove her pain. Nevertheless, I was able to see our child born. The Spanish have a nice expression for giving birth, *dar a luz* they call it, giving light. And Kitty, being given light, was an amazing experience.

"I'll call you when we're ready," the gynaecologist said, when I asked to be present. He was a big man with competent hands. "Until then, you must wait outside."

I waited by the door of the delivery room, bound in hospital greens, until a nurse directed me into a scene of quiet activity. Virginia was blissfully dreaming, the anaesthetist by her side. Other nurses stood ready with bowls, cloths and suction tubes. Kitty's head had just appeared and the gynaecologist sat ready to bring her into the world. He grasped Kitty, turned her a little and, when she was halfway born, glanced over his shoulder.

"Boy or girl?" he asked me, with a grin. "What do you think?"

I was too dumbstruck to reply. The gynaecologist's grin grew wider. His task was almost over, this was his release. "Let's see," I managed to croak.

"*Bueno.*" He completed the job, brought Kitty out. "What have we got here? A girl." He laughed and handed her to me. "She's perfect, no?"

I stood overwhelmed, the squawking bloody creature in my arms, not knowing what to do. Then hands, more capable than mine, took Kitty to be washed and cleaned. I went over to Virginia as she opened her cloudy eyes.

"A girl," I said.

"Wonderful." Her face burst with happiness. "A little girl."

"Yes."

"And we'll call her Kathryn?"

"We will."

We agreed to have a second child soon after we bought the house in Comillas. A number of reasons prompted this, the most significant being that moving to a town where there were no other English children, Kitty might feel isolated. She would be without the brothers and sisters, cousins, aunts, uncles and grandmothers that weave the fabric of a Spanish family.

"We'll be quite isolated there," I said to Virginia, as we waited for the Majorcan house to sell. "I know we want to get away from ex-pats. But this might be going too far."

"Do you think we've OD'd?"

"Perhaps we should have another child. Add to our team. Anyway, this is a good country to have children in."

"You're right about that."

Cooing women and smiling men would, more often than not, surround a babe in arms, bend beamingly over a pram. Our neighbours in Majorca swept down on Kitty and bore her away saying, "Who loves you most of all." She'd be taken next door, fed things we tried not to think about and returned later, burping happily.

In restaurants waitresses pounced on her at the table, gave her a tour of the other customers, took her into the kitchen, brought her back chuckling.

So, with the gods approving once again, the moon in a favourable mood, along came Michael. Once more, Virginia had another bad experience, again she was anaesthetised, this time with an epidural. I was present, but on the second occasion there was no light-hearted banter, no games of boy or girl. As the gynaecologist worked he didn't chat about his garden peas or the size of his tomatoes. Nor was I handed the baby to hold, but was pushed firmly aside as everyone in the delivery room moved as rapidly as possible. Michael was born with the umbilical cord around his neck. His face was blue. He wasn't breathing.

"He'll be all right," the gynaecologist muttered. "Don't worry."

I worried. Overwrapped and incompetent, I waited anxiously as they bent over the pale figure of the tiny boy. For tight moments there was only the sound of instruments, the murmur of strained voices. Then Michael screamed and the tension broke. Faces eased, movements slowed, the gynaecologist nodded and Mike was placed in an incubator. I turned toward Virginia, who looked up dreamily, hoping to hold her child.

"What is it?" she asked, smiling. "What have we got this time?" We could, of course, have been told earlier, but it seemed more exciting not to know. "Is it a boy?"

"It's a boy. Can't you hear him?"

"Can I have him?"

"In a minute." I took her hand. "They're just cleaning up."

"Is he all right?"

"Yes, he's fine."

And he was. Although for some years in winter Michael suffered from house-shuddering coughs, deep croupy barks that drew us from our bed, but he seems to be over the worst of that now, is as active as any of his friends.

At last the cottage in Majorca sold, and we were able to leave. For months we'd waited impatiently while buyers came and went, put down deposits, then failed to produce the rest of the cash. We talked, bargained and, in the end, arrived at a deal so complicated I wonder how it ever worked. Nevertheless, the moment finally came to depart, to join the furnishings we'd sent on ahead. Only the travel details remained to be sorted out.

"You take the cats," I suggested. "Go by plane. I'll bring the dog in the car."

"You mean, I'm flying with two children, seven cats and a change of clothing?"

"I'd take a couple of changes. Anyway, I'll make a cage for the cats."

Virginia shook her head doubtfully.

"I can't think of any other way of doing it," I said. "I can manage the dog in the car, but not seven cats. And, obviously, the children will have to be with you."

"Obviously."

"At least you'll get there fast. I'll be two days on the road. And a night on the ferry to Barcelona."

"We'll have to tranquillise the cats."

"What about the children?"

"I'd get on with making the cage, if I were you," she replied crisply. "The cats are getting nervous. They know that something's up."

As far as animals are concerned we're softies. The sight of some poor abandoned dog touches our hearts. Any cat that pokes its whiskers around the door is welcome to a meal. In Majorca, amongst the local moggies, the word that we were an easy mark went around like wildfire. There was a time when we regularly fed ten, seven of which we called our own. We had strangers give birth in our wardrobes, mothers with trails of kittens sitting on the doormat at breakfast time. The first night I ever spent with Virginia was disturbed by a quiet shuffling in a corner of the room. I put it down to a rejected lover until I was introduced the following morning to Mr Pig, a multi-coloured long-haired guinea pig, who moved in with me when she did. When we went to Mexico he retired to a Norfolk farm.

In Mexico it took little time to acquire a pair of *gatos*. We were invited to spend a weekend in a palatial house on the cliffs above Acapulco. There, among white-walled corridors, gracious arches, wood-beams heavy with all the grandeur of Spanish colonial architecture, a silver-grey mother paraded her kittens over orange-tiled floors.

"What will happen to them?" Virginia asked the housekeeper, a small woman with dark hair plaited back in a braid. "You'll find homes for them, I suppose?"

"Homes, *señora*?" The housekeeper smiled. "Who wants more cats in Acapulco? We'll take them to the country and leave them. That way they have a chance."

"Wouldn't it be better to put them to sleep?"

"Kill them, *señora*? How could you be so cruel?"

We took two. One an orange male whose eating habits rapidly led him to be called Groundhog. The other, a gentle little lady, came to be known as Miss Mouse. They flew with us to Majorca, pausing while we spent a week in New York, gazing out as snow floated past their sixteenth-floor hotel window. Groundhog died beneath the Mediterranean sun. Miss Mouse was part of the package we took when we left Majorca.

"I hope everything's going to be all right," Virginia muttered, as we bundled the cats into the cage the day she left.. "God knows what they'll think at the other end."

"They'll be all right. You're good with animals."

"It was the neighbours I had in mind."

The taxi-driver was the first to protest when Virginia arrived at Santander airport on a freezing December afternoon. He took one look at the moveable cattery and complained loudly, wondering where it was going to fit. Finally, the cage was strapped on the roof where the numbed creatures, emerging from their tranquilised daze, yowled in the biting air. Once in the cold and empty house they stared pitifully at each other and remained close to their cage. They cheered a little when I arrived two days later with our mongrel, Bienvenido. His, at least, was a familiar face.

Bienvenido was just about the most costly dog in Majorca. His over-inflated value was largely due to his association with a Boxer bitch. Together they went on a five-day rampage, chasing sheep on a local farm. Sheep-bothering was one of Bienvenido's favourite pastimes. Being a little chap he never did much harm, but his Boxer lady, with her fine sharp teeth, played a far more deadly game.

One morning a tractor roared up our little lane, stopped beside the house. "Your dog's killing my sheep," an angry farmer shouted. "What are you going to do?"

"Actually," I replied evasively. "He's not my dog. He belongs to the neighbours." So he had until they'd gone to Palma leaving him locked inside an empty house. After two days he broke open a shutter and moved in under our car. Very soon he was sitting by the fire. "You know, Rosanna..."

"She's gone. Now the dog's yours." The farmer waved a hand up the hill. "He's with the Belgian's bitch. They've killed four sheep."

"You couldn't stop them?"

"We've tried. We've been out with shotguns all morning. We can't get close enough to shoot." He wiped his sweaty face. "The Belgian's not here. Come and get your dog."

"To shoot him?"

"We'll not shoot him if he's with you. And, if you pay for the sheep."

For hours I walked through close Majorcan scrub, pushing aside wiry grasses, spiny bushes tearing at my legs. I peered around knotted olive trees, with their silver grey leaves, some so old it's claimed the Romans planted them. I looked beneath the heavy roots of carobs, behind almonds coming into flower, but nowhere was there any sign of Bienvenido or his big-toothed Boxer lady. In as gentle a voice as I could manage I called the name of my then least-favourite animal. As Bienvenido means *welcome* in Spanish I must have presented a curious sight. Empty-handed, I returned home with a sinking heart.

"I don't think we'll see BV again," I told Virginia. "They're after him with shotguns."

She sighed and looked away.

Two days, two more dead sheep later, Bienvenido returned, a piece of ear missing, tail wagging, a pleased look on his face.

"What do I owe you?" I asked the farmer, as we sat in a bar between a silent television set, on which a woman was dancing flamenco, and a table of card players shouting in the smoky air. "For the sheep?"

"About three hundred pounds."

"So much?"

"They were good sheep." The farmer sipped his anise. "It'll cost the Belgian the same."

"That makes him a very expensive dog."

"I'll shoot him if you like."

"I can't afford that now. There's too much money invested."

We had a drink or two more and parted reasonable friends. The Belgian was less fortunate. When he paid, and I might add that neither of us ever saw as much as a chop for our money, he stayed late into the night drinking with the farmer. In the wee small hours, driving home, he ran off the road, crashed his car and spent weeks in hospital recovering.

Bienvenido came with us when we moved to Comillas. Being cow, not sheep, country it was less tempting than Majorca. In his final years he fell into the habit of limping down the road with a ninety-three year old neighbour. They'd stop by the public rubbish bins on the corner and piddle against the wall. I think they appreciated each other's company.

After a week or two in Comillas, where December can bring a heady mixture of snow and brilliant sunshine, when the Picos de Europa stand like ice-cream towers in the northern light, our cold house began to thaw. It had lain unoccupied for months, but once fires were lit, heaters installed, books unpacked and pictures hung, it began to seem like home.

Kitty had been enrolled in the local school. Each morning she trudged off busily in her pinafore, her satchel strapped to her upright back. Mike eyed the world from his push-chair, happy to receive every sweet-on-a-stick offered by those who came to chat or coo, among them an ageing priest who never failed to reach into the folds of his cassock to produce gobs of delight. *Padre Amable, the kindly priest*, was known to every child for miles around.

Soon we took to walking on fine evenings, exploring the town. After school, before the chill curled up from the sea, drifted down from the mountains, we wandered through Comillas' curving streets, crossed cobbled squares, poked our noses into bars for coffee, a *refresco* or a glass of wine, perhaps a *ración* of fried squid, anchovy fillets soaked in lemon juice and olive oil, or slices of rich garlic sausage. Something to pick at, as the Spanish say.

One sunny afternoon we found ourselves climbing toward the marquis's palace, the Palacio de Sobrellano, the grand monument Antonio López y López had established in honour of all he'd achieved. He lived to see the building designed, the first stone laid, but never set foot within it. He died before it was complete.

"Would you like to look inside?" someone asked, as we stared up at the gothic finery. We turned to see a solid man with a thick black moustache, someone I'd passed on half-dark mornings jogging around the port. Emilio, I learned, was the custodian of the palace, the keeper of the now unoccupied gate. We said we'd love to, and he took a large bunch of keys from a pocket. "Come on, I'll show you what it's like. In the great days, my family worked for the marquis. But, I must warn you, it's not what it was. It's owned by the *Diputación* now, the local government."

"There's no marquis here?"

"Not any more. He lives in Madrid." Emilio gave his keys a desolate clank. "But, come inside and see how beautiful it is."

"What's that?" Virginia asked, as we moved toward the palace, pointing at a slender spiral, elegant against the shadowed east, where gargoyles leapt from stone gutterings and four-armed crosses reached for the sky. "Is it a chapel?"

"Yes, it's the Capilla-Panteón," Emilio explained. "The church and the mausoleum for the marquis' family. He's buried there with his sons. His *señora* also. And some others of the family. The old are still here, but the young live elsewhere now."

"It happens all over the world."

Emilio shrugged, and led us up steps of fitted stone toward massive wooden doors. A turn of a key and we were in a high and noble foyer where marble pillars, pointed arches, a wide and splendid staircase were tinted honey-gold in the late December afternoon. It was momentarily breath-taking, a first sight of the treasures that lay behind closed doors in this little town.

"It's beautiful," Virginia said quietly. "What a shame no one lives here anymore."

"When the second marquis was here it was full of life. They were great days in Comillas. All the nobles came to the town."

"Didn't the King of Spain come here?" I asked.

"He came in the summer, with his family. His parliament was here. Laws were passed. There was a day when Comillas was the capital of Spain."

"Right here?" Through a window, gothic in outline, I caught a glimpse of houses among the hills, red roofs stretching into green. "It's not like that today."

"There's no marquis here today," Emilio said pointedly, and moved further into the interior, over parquet floors in shades of autumn brown, intricately patterned. Triangles, cones and crosses lay beneath our feet. He opened a pair of tall polished doors to usher us into a salon where frescos filled the upper walls, and two ornate chairs faced a green trumpet-shaped carpet laid out to welcome those who came to call. Light shone through stained-glass windows, filled the air with slanting colour. There were reds and blues and rich vermilion of saints, knights and shields. There were interwoven floral patterns, all the trappings of the majesty the marquis had brought home to rest. "This was where the second marquis received his visitors. His wife seated by his side."

"It's lovely," Virginia said. "What amazing chairs."

"They were designed by Antonio Gaudí. You've heard of him?"

"Yes," I replied. "He's famous for the cathedral in Barcelona."

"*La Sagrada Familia*," Virginia said. "The one with the wobbly towers."

"We have a Gaudí here also," said Emilio. "The Capricho. There are only three buildings designed by Gaudí outside of Catalonia. And one's here."

"In Comillas?"

"Yes, we have much fine architecture. Look." He lifted an arm, indicating the paintings on the upper walls. "That's the seminary, the pontifical university. It was built with money from the marquis. And there..." His hand moved toward a group of Spanish soldiers in white flowing blouses and pantaloons, red berets and sashes, being ferried in long-boats to a steamship out at sea. "Those are troops the first marquis sent on his fleet to Cuba, to put down a revolution." Emilio smiled proudly. "For that Antonio López y López was made the first Marquis of Comillas. Come, I will show you more."

We followed our articulate host from room to room on the spacious ground floor, through doors of walnut, oak and cedar, beneath ceilings in gold and bronze, where hours of work had created delicate rectangles of flower, petal and leaf. There were massive ornate fireplaces with superb surrounds, chimney-pieces of carved and polished wood that gleamed in the invading twilight. Some carried sections of worked marble, others held exquisite tiles, one a mass of golden daffodils. From every side coronets, escutcheons, dragon-tailed beasts or floral clusters stared out into the now-silent rooms.

"*Modernismo*," Emilio informed us. "It's what the Catalan masters designed."

"Neo-gothic, we call it."

Emilio shrugged indifferently. "The wood came from the Philippines or the Americas," he continued. "Transported on the marquis' ships."

"What was he doing in the Philippines?"

"Making money," Virginia suggested.

"From tobacco," confirmed Emilio. "He had the biggest tobacco company in the world. In Cuba and the Philippines."

"Is that where his fortune came from?"

"From that and the ships. And other things." Emilio moved toward the sweeping staircase. "Come up, there's more to see. Even if it's not as impressive as below."

We went up into finely finished woodwork, sweeps of delicate parquet floors, through empty bedrooms, lacking life and character, sombre shadows of what they once had been. Long ago, with the swirl of a gown, passing between satin-covered furnishings and heavily-draped bedsteads, the rooms would have blossomed as vividly as the great salons below. But on that afternoon they were vacant shells, shapes where no voices echoed or fabric swished.

"Up here," continued Emilio, climbing a narrower stair. "Is where the servants were."

He led us into a darkening attic, the ceiling low, the windows small. Here, with few dividing walls, the servants slept when their tasks were done, when their masters needed them no longer. Here, like hay above humbler dwellings, they kept their betters warm.

"Little one, I will show you something." Emilio reached down a heavy paw, took Kitty by the hand. "There've been people working with ceramics. Perhaps they left something behind."

"It must be a curious feeling," I said, as he steered her away. "To have a palace all to yourself."

"Very nice of him to give us a private tour. It's just a pity the place doesn't have a lift. Those stairs…" Virginia moved Michael on her hip. "With all his money, the marquis might have thought of that. However, I don't suppose he ever carried a child in his life."

"I doubt it. He sounds like a bit of a pirate to me."

"A pirate who bought his booty home." Virginia turned her head "Here's Kitty. Now, what's she got?"

"Look." Kitty held out a piece of biscuit-baked clay. "Emilio gave it to me."

"What is it?" the burly custodian asked her gently. "What's it called?"

"*Una…*"Kitty hesitated, caught in the language zone. "*Una froga.*"

"*Rana,*" Virginia supplied. "Frog is the English name."

"At least she got the gender right," I remarked.

"*Bueno?*" Emilio broke into the foreign interchange. "Now, we leave, no?"

He took us down, out of the ornate building, into the grounds where heavy magnolias were settling for the night; where oaks stood slender in the coming dark and rusting cannons lay in mock defence; where the cold had begun to gather on the ground. We thanked him and walked home briskly, looking forward to lighting the fire.

"The people here, it takes a while for them to open up," I said.

"They don't say much. But when you tell them you've come to stay they do." Virginia steered Michael's push-chair between two parked cars. "Perhaps you should write about them. Could be interesting. After all, *Comillas* means *inverted commas*. Seems a good place for a writer."

"I'm not sure what I'd do."

"Just write about the town. It's full of history. It functions well, and that's a change these days." She was right. Bread was delivered daily, rubbish was collected six times a week, only on Sundays did the dustmen rest. And many of its old-time touches had been retained. The blacksmith made his own horseshoes; there was a boot maker who mended leather goods. "There's a lot in this little town. And there isn't much written about Comillas. I've looked."

"I'll think about it."

"I'd do more than that, if I were you."

Later, Michael and Kitty in bed, as we sat before our fire I thought about what she'd said. Today another door had opened, another curtain had been pulled back. Whether anything came of the book or not, it would give me a genuine excuse to probe, a reason to question without causing any offence.

"I'll try," I murmured, as I watched the flames flicker, the embers die. "To get something together for this guide book you were talking about."

"Good," replied Virginia, looking up from her cup of warm milk. "I don't think many people know about this place."

"I suppose not. We didn't before we arrived."

"There, that's a start. Begin by saying how we got here."

I looked back into the fire, at the fuel that came from a curving beach, one of the sickles of sand along the coast where our firewood washed in free. There are few tasks more pleasant on a winter's day than collecting firewood in the sun. The locals say the practice warms you twice, once when you're collecting, the other while you watch it burn. Firewood hunting can become obsessive, a good chunk is hard to resist. The picking up of pieces as you went along could be like putting together the story of Comillas, the story of how splendid buildings came to be established, of how a man whose mother sold fish beside the church wall became the richest man in Spain and brought the king to stay.

"There's something I've got to tell you," Virginia said abruptly. "The loo's blocked again."

"Oh?" I blinked, back in the real world. "Have you tried clearing it with a broom?"

"Until I thought I'd break it."

"Then, I'd better give Cuadri a call."

"Yes," replied Virginia, a determined look in her eye. "You'd better."

3

The Master Builder

"We have a tradition of construction here," Cuadri, the builder, grunted in a Spanish so guttural I only picked up a word or two. Fortunately he repeated himself frequently. "Carpenters, stoneworkers, they came from all over Spain. From Barcelona also. Great artists, many of them. So much talent. They came to work on the buildings the Marquis of Comillas gave to the town."

"That was in the nineteenth century, no?"

"Of course, but the tradition lives on," Cuadri said crisply and limped away. He'd fallen from scaffolding years earlier and had been lucky to survive. Now he walked unevenly, drove everywhere, never climbed a ladder and shouted instructions to his men loudly and obscenely from a distance. He was a curious mixture of overseer and designer who could rip the contents out of a house then rebuild the interior, using beams and flagstones, some hundreds of years old, with surprisingly modern concepts of space and style. Yet, I have seen him reduce grown labourers to tears when they were working on our house. "What was it you wanted this time?" he asked. "What can I do for you now, Señor Ken?"

"The lavatory. It's blocked."

"Call the plumber."

"I have. He could do nothing."

"*Bueno*," Cuadri grunted. "Then we'll have to dig."

Cuadri had been recommended by the man who sold us the house. "His labourers are the best," the ex-owner said. "They've done a lot of work for me. All of it good."

This proved to be true when Cuadri altered our house, although there had been little we wanted done. A window was added over the stairs to let in more light; the kitchen opened so it was no longer a place of retreat on winter evenings. Cuadri always listened to our requirements, considered our ideas, over-rode many with suggestions of his own, then brought in his men. The more experienced of his craftsmen immediately got to work, impervious to his vocal assault.

They nodded silently and put their skills to use. The younger, less hardened, began their day with a tremble as their boss shouted himself into the morning. In the end, however, when the work was done, neatly trimmed, finished and most of the mess cleared up, everyone went away smiling, the insults overlooked.

Cuadri had a passion for digging up, breaking down, getting to the base of everything before starting to reconstruct. "We'll have to dig," was his immediate response to the plumber's failure to fix the *water*, as the Spanish call the loo. "Dig and clean it. Then put it back."

"It's the back bathroom," I protested. "The pipes run under the hallway."

"That's no problem. I have a mechanical digger."

"I'd rather not," I said. We had once taken up part of the hallway when a water pipe burst. For days we crouched over the floor listening, until we located the leak. Then I removed two tiles and had the broken pipe replaced, but even that small exercise had given us more mess than we cared to repeat. The idea of Cuadri's men with a jackhammer tearing up the passageway was something I was keen to avoid. "Is there no other way? A pressure hose? Something like that?"

"*Bueno*." Cuadri shrugged doubtfully, seeing a favourite pastime fade. He limped the length of the hallway, lifted a thoughtful finger. "I have an idea. A *bomba*. Big. A big pump like the farmers use. To fertilise the fields."

"A...?" Unable to imagine what *muckspreader* might be in Spanish I went back to basics. "A machine to throw shit?"

"That's it." He nodded approvingly. "To fertilise the fields."

"What's he saying?" Virginia's head came out of the kitchen door. "Did I hear right?"

"He wants to bring in a muckspreader to unblock the loo."

"What sort of mess is that going to make?"

"This...?" I moved an uncertain hand in Cuadri's direction. "How would it be used?"

"We connect the *bomba* to the *water*," he explained. "Then, we turn it on. The pressure will make what's causing the blockage wash away. Into the sewer. There'll be no more problems. All will be clear, you'll see."

"You have one of these shit machines?"

"Me, no." He smiled at my ignorance. "I'll get one from a farmer."

"When?"

"Tomorrow. The day after tomorrow. I'm not sure."

"Does he know what he's doing?" Virginia asked dubiously as Cuadri limped out the door with a wave and a smile. "God knows what sort of pigsty we'll end up with."

"Seems better than ripping up the hallway."
"I wonder."

Two days later Cuadri returned. With him were several labourers, twitchily awaiting orders. Behind came a tractor-driven muckspreader, a scabrous tub-like machine, covered in the backwash of its function, reeking of the cow-yard.

"It's here." Cuadri wound down the window of his car. He seldom got out unless it was necessary. "Iván will put the *bomba* to work."

"Iván?"

"The farmer. In the tractor. He'll run the *bomba*."

Iván, so tall his overalls barely reached his boot tops, emerged from the tractor, glanced around indifferently then lit a cigarette. His eye caught Cuadri's and he lifted his head asking, without a word, where to begin.

"In the bathroom. At the back."

"It won't reach." Iván scratched an unshaven cheek. "The tube. It's not long enough."

"The tube," Cuadri told me. "Won't reach."

"How about through the window?"

"Ah, through the window? The bathroom window? Perhaps." Cuadri returned his attention to Iván. "The bathroom window? Will it reach through there?"

Iván shrugged.

"How do we get to the window?" Cuadri asked me. "Through the garden?" I nodded. "Over there," Cuadri called to Iván. "Come into the garden."

The three-way conversation continued until Virginia emerged to ask what we were doing. When told she closed her eyes. "I'm going out. I hope to God it's done when I return."

Cuadri listened to the interchange, eyeing me curiously.

"She's afraid there'll be a mess," I explained.

Cuadri shook his head, as if to say that was all one could expect from a woman. "We connect the tubes," he shouted at Iván. "Through the window."

For half an hour there was a flurry of activity. The muckspreader was backed up to the gate. Tubes were connected, still found to be short, another was gathered from the farm. It had no fitting so was bound into place with an old towel from the garage. Cuadri's labourers worked as fast as they could, skipping to instructions shouted from the garden seat, where their *jefe* had installed himself. Iván remained beside his tractor, smoking steadily, saying little, shrugging from time to time. Finally the tube was pushed through the window, down into the hole in the bathroom floor where the lavatory had been removed.

"*Bueno,*" Cuadri called. "We're ready."

"There's just one thing," I said.

"What's that? We start the *bomba* and *zas*. The water's not blocked any more."

"There's going to be a lot of pressure, right?"

"Of course, to clear the problem."

"It'll go through all the water pipes, no?"

"It has to. Who knows where the blockage is."

"Then we'd better cover the outlets in the bathroom."

"Of course," Cuadri replied firmly, as if the idea had been his own. He climbed to his feet and shouted at his men. "Close everything. In the bathroom. All the outlets must be closed."

"And we'd better keep them closed," I suggested.

"Of course. We'll hold the plugs in. If not we'll have a problem."

"I'll give you a hand," I said. "There's a bath, a bidet, a washbasin...."

"As you like. But we have many workers."

"All the same, I'll help."

Cuadri watched through the window as I went into the bathroom and crouched by the washbasin, one hand on a plug. Three workers were there, forcefully blocking outlets. When he was satisfied everything was under control the master builder turned to Iván.

"*Bueno,*" he shouted. "We're ready. Start the machine."

Iván grunted, pushed the starter. There was a thunderous roar. The muckspreader shuddered. The tube swelled under pressure. Hands pushed down plugs. There was determined concentration on every face. For the briefest moment all seemed well. Then disaster struck. Beside me the drainage pipe for the washing machine exploded. An unspeakable mixture from the depths, the interior of the muckspreader, and whatever it was that blocked the loo, shot into the room, hit the ceiling and bounced back to cover me from head to toe. We had forgotten about the washing machine. Unfortunately, it hadn't forgotten us.

There was a moment of amazed silence before I staggered to my feet cursing in English, fractured Spanish, anything that came to mind. I wiped muck from my eyes, grabbed a towel, protesting our stupidity, while the others in the now-foul bathroom stared at me trying, unsuccessfully, not to laugh.

Cuadri's head came in through the bathroom window. "All right?" he called cheerfully. "Everything all right? It must be cleared now. Iván says all the water has been pumped. All of it. It must be clear. The problem solved, no?"

"The problem…God damn it, the problem…" I yelled, then joined the others in their laughter. "Yes…" I spluttered. "The problem's solved. All we need now is to clean up the shit."

"That was…?"

"From the washing machine."

"Ah…" For a moment Cuadri seemed about to say more, but shook his head and moved away. He walked down the garden path without any trace of a limp, muttering, "Ah…"

By the time Virginia returned the bathroom had been scrubbed, I showered, and competent hands were replacing the loo. Cuadri was back on his garden seat, looking like a contented gnome. Iván had driven his muckspreader away, its task complete.

"Have they finished?" Virginia asked, her nose twitching. "What's that ghastly smell?"

"There was a backwash," I tried to explain. "From the washing machine."

"My God, is it all right? They haven't ruined it, have they?"

"The washing machine's fine."

"And you?" Her eyes went over me. "You've had a shower."

"I had to. I caught the lot."

"You mean…?"

"From head to toe."

"Good God." She giggled. "You're all right, are you?"

"Yes, but the bathroom smells a bit."

"Don't worry about that. I'll go over it with bleach." Her nose twitched again. "You too, if you like."

"I don't think that'll be necessary," I replied.

Some days later, as I settled the bill over a glass of wine, Cuadri, carefully avoiding any reference to bathrooms or *bombas*, talked about his town. "Sometimes we've had to move to work, you know. When there was little here, we looked for it in other countries. In France or Germany. Anywhere, where there was work."

"That's what the first marquis did, isn't it?" I asked, recalling what Emilio had said when showing us the palace. "He went to Cuba to make his fortune."

"I, too, have been away." Cuadri smiled, content with the comparison. "For seventeen years I worked in France. Then I came back to Comillas."

"With your fortune?"

"*Bueno*, not exactly. But I learned some things. I came back with the knowledge and the experience I apply here."

"Does that make you a *jándalo*?" I asked, using a recently encountered word. "A *jándalo* from Comillas?"

"You know about the *jándalos*?"

"A little. My neighbour, Antonio, talked about them. Can you tell me more?"

"I'm not an historian." Cuadri shrugged. "For that you must talk to Eladio. Do you know him? Eladio, *El Libro*, who lives in the Corro?"

"Eladio the Book?"

"Him and one other. *El Rey*. They know all the history of Comillas."

"The Book and the King? Not many seem to use their names here. You're Cuadri. And there's Toto, Pepón, Neluco, Chucho, Chuchi and Chus. Why?"

"Many names are the same. Many have the same name as their father and mother. Some are called Segundo, if they are a second son. Or Domingo if they're born on a Sunday. And when the names are the same, we want to know who we're talking about." Cuadri waved toward our *barrio*, the tiny suburb in which we lived. "In three houses there are three Pilars. One is Pili, one Pilarine, and one Pilina. So you know who you're talking about. You understand?"

I nodded, nicknames seemed essential. Kitty talked about her friends at school, of how Inmaculada had come top of the class, how Dolores had been bad. She spoke of Asunción, María Jesus and Remedios. To me Immaculate, Pains, Assumption, Mary Jesus and Remedies sounded strangely out of place. I found Asú, Chus and Reme much easier to use.

"But *jándalo*, what's that mean?"

"Someone who went to Andalucía." Cuadri finished his wine, left a little in the glass, a practice I'd noticed amongst men in local bars, as if to say they didn't need it all. "You must talk to Eladio, *El Libro*, he'll help. I've never been to his house. But they say there are more books there than you could ever read. Books to last a lifetime."

Eladio the Book was a tall man in his seventies with the out-of-focus gaze of someone who finds more on the printed page than in the world around him. He shook my hand softly when I introduced myself in the street, telling him I had an idea for a guide about Comillas and was looking for information. He agreed to talk about *jándalos*, and invited me to his apartment the following day. When I arrived I found half a dozen well-thumbed books laid out in preparation.

"The *jándalos* have a long history that began with the liberation of Seville," he said, after welcoming me inside. "When the city was freed from the Moors, men from Cantabria participated. They were key to the liberation. It's part of our history. We live with it today. You hear children in the street saying, *Hay Moros en la costa*? In other words, is anyone coming?"

"I've heard Kitty and her friends say that"

"*Bueno*, Seville was held by the Moors for more than five hundred years. Then, when it was liberated by Fernando the Third, the king who was called *El Santo*, men from Cantabria took part. Sailors from this part of Spain have always had a great reputation. In the last century they were known as the Wizards of the North. Marvellous men. Very brave. The sea was in their blood."

He settled more comfortably into his leather chair.

"To liberate Seville they sailed west along the coast. Past Asturias, Galicia and then south. They went down the coast of Portugal, then east toward Seville. The captain of the fleet was…" He glanced at an open book by his side. "Admiral Bonifaz, a mountain man who came not far from here. Their voyage was difficult. There are gales along the coast that can make the water boil. The storms come in like thunder. Men have drowned by the dozen in one sweep of a wave. However, Bonifaz and his ships arrived safely at the mouth of the River Guadalquivir. The river that is part of Seville."

"And liberated the city?"

"Well, it wasn't quite as simple as that." Eladio smiled and reached for another book, turned it in my direction, tapping a picture of a shield. "See that tower? The chain? And the ships that are sailing toward it? They are the fleet from Cantabria arriving in Seville."

I peered at a tall round tower, standing protectively beside a river-mouth. From it a gigantic chain ran to the opposite bank, its shackles seemingly impregnable. Racing toward it was a galleon, sails filled with all the force of a God-given wind. In the four corners of the picture cherubs blew additional breaths. Below, the face of an angel was carried by heavenly wings.

"That's the Cantabrian shield," Eladio explained. "It's on every official document, on all official buildings. It celebrates the role men from Cantabria played in the liberation of Seville in one thousand two hundred and forty-eight. They sailed where no Moor thought they'd enter and broke the chain apart." His hands spread in appreciation. "For that, Cantabria was thanked by the king. Land was granted. There is part of Cantabria in Andalucía today which flourishes. Vineyards, hostelries that serve pure Cantabrian food. Men have been travelling to that part of Spain ever since the Moors were banished. Seeking their fortunes, making their names."

"Known as *jándalos*?"

"That's what those who went to Andalucía were called. But there were others who went further. They were the *indianos* who travelled to the Americas.

"Antonio López y López, the first Marquis of Comillas? Was he *jándalo* or *indiano*?"

"He was both, but especially *indiano*. One of my dictionaries defines an *indiano* as someone who returns *rich* from the Americas. The first Marquis of Comillas was certainly that. He came back enormously wealthy."

"The richest man in Spain?"

"So they say, he certainly seemed as rich as a man could be." Eladio paused a moment, his eyes thoughtful. "Now, this guide you want to write? Is it only about the marquis or will there be more in it?"

"I'm not sure yet."

"Well, if it has a lot about the marquis here's something else you might find interesting." He picked up another book. "This is the other side of the coin. Written by his brother in law. And it paints a darker picture of the great man's achievements."

The volume he handed me was small, incompetently bound. The pages were photocopies of an original, with dark patches staining the sheets, some angled as if done in a hurry.

"I copied it from a friend. There are very few available. Many were destroyed. They said it was not a *libro* but a *libelo*. Not a book but a libellous document. As you'll understand, most of what was written about the marquis was hagiography. The authors were the grateful ones. Especially the Jesuits who'd been given the Seminary. They were very, very grateful." Eladio shrugged eloquently. "There are many books about the marquis, but I suggest you look at this one too. I presume you read Spanish?"

"Reading is easier than speaking."

"Of course. It's also more dangerous. History, after all, belongs to the conqueror. Those who survive to write the books. But, you should remember that no man is ever as good as his admirers would have you believe. Or as bad as his enemies paint him."

"What do you think of the marquis?"

"Ah, that's another matter." Eladio sank deeper into his chair. "However, I've talked enough for one afternoon. I don't want to bore you. It's your turn now. Tell me something about yourself. Are you Scottish, with a name like that?"

"The name came from Ireland originally. But, my father was a New Zealander, my mother Australian. I was born in Fiji."

"Why was your family in Fiji?"

"My father went there as a young man. He was a sort of *jándalo*, I suppose. He went to the islands to see what he could find."

"Fame and fortune? Is that what he found?"

"Well, he found my mother, although it wasn't there."

"Tell me about it."

So I told Eladio about my parents, speaking slowly in stumbling Spanish, finding a certain freedom in another language, a release from the accustomed meanings of words I knew. Once I began, the story came easily and I talked about the young man my father had been in Fiji and Samoa, of how he had returned to the South Island of New Zealand, to the small town where he was born, to meet a wealthy Australian family on holiday there. He took them fishing, laid their lines and showed them how to tickle a trout.

"Your mother was with that family? They fell in love and married?"

"It wasn't as simple as that. Like the city of Seville, there were chains to prevent an invasion. My grandfather was a Jew, he didn't want my mother to marry a Protestant. For eight years he managed to keep them apart."

"That's a long time. It's surprising he wasn't successful."

"He might have succeeded if it hadn't been for my grandmother. She was a loving woman who wanted to see her daughter happy. She posted letters, collected mail and said nothing to her husband, even though he sent my mother off to Europe, hoping that a voyage to the far side of the world would keep my father out of mind."

"But it didn't. Or you wouldn't be here."

"That's true enough. I'm living proof of the failure to keep them apart. You see, although my grandfather thought he was being clever when he booked his daughter for a *second* trip to Europe, on a route that avoided New Zealand, he didn't know that by then my father was in Fiji. When the ship stopped at Suva my mother got off, and immediately they were married."

"Very romantic." Eladio smiled. "So it ended happily?"

"Not really. My grandfather was furious. He made life as difficult as he could. Although he was wealthy he gave them nothing, even cut her out of his will. My mother gained a husband but lost a father. I don't think she ever recovered from that."

"Parents? *Dios mío*, they have so much to answer for."

"I suppose they have. Curiously, something similar happened to Virginia's parents. There was less family interference in their case, but the grandmother didn't approve. Virginia's father went to South Africa, her mother followed, and they married."

"It's not surprising you've come to Comillas. You were born with travel in your genes."

"Perhaps we were."

Walking home, I paused on the cobblestones by the Fuente de los Tres Caños, the Fountain of the Three Spigots, site of the first water supply to the town. The Fuente is a highly decorated monument with three maidens, hands clasped to their breasts in attitudes of thanks, above three functioning brass taps. The first fresh water was brought here by Joaquín del Piélago y Sánchez de Movellán, a member of another noble family with another rolling name, who made his money elsewhere and gave part of it to the town.

The Fuente is a tranquil plaza outlined by acacias. Old men sit in the morning sun and grandmothers guard their *nietos*. Until quite recently the school was part of the open square. Then, when the bell rang pupils poured out, pushing, shoving, yelling. And those who came to collect them moved forward to take their charges home to lunch. Now, a new school has been built on the outskirts of Comillas, and the rush of youth has gone from the centre. But, on the day I paused after visiting Eladio, it was as it had been for more than a hundred years. I was enjoying its tranquillity when a voice spoke in my ear.

"It's pretty, no?"

I turned to see a man, wearing a black *boina*, the familiar Spanish beret. I knew him as Toto, one of those I nodded to when we passed. "It was where my grandmother used to come with a bucket. In those days there was no water in the house."

"Times have changed."

"For the better? I don't know. They used to come and talk, exchange gossip. Tell each other the latest news. Today they sit in front of the *tele* watching *culebrones*. Those *telenovelas* that are like a snake with no end."

"But people still come. They're here every day."

"But it's not what it was. Before, they used to meet for a reason. To collect water. To take their laundry to the public washing tubs. You've seen the tubs? On the road to Cabezón, near the slaughterhouse. They used to wash there and talk about their lives." Toto sucked air through well-spaced teeth. "They don't use the old tubs now. All have electric machines."

"What's wrong with change?"

"*Bueno*, change is all right if you don't lose anything. You see that?" He glanced at a shield on the fountain. "That's the *escudo* of Comillas. It is of a time when we were strong."

I looked at the stone engraving he'd indicated. It was another version of the liberation of Seville, with the Moorish tower and the big-shackled chain. The boat snapping the barrier was a simpler vessel than the one Eladio had shown me. Not a galleon in full sail, but a fishing boat with triangular sheets and oars dipping into the sea.

"That's what we were. Now, we're different." Toto glanced at a child bouncing across the cobbles in an electric car. "We spend so much money I don't know how we live. If you get too much you lose something. That's what I think. The cost of things these days, it all goes up. Except me." He laughed crudely. "That's what my wife says, anyway."

"What do you do?"

"At the moment I am *en paro*. I have no job. Before, I worked in the mines. In Torrelavega. *Hombre*, that was a life of shit. I hurt my back, so they gave me a pension. Not much. Now it's worth even less. What can I say? Things are not what they used to be."

"Life today is good in Comillas."

"It is true that no one's hungry now. Before, there were times when life was bad. After the war, you know, the streets were always clean. Anything that was thrown away was picked up. Pieces of orange peel, cigarette butts. Whatever it was, someone had a use for it. But not any more. Now we throw our rubbish in the street and it stays there until the sweeper comes. Maybe, we *are* better off now. At least, there's no hunger." He glanced at the child and his expensive toy. "And the children have a future. That's good. It's their world today." Toto took a final look around the square, nodded toward a bar. "A little glass of wine? I invite you."

"Thank you, I'd like that very much."

"How'd you get on?" Virginia asked later. "Was Eladio the Book any help?"

"And Toto the Miner. Hard to say who told me more."

"Toto?"

"You've seen him around. He's married to that woman with the brown dog. She's always at the Tres Caños."

"Oh, Mrs Red Setter." Virginia's identification usually related to a person's pet. We knew someone as Daddy Black Hens, a woman as Mummy of the Ginger Kitten. "Did he say much?"

"Quite a lot." I thought of Toto, the way he talked, sipped his wine, left a little in the glass. I saw Eladio settle back in his leather-bound chair with his books. Each was part of a town where the past crept out of the stonework. "They're proud of their town."

"I get that impression too. Although Lisa, in that little clothing shop, says they don't give a cucumber about anything. *Ni un pepino*. That's the expression she used."

"A good expression, I must remember it. Oh, and something else. Antonio said he'd take me octopus fishing tomorrow afternoon. It's one of those exceptionally low tides."

"If you get anything I'll try cooking it the way they do in Galicia."

"How's that?"

"Boiled with black peppercorns and bay leaves. Then served cold, on sliced potatoes, sprinkled with paprika."

"Sounds delicious. I'd better bring one home."

4

Fantasies and other Things

"That is El Duque," Antonio, our neighbour, said as we walked back in the evening from the coast, our eyes on the outline of a fairy-tale mansion against an orange sky. "Everyone calls it El Duque, but really it's the Prado San José."

"Another of the marquis' buildings?"

Antonio shook his English-capped head. "Not directly, although you could say he was responsible. When you bring the King of Spain to Comillas much of the world will follow."

"And build their houses?"

"Of course. El Duque was constructed for the Duke of Almodóvar del Rio, a family from the south. These days there's one old lady who visits for some weeks in the summer. But, after the king had come, it was full of life. There were peacocks on the lawns. The gardens were beautifully kept. There were many servants."

We gazed at the building lit by the late sky. It was tall and ample, the high-pitched slate roof filigreed with wrought iron. The walls, where not covered with ivy, were white, and a grand expanse of window reflected the evening light. It was a chateau that could have been in a shadowed forest, surrounded by witch's mist.

"They say the architect was from Austria," Antonio said.

"It does look like something from the Vienna Woods."

"Would you like to see inside?"

"Love to." I held up the octopus I carried. "Should I take him home first?"

"No, we'll leave our catch by the door." Antonio had a pail of *barbas*, little whiskered rocklings he'd caught with short hooked lines poked into cracks along the shore, using garden worms as bait. "They won't get far while we're in El Duque."

I stared a little longer at the elegant building, the carved ridge, the little spires lifting from its conical towers, and for a moment thought I heard the sound of violins, saw women in their crinolines amongst peacocks on the lawn. The images were vivid, moved in perfect harmony with the splendour of the chateau.

The magic moment recalled another, when the sky was also a dying red and I heard music, the lilt of laughter, the tinkle of clinking glasses. It must have been twenty years earlier in London, on a summer's Sunday afternoon, when I set off for a pop concert and ended on an hallucinogenic journey across Hampstead Heath with a girl called Maureen, a kind and understanding friend.

Before leaving my flat to collect her, I'd eaten a small amount of hashish in the belief it would enhance my appreciation of the music that lay ahead.

"Dodgy," Maureen murmured, when informed. "Maybe I should drive."

"What a great idea."

We went north as the sun came down, a fireball in the sky. Its eye took hold, and I knew I'd never make the concert. There was too much activity surrounding me. Passing cars assumed individual characters, colours jumped on every side. The bonnet of our vehicle was a wide green sweep, its sun-specks a field of stars. I couldn't keep still.

"Would you mind if we didn't go?" I asked.

"I was wondering when you'd say that. What do you want to do?"

"Walk this off. Hampstead Heath's not far."

"Got to you, has it?"

"More intensely than I've ever known."

"Don't worry, you'll be all right."

Maureen parked the car on the edge of the Heath, and we began a trip that ran through every corner of my being, mixing fantasy with dread, brought me close to the land where madness lies.

"You all right?" Maureen asked, as I hurried over grass that held too many daffodils, around bushes and the secrets they hid. "Slow down. You'll be all right. I'm here."

"Hold my hand."

"I'm holding it."

I looked down. "So you are." We turned a corner. I went cold and couldn't move. Before me, full of menace, a black panther crouched on a tree. "Wait."

"What's wrong."

"That panther."

"What panther?"

"Climbing that tree?"

"There's nothing there."

"There is. I can't go past."

Maureen sighed, then nodded calmly. "All right, don't worry," she said reassuringly. "We'll go another way."

"You can't see it, can you?"

"There's a bit of black on one side, that's all."

"There's no panther?"

"No, but you didn't take me on this trip, remember." She gave my hand a tug. "Come on. Let's go on over there."

We walked higher up a slope, turned a corner where bushes grew thickly, the pathway thinned, and music filled the summer air. "Listen, don't tell me you can't hear that?"

"Nope." Maureen shook her head. "What's getting to you now?"

"There's a party in that building. Very elegant, very smart. People are laughing. Drinking. I can hear their glasses tinkling. Violins, strings. Very gentle. Very nice."

"I wish you'd given me some of that hash."

"You mean there's nothing there?"

"Not for me, there isn't."

"Up there on the terrace?" Over the tops of the bushes I could see a balustrade, slender columns, traceries of graceful architecture. "It looks Italian."

"See anyone you know?"

"No, but I can hear them. Voices, glasses, the sound of music."

"Julie Andrews anywhere around?"

"No, I mean…" I started to laugh. "Come on, don't tell me it's all inside my head."

"Seems to be."

"No music even? There's nothing from anywhere? Not even a trannie in the park?"

"Nothing."

"What a pity. You'll never know what you're missing." I rubbed my hands over my face, beginning to come down. "And the building? What's it look like to you?"

"An old brick wall. Now, you ready to move on?"

We walked again, the real world beginning to return. The trees lost their menace, the walls were simple, unadorned, no voices sang. Finally, we found a beer garden and, as the day slowly turned, drank golden lager in comforting glasses touched by the lingering colour of the sun.

"I was right out of my head," I said. "Thanks for being so patient."

"You weren't that bad. Some of it was quite funny."

"Maybe." I filled my mouth with lager, it tasted like pure bliss. "Not a clever thing to do."

"Specially if you didn't know it was going to get to you like that." She picked up her bag. "Never mind, we all do silly things. Come on, I'll drive you home."

I looked back as we left, down the sweep of the hill, saw nothing but the gentleness of a summer's evening, the ending of a day. Yet somewhere voices lingered, the sound of strings remained and everywhere were traces of a glittering world hidden in an old brick wall.

Memories of the afternoon on Hampstead Heath returned as I stared at El Duque, stark against an orange sky. Walking with Antonio toward the chateau, with its bulging bay windows, I could almost hear the sound of music once again.

"It is a great house," he said as we approached through trimmed hedgerows, flower beds laid out like jewellery on the manicured grass. "I do the gardens. Chus keeps it clean. She's there now, so we can go in."

Antonio was referring to his wife, María Jesús, known as Chus. She was a small neat woman who kept everything very clean. Their own ground-floor apartment, in a house one remove from ours, was spotless. Each day she could be seen on hands and knees scrubbing the little pathway that led in from the road. The butane-gas bottles she left out were always polished. Comillas, like most small Spanish towns had, until recently, no piped gas. Most of the chips that were fried, cups of coffee made, nearly all the paellas were cooked on bottled gas. The gas-man still delivers weekly, his lorry shuddering up the lanes. Empty orange gas bottles are put out to be exchanged, but Chus' really shine. Cleaning is part of her life. Her kitchen glows, each few years she unpicks their mattress, leaves the flock out in the sun and, when it's dry, restuffs it, sews it up again.

She was at El Duque when we arrived. "Chus, *mujer*," Antonio called. "We want to see the house. Is that all right?"

"Of course," she replied from the top of the steps, wiping her hands on a cloth. "Come in. I've almost finished here."

Leaving our catch outside, we walked into the evening-dim interior of the splendid mansion, into a climate of dark woods and patterned wallpapers, high decorated ceilings and solid wooden floors. What struck me immediately was a giant wooden staircase, so overwhelming it dominated the entrance hall. Each section had been hand-carved before being fitted into place. There were newel posts bearing pineapples, rosebuds and tulips, balustrades with curlicues bursting into blossom and thrusting leaf. Only the stair-treads were unadorned, they'd been worn into simple curves by generations of passing feet.

"A very impressive staircase," I said. "Where does it lead?"

"Up to the grand salon."

"I suppose they needed the space in those days. The clothes they wore."

"Especially the women with their skirts."

"Was the King of Spain ever here?"

"I don't think so. This was built after his visit."

"When does the old lady come?"

"Later. When the weather's hot."

"Think she'd mind if I talked to her. Asked a few questions about the past?"

"None of them mind talking about the past," Antonio replied. "It's where many of them live. But, there are others who know more about the king. For example there's a viscount, Santiago, who comes each summer. His grandfather was close to the royal family."

"Do you know him?"

"Well, I wouldn't say we know people like that. They're of another class. We work for them as servants, the way Chus is working here. You see, we live in different worlds. *Papados*, we call the summer people. The fish that immigrates north when the sun shines."

"Where would I find him? This immigrant viscount?"

"He lives in a house by the Estatua."

"Thank you," I said, becoming accustomed to being passed from hand to hand. "I'll get in touch with him."

"Good. Now, I'll show you the rest of the house."

We toured through vacant rooms that smelt of fresh polish, the absence of life. Antonio pointed out family portraits, majestically hung on panelled walls, showed me a set of delicate dinner-ware in gold and crimson, standing unused in a glass-fronted cabinet. I was reminded of the marquis' palace, of the emptiness that confronted us there. Yet, the same quiet sounds, the flickers of life that once filled the palace, also occupied this chateau. I thought of Hampstead Heath, and realised there's always a whisper waiting in the bushes, in the corner of an empty room, ready to trigger your imagination whether you've taken something hallucinogenic or not.

Some weeks later I stood before an arched wooden door, its panels cracked by countless summers, part of a rambling thick-walled *casona*, as large country houses are called. Beside the door was an enormous heraldic shield, on which a knight rode splendidly over lesser mortals. I pushed the bell, and a maidservant dressed in a black pinafore, black shoes, black stockings, a white cap and apron let me in.

"Enchanted," Viscount Santiago said when I was shown into his study. He rose, offered me a long-fingered hand. "How nice to see you."

"Thank you." I took the straight-backed chair he indicated, beside the table he used as a desk, in a long room where roof beams were studded with worm holes, and heavily framed portraits from his past stared uncompromisingly down. "It's nice to be here."

"Tell me about yourself." The viscount leant back in his chair, unbuttoned his navy yachting jacket, folded his hands behind his head. He appeared to be in his forties with a lean lined face, a greying moustache, untidy longish hair. "What's an Englishman doing in Comillas?"

"Living here" I replied. "Do *you* speak English, by any chance?"

"My English is good, but I prefer Spanish." He smiled broadly. "That allows me to have, what do you say, the hand on top? Would you like a cup of tea?"

"Yes, please."

"Elisa," he called. The maid arrived promptly. "Tea. Earl Grey, I think. To make our English guest welcome."

As he spoke I wondered about the man on the far side of the desk. He appeared at ease, yet withdrawn, as if reluctant to respond. My eyes went to the books lying between us like a barrier. There was a biography of a banker indicted for fraud, a thick volume on the government's problems with Basque terrorists, three editions about the Common Market. None appeared to have been opened, the Basque book still bore its plastic wrapping.

"How can I help you?" he continued. "What do you want to know?"

"As I explained on the telephone, I'd like to write about Comillas. But there's not much information available. There's a lot about the marquis but little about the town."

"The marquis *is* the town."

"I'm beginning to realise that."

"Did you come to Comillas especially to write a book?"

"No, I knew nothing about the place before I arrived."

"Interesting. But now you're going to write a write a history of Comillas?" The viscount seemed vaguely amused. "To show us how it should be done?"

"I've nothing planned yet. At the moment I'm listening, getting opinions and ideas. Memories. Little things that may never have been recorded before."

"And you've become fascinated by the marquis, no?"

"As you say, he seems to be the town."

"But marquises, like towns, are made." The viscount raised his voice significantly, then paused as the maid returned with a tray on which a silver tea-set sat beside a plate of sweet biscuits, a jug of milk, a bowl of sugar, slices of lemon. "Leave it on the desk, Elisa," he said. "I'll pour." His gaze came back to me. "Milk?"

"Please."

"Now, as I was saying, marquises are made. I'm not referring to titles or fortunes. I mean as people of taste and culture. People worthy of becoming part of the society they move into." He passed a cup across the table. "Do you understand me?"

"Practically every word you say. Just keep speaking slowly and clearly."

"Thank you, but I was referring to the sense rather than the diction."

"I got that too."

"Good. A marquis who is, shall we say, fresh to the honour, might need certain guidance. As far as the first Marquis of Comillas was concerned, he couldn't have made the town quite the way he did if it hadn't been for my family. It was we who introduced him to the refinement. To the sophistication that gave Comillas the beauty it possesses today."

"Sophistication from Barcelona?"

"Precisely." The viscount touched his moustache thoughtfully. "I come from a family that has, for generations, been a patron of the arts. It was we who first gave Gaudí an opportunity to prove himself. Without us, he might have remained unknown."

"Antonio Gaudí, the architect?"

"Yes, our interest in Gaudí began with a glove display he designed for the Paris Exhibition in eighteen seventy-eight."

"That seems a long way from a cathedral in Barcelona."

"*La Sagrada Familia*?" He smiled. "Well, he had to begin somewhere. An ancestor of mine saw the glove stand and was impressed. When he returned to Barcelona he contacted Gaudí, and so the association began."

"What brought Gaudí to Comillas?"

"Gaudí never came to Comillas. El Capricho, the summer house, was constructed for a member of the marquis' family. It was designed by Gaudí, but he never set foot in the town."

"Who was the Capricho built for?"

"I've no time to go into details. It's enough to say that the marquis' family and mine were joined in matrimony. It was through us the marquis came in contact with any refinement he possessed. He might have turned himself into a wealthy man on his own, but it was by knowing us that us he gained his polish."

"Your family gave him taste?"

"Absolutely. We transformed him completely." The viscount picked up the plate of biscuits. "Something to, what do you say, dunk?"

"No, thank you. Tell me about the marquis' association the king."

"Very well." He reached for a sugared biscuit, dipped it into his cup. "It was in the year eighteen eighty-one that Alfonso the Twelfth, King of Spain, made his first visit to Comillas."

As he spoke Viscount Santiago relaxed a little, lit a cigarette. By 1881, he told me, Alfonso XII owed a great deal to Antonio López y López, the man he made Marquis of Comillas. Several years earlier there'd been trouble in Cuba. An uprising, which ultimately led to the abolishment of slavery in the colony, was turning the island into a nightmare. What had been known as the Pearl of the Antilles, the richest jewel left in the Spanish crown, was on the verge of chaos. Armed gangs were threatening citizens' lives, protection money was demanded by the police and, it was widely rumoured, rabid dogs roamed freely in the streets.

"Sounds like a typical South American scene."

"Perhaps, but in this particular case the King of Spain was involved." The viscount sighed. "Poor man, he'd had an unfortunate life. His mother, Isabella, ascended the throne at the age of three. That led to the Carlist Wars. Alfonso himself became king at seventeen, when his mother fled to France. His first wife died childless, his second bore him only daughters."

"Didn't he eventually have a son?"

"After his death. The father never saw his heir. One of the prides of a Spanish male is to produce a son. There are many who have four, five or six daughters before one is born. Anyway, Alfonso was just beginning to see order restored in Spain when trouble began in Cuba."

"Where Antonio López went when he left Comillas?"

"Exactly, he made his fortune there."

"From what?"

"From whatever fortunes were made in that time and place." The viscount's long-fingered hand came up, preventing further questions. "Be patient, and I'll tell you more."

He settled further into his chair, delivered his version of the past, pointing this inquisitive Englishman in the direction he ought to be going. He described how Antonio López, the successful entrepreneur, whose mother once sold fish beside the church wall, came to the rescue of the king. He supplied funds, and ships to transport troops to Cuba, to settle the insurrection. Largely through his efforts the Cuban uprising was contained, the Peace of Zanjón signed, order and a simmering tranquillity were restored to the colony.

"The king was grateful?"

"Pouf." The viscount blew a long plume of cigarette smoke. "He was more than grateful. He made the man a marquis on the spot."

"And came to Comillas for the summer?"

"A holiday in Cantabria was exactly what Alfonso needed. And, of all the offers he received, he accepted that of Antonio López y López. He wasn't a well man. His chest was bad. Now, I'll tell you something I don't believe I've ever mentioned to anyone before. Certainly, not outside the immediate family."

"What's that?"

"When the king was here that summer he made a journey into the mountains. The Picos, you must know them."

"Yes, they're beautiful."

"You've obviously seen the clear streams. The valleys. The wildflowers in the summer. They *are* truly beautiful." The viscount closed his eyes a moment. "The king thought so too. He went on a journey, with mules and horses, and did a lot of walking. It was then he coughed up blood."

"What?"

"Blood. It was the first sign of the tuberculosis that killed him. It was my own great grandfather, who told us about the incident." He shrugged. "We kept it in the family. It wasn't the sort of news for all the world to know."

"Certainly not in those days."

"I suppose it would be different now. Anyway, when Alfonso and his family came here in eighteen eighty-one the town was turned into a showplace fit for royalty."

The viscount lit another cigarette and repainted the tapestry of the time. When the marquis had the king to stay his Palacio de Sobrellano hadn't even been designed. He was living in what is now a red-walled house at the foot of the town known as Ocejo. Ocejo had been a noble enough mansion when Antonio López bought it, but for the king's visit it was refurbished from the heavy green tiles on its slanted roof to the depths of its capacious cellars. Twenty-two wagons full of expensive goods arrived from Torrelavega, a large town twenty kilometres to the east. They were loaded with hand-carved furniture in oak and ebony, some adorned with ivory, others with bronze. There were chairs and vanity tables, footstools and the dressers the Spanish call *tocadores*, where finishing touches could be put to royal lips and cheeks. Beds and wardrobes, French-polished to a brilliant shine, upholstered in silks, muslins, cretonnes and satins were all trundled toward Comillas. There were paintings to brighten Ocejo's walls, an organ, a piano, and dozens of pretty toys and ornaments to occupy royal hands, to rest tired regal eyes.

"You can't imagine the work involved," the viscount said. "And the expense, it was enormous."

His tale went on, grew in extent and detail. Three hundred painters, decorators, carpenters and metal workers came to organise, to toil throughout the town. Every house in Comillas was painted at the marquis's expense. Gardens were dug, trimmed, planted at feverish speeds to make certain the flower beds, the decorative borders around Ocejo, were in full bloom for the visit. A stable for thirty horses was constructed, beside it a coach-house holding ten grand carriages. However, the most impressive vehicle of all was a mobile bath-house mounted on rails at the head of Comillas' curving beach. There, among the pines, a bungalow with a curtained veranda and four changing rooms stood waiting for the royal party to arrive. In it the king, the queen and the princesses were to put on their bathing costumes before being borne down to the water's edge, to descend into the sea without displaying as much as a royal ankle.

"Very different from today," I said.

"My God, those *cabrones* from the Press would be everywhere. They never leave anyone in peace. Those bastards should be whipped."

As I listened, I wondered if his anger had anything to do with a member of the nobility who'd been photographed, quite literally, from under the table, not wearing knickers. Her revealed pubic hairs sold a million copies of a racy magazine.

"They should have their balls cut off." He shrugged angrily. "Anyway, did I tell you that for the king's visit Comillas had the first street lighting in all of Spain?"

I shook my head.

"All around Ocejo electric lights were erected. The marquis had a special steam engine installed to drive the generator. So, it was here, in Comillas, that the first electric street lights in Spain were switched on. That was something, you'll agree?"

"Yes, that was something."

"And Gaudí built a kiosk in the garden. A summer house for the royal family to sit in. It was beautifully designed. A fantasy. Like the whole vacation in Comillas, something not quite to be believed." The viscount leant forward, a finger raised. "That was where the member of the marquis's family first saw Gaudí's work. And thought of the Capricho for himself."

"It grew from a kiosk."

"Of course. Everything's connected. Like elsewhere in life, everything's connected in Comillas. One thing begins, another follows. Someone came, made something, and something else grew from that." He smiled briefly. "That's what you'll find if you keep asking your questions here. Everything's connected."

"What about…?" I began, but the viscount abruptly stubbed out his cigarette, looked at his watch. "Sorry, I can't talk to any more. I haven't got time."

"Well, you've been most helpful."

"Perhaps on some other occasion we may talk again." With the fingers of both hands he combed his moustache. "If you have any more questions, call me."

"I'll do that."

I shook his hand. We smiled. Elisa, the maid appeared and I found myself in the street again beside the shield with the helmeted knight, the humbler creatures below. I walked toward the park where the statue of the Marquis of Comillas dominated everything for miles around. I stood a moment looking up at the image of the man who'd done so much. High on his tower he gazed out over wide blue water, calm and flat and unlimited, little changed since the king was here in his bathing house, shuttling down the sloping sand, shielded from public gaze.

"What was he like?" Virginia asked later. "Say anything interesting?"

"A great deal. More than he intended to. He was edgy to begin with. I think he was concerned about what I might write."

"Why should that worry him?"

"I was intruding. I've had the same reaction from some of the others, the ones Antonio calls the summer aristocracy. They're nice and helpful, but they'd rather you went away."

"The locals say they live in another world."

"It's got a lot to do with the way the marquis made the town. It was his little kingdom. Everybody respected him. Nobody asked any questions. And people like the viscount believe they can do the same today. It's part of their inheritance."

"That's why they've got their club."

"Just like the Majorcan ex-pats. They've got a club, they have their parties. They share gossip, play tennis, swim together. It's their way of keeping apart."

"Anyway, what did he say about the king?"

"Let's go outside and I'll tell you."

I poured drinks and we went out into our little triangular garden where I talked about the visit of the king, the splendour Comillas had seen in the summer of 1881. I told her about the craftsmen who arrived, the wagon-loads of furnishings that trundled in to fill Ocejo, the house that became a palace and a parliament. I mentioned Gaudí's kiosk and the bath-house on its rails, the trappings, the adornments, the arches that were raised. Toward the end Virginia began to laugh.

"Amazing," she said. "The circus came to town."

"Only the elephants were missing."

"Oh, I imagine there were plenty of them."

"You're talking about the size of certain Spanish ladies?"

"Don't be rude. By the way, did I tell you I'm thinking of starting an aerobics class?"

"You'll do it well. And there should be no shortage of customers."

"You're being rude again."

"No, but it's funny when you come to think of it. We land here and somehow it's right. I'm not sure why, but it is. I've got things to do. The children are happy. Kitty's fitted into the school and Mike's walking. It's nice."

"It is."

"The viscount said something else. He said everything's connected here."

"That happens everywhere."

"I know, but here you can see the links. A boy leaves, goes to Cuba, marries a girl from a family in Barcelona, makes a fortune and brings some of it here. With that, the Comillas-Barcelona connection's under way. The town becomes a centre of *modernismo*. Spanish architecture in its flowering. We have one of only three pieces by Gaudí outside Catalunia. And think of the impression the king made. His visit brought craftsmen who've never left. They moved into the town and lived on. There was a poet, they say he knew Lorca, who was born here because his grandfather came to work on the marquis' palace. And what about the effect that seminary up the hill had when it was full. Hundreds of students all over the place. The Jesuits who ran it. The townspeople who were employed there. It's an amazing complex. I haven't been able to look inside yet, it's closed most of the time."

"I dare say you'll get a chance."

"I hope so. The place is a treasure trove."

"You're talking well. Would you like another scotch?"

"Very much." I handed her my glass and smiled. "I hope you do well with your aerobics class. At least you might get something going. All I do is sit around and talk."

"Fun though, isn't it."

"It certainly is. Curious, you know, how we've become involved. Your aerobics class, for example. Who knows what long term effect that might have on certain people. It could change their lifestyle completely."

"I doubt if it'll go that far."

"You never know. I read once that a whole weather cycle can change because a flock of seagulls takes to the air. Up they go, causing a current. Something magnifies it, it feeds on itself and before you know it you've got a storm."

"Fascinating. But what's that got to do with my classes?"

"They might turn into a flock of seagulls. Change the climate here a little."

"What a responsibility, I'll have to think about it. In the meantime I'll get you a drink."

I watched her walk down the garden path. Beyond, the shape of the marquis' palace was turning golden in late afternoon sun. Beside it rose the delicate spire of the Capilla Panteón, and to the left I caught a glimpse of the Moorish tower of El Capricho, Gaudí's monument, tinted orange, its tiles softly glimmering. I turned as I felt the beginning of a breeze come down the wall to brush my cheek, and there was music in the air. It was the sound of church bells saying it was time for evening Mass.

5

Going to the Flowers

"That's the church bell," Virginia said. "I wonder if it's for Pilarine."

It was spring, another year was filling in, time was passing quickly. At night frogs croaked in the garden, issuing a trumpeting note, in the early morning birds began their calls before light filled the inky sky. On the hillsides wildflower sprang. Crocuses, giant daisies, wild orchids, cow parsley, layers of red and white clover and shining poppies moved with the turning days. There was new life all around us, yet, in a house down the lane, Pilarine lay dying.

"You told me she was bad yesterday," Virginia said, as the church bell tolled another solemn note. "I think the bells must be for her."

The day before I'd been asked to phone a son in Canada. Pilarine's daughter had tried to make contact but her brother hadn't been at home, and the person who answered spoke no Spanish. I made the call and, before leaving the house went to see the old lady, who lay eyes closed on the bed, her breathing shallow and harsh. When I told Virginia about the condition she sighed.

"It must be awful for the others," she said simply. "They're all so very close."

"Even the son in Canada. He comes back every year."

"I hope he calls soon."

He did, and spoke to his mother, but the next day was her last, and the bells we heard *were* for Pilarine. Death notices were printed, appeared on doors of bars and cafés announcing she had died peacefully after receiving the last rites, a final absolution. They said she was mourned by all who loved her, and gave the hour of the funeral service.

We went to the service in the big open church in the centre of the town. We knelt in pews beneath a high domed roof supported by four square columns. There were no touches of *modernismo* here. The reach of the Catalan masters of the neo-Gothic, of Art Nouveau, stopped outside the door. The pews were not designed by Gaudí, no heraldic shields of coloured glass let in the outside light. But the temple was large and simple, alive with those who had come to pay their respects to Pilarine, to accompany her on her final journey in the procession that made its way across the foot of the town, up the hill to the cemetery, where the white marble angel, leaning on a sword, waited for those who entered.

The first Spanish cemetery we walked through, on a sunny November afternoon, was in Majorca. One All Soul's Day we followed a group of fellow villagers carrying bunches of flowers, the women dressed in black, as they went to pay their respects to the dead. Like many country cemeteries the thick-walled enclosure lay behind locked gates. High green shutters added to the seclusion, gave depth to the privacy of the niches laid one above the other, the stacked resting places of those inside.

"It's pretty?" said Kitty, then only three. "All the flowers."

"It is," replied Virginia, pregnant with Michael, beginning to move with a rolling walk. "Especially today, when everyone brings them."

"We haven't got flowers."

"We haven't got anyone buried here."

"They're not buried, Mummy. They're put in the wall."

"For a while, yes."

"What happens then?"

"I'm not sure." Virginia looked at me. "Have you any idea?"

"I asked Tomás about it the other day. I was working in the garden when he leant over the fence to give me some advice. He said as long as the niche is paid for, the bones stay. Get behind in the payments and they go to the bone-yard."

"Where's that?"

"Round here somewhere. It's still hallowed ground."

"What if they need more space in the niche?"

"They bag up the bones, put them in a corner and add the next coffin."

"What about the flowers?" Kitty asked.

"Someone comes along with new ones from time to time."

"They're pretty." Kitty paused thoughtfully. "When I go to the flowers will someone bring me new ones too?"

"When you *go to the flowers*?"

"What a nice phrase," murmured Virginia.

"Will you?" Kitty's voice was determined. "Will you bring new ones?"

"Of course. But I expect we'll go to the flowers long before you do."

The phrase passed into our language, became a gentle way of describing the deaths of many little creatures, some friends and a relative or two who've gone to the flowers since that sunny afternoon when we walked among white and purple blooms on All Soul's Day in Majorca.

Now Pilarine had gone to the flowers, and we were part of a long procession winding its way to the cemetery high on the hill. A cemetery that, from a distance, still looked like the church it once had been. Its Norman arches had first been erected in the eleventh century, and had served as Comillas' centre of worship for almost five hundred years. Its tower had been a sighting point to bring fishermen home. Those same fishermen who went north to Greenland hunting whales, who swept down to Seville to help free the enchained city from the Moors, would set their eyes on the church as a guiding beacon. It had been a house of God with twin purposes, both of which steered the people of the town.

"It's lovely," said Virginia. "A nice place to end up in."

We followed the others through wrought-iron gates, walked beneath an arch that bore the distinctive floral emblems of the architectural *maestros* who came from Barcelona. Luis Doménech, the man who added wry detail to the Seminary, refurbished the cemetery in the 1890s, designed the walls that bound it, placed at their corners pinnacles with fish-scale tiles and four-armed crosses. Doménech restored it with the marquis' money, another prize the swallow immigrant brought home to embellish his nest.

"It is pretty, no?" A cheerful voice, in accented English, whispered. "You like?"

We turned to see a creased and smiling face, a mane of long white hair. It was Marcello, a man we first encountered in a wind-swept corner of the Corro the winter we arrived, seated beneath an umbrella painting a bleak and empty scene.

"Yes," I replied. "Pilarine will be at peace here."

"She was a good woman. For years I know her."

"We got to know her well too." I recalled the trim figure, wedded to black since her husband died, sweeping the steps each morning, weeding her patch of garden, talking to her dog. "She always had a smile."

"That is why so many people." Marcello indicated the crowd. "The mayor too."

"I noticed that," I said. The round-faced mayor had prayed before the altar, walked with the family from the church. "It shows how popular she was."

"Her husband too," Marcello murmured as we moved toward the family crypt. "You see, it is big the *sepulcro*. For the old families. For many generations."

Our eyes went around the cemetery, over the names, so many of which were the same, past ostentatious marble sculptures mounted on the surface tombs, to the simpler niches in the walls where plaques identified those who lay within.

"I remember in Majorca, when a person died, the first night the family would sit around the corpse saying they'd meet again in heaven. Does that happen here?"

"No." Marcello shook his white-maned head. "But, I'm not of here. I am foreigner."

"Really?" I looked into his twinkling eyes wondering if he was joking. I'd heard people say you could be considered foreign if you came from a town a mere kilometre away so close were Comillas' bindings. "Where are you from?"

"Canfranc. In the north. You know it?"

"Canfranc?" I turned to Virginia. "I know it well, don't I?"

"Too well, for so short a stay."

I'd gone to Canfranc, a tiny town in a cold corner of the Pyrenees, on the border between Spain and France, quite by chance. Nowhere had been further from my mind when I checked out of a hotel in New York, caught a cab to Kennedy Airport with the snow bucketing down. At the time that had seemed a good omen, I was on my way to France to ski with Virginia and her father.

But at Kennedy my plans began to go awry. All landings had been cancelled, and few aircraft were taking off. My flight to Paris was among those no longer scheduled. However, certain options were available so, in a burst of confidence, I took off for Madrid in the belief that the following day I could catch a train to France.

I rang Virginia before I left. She was in Barèges, at a small hotel run by a sturdy man with legs of iron, who had once been French downhill champion. "It should be all right," I told her. "We could meet in Pau."

"Fine. Daddy will drive me down."

"What's the snow like?"

"Beautiful. We've had powder every morning."

I boarded the aircraft and settled in. I might mention that, by my standards, I was unusually well-dressed. I'd signed a contract for a new novel in New York and, on the strength of it, bought a beautiful tweed jacket, trousers in soft corduroy, a smart shirt with a pale blue stripe. I was to arrive in France appearing successful and urbane. Looking back, I think that was the last time I dressed up for anything.

The plane arrived in Madrid. I took a taxi to the station, and bought a ticket on a train due to leave for the north in an hour or so. I would have to change at Zaragoza to a smaller line which would take me to Canfranc. There, a bus was to carry me across the border to Pau. While waiting I had breakfast in the station cafeteria, sweet rolls and milky coffee, then went for a wash. Even though I didn't bother to shave, and although my shirt was not quite as pristine as it had been, I still seemed to be quite presentable.

It began to rain as the train pulled out of Madrid, by Zaragoza it was pouring down. When we reached Jaca, the ancient capital of Aragón, a dull complex of factories and high-rise flats, the railway carriage felt closed and damp. There was a long delay in the station while men in wet slickers walked up and down the platform shouting at each other, occasionally exchanging a word or two with a passenger, then shaking their heads unimpressively.

"What's wrong?" I asked the man sitting opposite. He was unshaven, wore a black beret, a grubby brown suit, and was unwrapping a bread roll in resignation. "Why have we stopped?"

"*Derrumba*," he said, a word that could mean anything from the collapse of a building to a cave-in. "Very bad."

"What do we do?"

"*Esperamos*," he replied, taking a bite of the roll, filled with *chorizo*, spicy Spanish sausage. "We wait."

I waited, envying the man his roll. It smelt delicious. My breakfast was a thing of the past. Just as I was about to go in search of nourishment, we were ushered off the train, told that a hillside had been washed away, that the line was impassable, but busses would arrive soon to take us on. I pulled a light anorak out of my bag. It gave little protection, but was all I had.

I found a phone box and made a call to the warm little hotel in Barèges where there was lovely powder snow. Virginia, at that moment, was enjoying it. I spoke to the ex-champion in a mixture of Spanish and French that would have caused a schoolboy to blush. When I made myself relatively clear he broke into gales of laughter.

"Tomorrow, you come. *Mañana?*"

"*Mañana*, it is."

"I tell Virginia. My God, *mañana.*"

When the busses finally arrived, and we were bundled aboard, I found myself beside a woman in black with saddened eyes. The windows steamed over as we pushed on through winding roads in a haze of cigarette smoke and static conversation. I exchanged a few words with the woman but she was not inclined to talk.

Finally the bus stopped. "What's happened now?" I asked.

The woman turned to me, made a movement with her lips, a turning down of the corners to form an expression that wondered how she could possibly be expected to know.

I leant past the woman, wiped steam from the window. Outside I could see men wearing waterproof capes, old jackets. One had a sheet of plastic over his head. They were shovelling at a pile of mud that had slumped onto the road. A farmer in a shapeless felt hat, with a dispirited donkey, stood staring at the mess. After a while the bus driver turned to the passengers and told them not to worry, we'd be moving soon. A bulldozer was on its way from a nearby village. It shouldn't take long. We'd be in Canfranc before dark.

It was after midnight when we got there to find the streets deserted, rain coming down in slanting lines, making silver streaks in the headlights of the bus. We were deposited beside an enormous station some mayor or benefactor had once built as a final punctuation to the line. It was a showplace of platforms and arches, great entrances and spires, an out-of-place monument at the end of a country branch. Now, late on a windswept winter's night, it was tomb-like. Our voices echoed, the few lights cast long shadows, its bareness was intense.

I went to all five hotels in Canfranc but couldn't find a room. In the half-empty bars the loiterers, the final drinkers, sat in small groups, gathered around dying fires, huddled beside pot-bellied stoves. In every case the barman shook his head. They were all full. It was the skiing season. The snow had been good. There was powder on the slopes.

I said I'd heard about it.

Finally, the cold penetrating my once-smart, inept New York gear, my former shiny shoes covered with mud, I returned to the station, to the dark and echoing emptiness, where the damp came out of the stonework and the rain dripped steadily down, hoping to find somewhere to sleep. I curled up on a bench in a corner, my bag under my head, the light anorak pulled around me, envying Virginia in her warm hotel.

For a while I shivered alone, then a cat jumped up beside me. It was a grey cat, with an over-abundance of hair that I discovered later when I tried to remove it from my clothes. The creature snuggled in and we shivered together for what seemed like an eternity. My bag pushed into my neck, the wooden bench grew harder, the cold crept deeper into my bones. It became increasingly clear that this was no place to spend what was left of the night.

"Let's talk to the police," I said to the cat. "Perhaps they've got a nice warm cell."

The cat rubbing itself against my legs, I set off along the station, my footsteps ringing as I tramped along a great open platform, where the wind came down from the Pyrenees, and the dreams of some long-dead architect lay frozen in puddles at my feet. In a corner, almost hidden in the curve of an arch, I found a red and yellow Spanish flag indicating an office of the Guardia Civil.

A corporal, sitting behind a desk reading a sporting paper, a cigarette between his lips, stared at me for a long time before he enquired what I wanted.

"Somewhere to sleep."

"It's late." He glanced at his watch. "The hotels?"

"I went there. They're full."

"It's the skiing season. Good snow, this year."

"Perhaps, but I've just arrived from New York."

He glanced at my feet. "With the cat?"

"The cat's not mine. I thought it was yours."

The corporal shook his head patiently. "Where are you going?" he asked.

"To France." My Spanish would never have survived further explanation. There was no way I could have handled cancelled flights, interrupted train journeys, mud-bound bus trips. "Pau."

"There are no busses now. Tomorrow, if the road is good." He laid the sporting paper on the table. His eyes went over me again. My hair was a mess, my anorak stained, my corduroys were covered with cat hair, and the animal was sniffing at my muddied shoes. I think the corporal wanted to laugh but was too polite. "Perhaps I can find a bed. One of the hotels keeps a bed for the Guardia in case of emergency."

"I am an emergency."

"I can see that." He smiled and went to a coat rack, took down a heavy jacket, put on his cap. "Come. We'll see what we can find."

We walked back along the station platform, our footsteps echoing in the cold and clanging dark. I said good-bye to the cat. We crossed the muddy road and went into one of the bars I'd visited earlier. Few of the inhabitants remained. The barman glanced up, greeted the corporal cheerfully, immediately poured him a glass of pink wine. He turned to me as if he'd never seen me in his life, then poured me a glass too. I must have looked as if I needed it.

For several minutes the corporal and the barman shared a rapid conversation, which ended when the barman reached beneath the counter and produced an old-fashioned key tied to a block of wood. He handed it to me.

"Now you can sleep," said the corporal, lighting another cigarette. "Good night."

Very shortly after that I was tucked up in bed and, even though I was wearing most of my recently purchased clothes, and the sheets were damp, the air freezing, the paint on the walls peeling off in layers, I slept like the proverbial log. The following day I caught a shabby blue bus, which crawled slowly over the mountains, to be met by Virginia and her father in Pau.

"My God," she said, her eyes going over my soiled appearance, the unkempt shirt, the cat hair on my trousers. "What happened to you?"

"I thought I'd dress for the occasion."

"Could have been a mistake."

"Where did you spend the night?" her father asked.

"Canfranc."

"They've got the most marvellous station. You notice it?"

"All too well. I tried to sleep there."

"No hotels?"

"Not at first. In the end the Guardia found me a room."

"Good chaps, the Guardia. If you treat them well."

I agreed, and asked about the powder snow.

After Pilarine's funeral we walked down to the little curving harbour, built centuries ago to shelter storm-bound whalers, and along the waterfront to a restaurant-bar where we sat above the beach as the sea frothed in.

"This is where the king had his bathing shed," I said.

"What bathing shed?" asked Kitty.

I told her about the royal visit and the curtained bath-house, built to hide royal ankles from prying eyes, while Virginia ordered ice cream for the children, coffee for us. We'd just finished when a voice called, "*Hola.*" We looked up to see Cuadri, more gnome-like than ever, limping toward our table. "You've been to the funeral, no?"

"Yes," I said. "I thought I saw you there."

"She was a good friend." He indicated a chair, asking if he might join us, then sat and peered at our empty cups. "What can I offer you? *Un vinito.* A little wine. Some *nekora*? You've tired *nekora*? It's very good."

We shook our heads.

"It's a crab, from around here, you must try it." He waved a hand at a waiter, ordered *nekora*, wine for himself and me, then turned to Virginia. "For you, some wine, too?"

"I can't drink alcohol," she replied.

Cuadri stared at her in disbelief.

"I don't know why. Two sips and I get a hangover."

"*Madre mia.*" Cuadri shook his head uncomprehendingly, aware of a further flaw in the female sex. "What a condition."

"I'll have a Diet Pepsi."

With a sad shrug Cuadri gave Virginia's order to the waiter, then turned his attention to the cemetery riding the hill. "You know it was once the church?" he asked.

"We've also been told one of the architects from Barcelona designed the walls," I said. "Did he put the angel there too?"

"Ah, no, that was made for the Capilla Panteón. You know it, by the palace? Even without the angel the Capilla is very beautiful." Cuadri smiled in appreciation of a job well done. "It's a cathedral in miniature."

The description was apt. The Chapel Mausoleum marked the beginning of the Marquis of Comillas' grand design and introduced the work of Juan Martorell, the Catalan architect who planned the temple to be intimate, yet architecturally sweeping in spite of its scale. A tall neo-gothic spire, elegantly ribbed, lifts high above a grey slate roof. Flying buttresses spring out from the body of the church, gargoyles are poised on stone gutterings; the floral-leaf patterns of Spanish *modernismo* are everywhere. The Capilla was to provide the final resting place for the marquis himself. Its first function, however, was the entombment of his elder son, already dead from tuberculosis, waiting embalmed in Barcelona.

"There are many sculptures in the Capilla," Cuadri said, as we waited for our *nekora*. "Only the angel didn't fit. And, you know, the pews were designed by Gaudí."

Later, I was to see for myself how beautiful the small cathedral was. Marble figures lie quietly in the still cool air beside hosts of angels. On the tomb of Antonio López y López a bronze sculpture depicts him putting out to sea on a long and final journey. In the early mornings, on brilliant afternoons, sunlight coming in through stained-glass windows falls on the stately tombs. Most of the sculptures are the work of another Catalán, José Llimona, with some of the marble so finely chosen it seems the veins of the dead are part of the stone, lying blue beneath a lifeless skin.

"Llimona also made the angel on the cemetery," Cuadri said, leaning back as our order was placed on the table. "For the Capilla Panteón. But it couldn't go in there."

"Why not?" Virginia asked.

"*Bueno*, you know, someone made a mistake." Cuadri moved an expressive hand. "Some measurements weren't correct. A guess, an estimation wasn't right. You've got to be careful. If everything isn't right, you have a disaster."

"We've had one of those." I said, recalling the day we unblocked the loo.

"*Bueno*." Cuadri took a mouthful of wine. "That was another matter."

"So, they put the angel on the cemetery instead?" Virginia reached forward, placed a bright red *nekora* on her plate, gave one to Michael and Kitty. "That seems appropriate."

"A good idea, no? Perhaps it's better there." Cuadri glanced up at the white marble figure, wings outstretched, leaning on its sword. On some mornings, against the mirror of the sea, it seems to be in full and heavenly flight. "Now it's for all the whole village. If not, it'd be inside the Capilla, not for everyone to see."

"I quite agree." Virginia began to undo her crab. After a moment she nodded approvingly. "This is delicious," she said. "Even goes well with Diet Pepsi."

I tasted mine. It was firm, delicately flavoured, went even better with red wine and crusty bread. As I chewed, my eyes drifted back to the cemetery, the angel poised majestically above the dead. Cuadri was right, it served a better purpose there.

We said good-bye to Cuadri, walked back along the cliff-line watching the waves crash in. Storms can be sudden along the Cantabrian coast, the *Cornisa Cantabria* as it's known, the ornamental moulding on the upper crust of Spain. They blow in from Galicia where the knife sharpeners come from.

Knife sharpeners are part of the town, can be seen riding slowly on their mopeds, blowing high and mournful notes on their pipes of Pan, asking for knives to sharpen, umbrellas to mend. They have the reputation of being precursors of bad weather.

"It's said you're weather men," I mentioned to one, as he expertly put an edge on our knives, using the grinding wheel attached to his bike. "You're here to escape the storms in Galicia."

"It's true." He moved his cigar from one corner of his mouth to the other. "We're not fools, you know."

The thrashing storms also bring the *oca* in, the purplish-brown seaweed that turns violet in the sun. Uprooted by churning waters, it's piled in heaps along the coast, where whole families used to harvest it, forking wet weed onto cattle-pulled carts. These days men with pulleys and tractors haul it up, dry it on the hillsides, forming violet chains against the green. Later, it's purchased by food companies and cosmetics industries for the gel that it produces.

"We can't swim there now," Michael said, staring at the crashing sea.

"You're right," replied Virginia. "The water's treacherous."

"What's treacherous?"

Both children had Spanish as their first language, were taught it at school. However, we insisted on English at home. *Speak English*, became a constant cry.

We had a satellite dish installed, watched a lot of English television, whose efficacy was evident when Kitty brightly said one day, 'Way to go, Dad.' But *treacherous* was then still in the learning curve.

"It's something you can't trust," Virginia told Michael.

"Like Hector?"

Hector, a school companion, was the bug-bear of the barrio. Like every other child who came and went he had free-range of the playroom, access to all the toys. But, unfortunately, he harboured a wayward streak. Toys disappeared. Bread money was no longer in its place. The cat water was pissed in. A fire was lit by the garage door. We spoke to him on several occasions with little effect. His head went down, his bottom lip came out, and he made no reply.

"Was Hector treacherous when he killed his cat?" asked Michael.

"Especially as far as the poor cat was concerned," Virginia replied. "But Hector's just a bad little boy. When we say the sea's treacherous we mean it can change suddenly. In the morning it's nice and calm. A few hours later you can have a terrible storm."

"Exactly like Hector," said Kitty.

Which was true enough. Some days he and Michael were the best of friends, on others at each other's throats.

"He was treacherous when he left that note," Michael said. "When he called me *hijo de puta*. That's very treacherous. It means, son of a...." He paused until satellite TV came to his rescue. "*Hooker*. Son of a hooker. That was very treacherous."

"His parents turned pretty treacherous too," I remarked.

"The woman went mad." Virginia shook her head sadly. "She went absolutely bonkers when we spoke to her."

The conversation with Hector's mother gave us one of our few disagreeable moments in the town. Assuming we were doing the right thing, we took Hector's *son of a hooker* note down to where she worked in a bar, hoping to catch her in a quiet moment, assuming she'd want to know what her child was up to. We couldn't have been more mistaken. When we mentioned his shortcomings she exploded in defensive rage.

"What do you mean by coming to where I work?" she shouted, her normally quite-pretty face twisted with anger. "Why not the house?"

"We tried the house. There was no one there."

"It's all your fault." Her voice rose. A solitary drinker at the end of the bar buried his face in the newspaper. "You're to blame. You shouldn't be here."

"We've been here for years."

"You shouldn't have come." She tore Hector's note in half. "This's nothing. It's just something children do. Anyway, he's right. That's what Michael is. What Hector says."

"I think we're wasting our time," I said.

"I had the feeling it wouldn't work," Virginia murmured. "It's all right," she said to Hector's mother. "Don't worry about it."

"How can't I worry? You're here. You've made this trouble. Coming to the bar. Living in the barrio. We had no trouble before you came."

"I am sorry. Forget it happened."

We left, her voice following us out the door. When we got home the telephone was ringing. Kitty skipped ahead, picked it up. She listened a moment, looked at Virginia who shook her head, then replaced the receiver. "That was her," Kitty said. "She said some nasty things."

"What?"

"Well, you told her Hector had done a pee pee on the doormat. So, she said she'd come up and do one in our mouths."

"I'll call her back," I said.

"No you won't." Virginia's voice was firm. "Nothing you say'll make any difference. Just leave things as they are."

For a time we had no further conversation with the parents. When we passed them in the street they sometimes nodded, on other occasions steadfastly looked the other way. As for Hector, he was back in the playroom within a day or two, his eyes locked onto a computer game, saying Michael was his friend. With the passage of time he's turned into a more acceptable youth, and his parents smile and wave as if nothing unpleasant had ever occurred, but I'll never forget the bitterness of his mother's words, the look of hatred in her eyes. Her image comes to mind when I hear townsfolk talk of the Civil War, their memories going back to a time when neighbour turned against neighbour, friend against friend. It was something no one understood, the townsfolk say. But it happened and the scars may never fade. And, inevitably, its endurance encouraged me to probe a little deeper.

6

The old Republican

The Spanish Civil War left many marks on Comillas. On a hill to the east, until recently converted into a housing estate, stood the wreckage of a stately mansion, a fine construction reduced to a ruin when the battle came through the town. After the war the parochial church had its conical tower replaced, the old having been torn down during the conflict. Jesús Cancio, Comillas' contribution to Spanish literature, a poet who wrote of the fire and thunder of the sea, was imprisoned by both sides in the local jail, a process that destroyed the man.

I asked Antonio, our neighbour, about the war one morning while collecting bread, in the hope he'd introduce me to some of those involved.

"What I'd like," I said. "Is to meet someone who actually fought. Someone on the losing side. Who was against Franco."

"A Republican?"

"Mostly they're called Reds."

"Anyone who was against Franco was a Red." Antonio smiled grimly. "And, anyone you talked to would be one of the lucky ones."

"Lucky to survive?"

"Not only for surviving the war, but for what happened after. Many were put in prison. The monument to the fallen, *El Valle de Los Caídos*, was built by Republican prisoners. There were a lot who died there." He pushed his English cap a little higher, scratched his head. "But I know of one, Gregorio. He might talk to you."

"Where could I find him?"

"I'll let you know."

While I waited, I went out each morning when the *panadero* blew his horn, where you can begin the day by saying *Good-bye*. *Adios* or *Hasta luego* are commonplace before anything else is uttered, although *Buenos días* and *Hola* are frequent greetings. But townsfolk often use each other's names when passing, making each small exchange something personal. And the gatherings beside the bread man's van are always rewarding. There are items of gossip to be exchanged, news of who is ill and who has died. Old ladies count their change several times, pause then count it again, a practice that takes twice as long since the introduction of the Euro. And there's frequently a new word to learn, a new phrase to add to the vocabulary.

"Chus," I said to Antonio's wife, on a grey and overcast morning, as women emerged wearing blue or red dressing gowns and carpet slippers. On wet occasions a few wore stilted clogs, *albarcas*, to keep their feet out of the mud. Chus, however, was always neatly dressed in skirt, blouse and cardigan. She crossed herself as she stepped out of the house. "*Buenos días*," I added.

"*De buenos nada.* These aren't good days, they're sad days. *Días tristes.* We have a rhyme, Don't take off your winter array until the fortieth of May."

"The fortieth?"

"Of course, well into June."

"I've heard days like this called days of hunger."

"That too." She shivered, put a hand over her nose, and hurried back to her door. "This is not good air to breathe."

A week later, on another sad and overcast day when even the birdcalls seemed subdued, Antonio told me he'd been in touch with Gregorio, the old Republican. "He's agreed to talk and suggested I take you to his bar."

"He runs a bar?"

"Well, it could be his, he's so often there."

"He sounds like a survivor."

"He's a grand survivor. Every day at three he's in the bar. He takes a whisky or two, smokes a cigar, and talks to people. Sometimes he'll dance. The Troubadour of Cantabria, they call him. He'd rather be known as a poet than anything else."

"Will he talk about the war? There are some who refuse to mention it."

"He said he would." Antonio looked away. "Even though he's reluctant. But, when I told him you were a writer, he agreed."

◆ ◆ ◆

We arrived at Gregorio's bar, high in the hills above Comillas, on an afternoon when a fine mountain drizzle cloaked everything in its shroud, stripped colour from the trees, turned roof-tiles a sullen ochre. Inside, the air was steamy. At a table a group of card-players thumped loudly, taunting each other as they won or lost. In a corner a television set played *Falcon Crest*. Lust and greed, in bitter Spanish, competed with the other voices in the room.

Gregorio sat alone at a table, his elbows on the formica top.

He was a small, neatly-made man whose face was smooth, little lined for his eighty-four years. His eyes were sharp, disappeared when he laughed or scowled. He wore a clean, striped suit that had seen better days and an open-necked shirt. Covering his short white hair was a black Spanish beret. As we arrived he looked up at Antonio, barely gave me a glance. When we were introduced he offered a small dry hand.

"Are you a poet?" he asked with a doubtful smile.

"I've had one or two published."

"Where?"

"In New Zealand."

"*New Zealand*?" He laughed. His eyes disappeared. "Then you're not like those from Cantabria who write about the mountains and the sea."

"They have them there too."

"But not as beautiful as the Picos." He reached toward a jacket pocket. Antonio's hand came forward holding three fat cigars. "Thank you. Just what I was looking for."

"*Un chupito?*" enquired Antonio casually. "A little drink?"

"*Pues*, a small *Jota Bey*," Gregorio replied, referring to JB whisky. "It's a good hour to take something." He lit his cigar with a kitchen match, saw that it was going nicely, then turned to me. "Antonio says you want to ask about the war. It was a long time ago."

"It's something that's still talked about."

"*Bueno*, in Comillas they talk about the war a lot. It was bad there. What was done by the Republicans to the church was a disgrace. And to the Jesuits in the Seminary. Then Franco and the Falangists came and it was bad again. They'll never stop talking about the war in Comillas."

"Very few are prepared to talk to me."

"They don't trust you, you're a foreigner. They don't know what you want." The old man smiled tightly. "What *do* you want, by the way? Are you going to write a poem about it? For, what did you say, Holland?"

"I'm trying to write a book."

"Then write about the good things, not the war. Wars are bad. They're made by politicians, who are all corrupt. And by the Church, which has no heart." Gregorio's short bursts rose above the pettiness on the TV screen, those of the cardplayers in the corner. "Anyway, what can I tell you about the war? When it came, I didn't know how to load a rifle. How to shoot. I put on my best clothes, polished my shoes, and left home to join the Popular Front."

He looked up as Antonio came back from the bar, put drinks on the table. Apart from the whisky he had a beer for himself, a glass of red wine for me.

"He wants to know about the war, like you said," Gregorio told Antonio. "But what can I tell him that's not in a book?"

"He wants to know how you felt."

"Bad, I felt bad." Gregorio picked his glass, drank quickly, then took a white handkerchief from a jacket pocket and wiped his lips. "How do you think I felt? I don't like *politicos*, but I didn't want to kill them. I've no time for the Church, but I wasn't fighting nuns."

"Why were you part of it?" I asked.

"It seemed the right thing to do. *Bueno*, I didn't know how bad it would be. What it would do to us. Anyway, I did very little fighting. And I was disgusted with what I saw. Some bad things happened." Gregorio glared at me, loathing the return of old and bitter memories. "Listen, I'll tell you how bad it was. I'll tell you, and then you'll leave me in peace."

"If it's painful, there's no need."

"I'll talk, but you must listen to the bad things. Things they don't talk about in Comillas, because they didn't happen there." He glanced at Antonio, who was staring into his glass. "You had to see it happen, to feel what it was like. *Bueno*, I'll tell you one bad thing and that'll be enough." Gregorio took his cigar from the ashtray, blew smoke across the table. "There were a lot of people on a boat in the harbour in Santander. The *Alfonso Pérez*. It was a prison ship."

"Who were the prisoners?"

"Those who didn't belong to the Popular Front. Who were not Republicans. They were Falangists, and…" He paused, swallowed the rest of his whisky, stared at his empty glass. Antonio took it, went to the bar again. "Those prisoners, they were killed. They were killed by others in the town. By their neighbours, by fellow Santanderinos."

"Why?"

"Because of the planes. Franco's planes came over Santander. They dropped bombs and many died." He grunted as his glass was replaced before him, gave Antonio a nod. "Some say it was the Germans from the Condor Legion. It was their bombs that drove the people mad. Made them do bad things."

"So the prisoners were killed in revenge?"

"It was very bad, you see. Many were hungry. Everyone was frightened. When they saw what the planes did to their families, to their children, it drove them crazy."

"That's not difficult to understand."

"It doesn't make it good." Gregorio turned his eyes away, gazed out through the misted window at the drizzling rain, over a children's playground where wet swings stood unused, empty seesaws glistened in the damp. "When the war came right into Santander it was worse," he added. "It was the others who did the bad things then. Then it was Republicans who were prisoners. It was like a madhouse. With Franco approaching, everybody from the countryside came to Santander. Farmers with their cows and horses. With pigs. Everything they owned. The streets were like a cattle market, a *feria*. You know what I mean?"

I nodded.

"Some escaped by sea. Hundreds got away. Basques who needed refuge after Bilboa was taken. Communists who were frightened. Any who thought they had a chance jumped into boats to escape to France. To Asturias. Many drowned."

"You didn't get into a boat?"

"How could I? The places on the boats were for the *peces gordos*, the fat fish. Who had money." He puffed on his cigar. "Officers, they went. And left us alone. In the chaos, they didn't care what happened to their men. Like animals they ran away."

"What happened then?"

"It was *fatal*. For two days, three, it was terrible. Days of chaos. After that, I was taken prisoner. They put us in the bullring in Santander. When I arrived the seats were occupied and I sat in the sand. Like a bull, waiting for the sword." Gregorio drank a little whisky. The room was quieter now. The card players made less noise. *Falcon Crest* had been replaced by animated cartoons. A cat chased a mouse through city streets. "I was lucky I wasn't shot. I was taken with others for a trial. Not a real trial. They put down my name, but I had nothing written against me. All the same, I was sentenced to three years prison."

"That must have been bad."

"Very bad. Completely *loco*. I told you, I didn't know how to fight. How to load a rifle. It couldn't have been worse. Guards came into the cells and read out names. Those with the names had to go outside. Some days they came back. Some days they didn't. They were shot. There was a man who was deaf. He never heard his name. Never went outside. That saved his life."

"Was your name ever called?"

"In the jail? Yes. I went out and worked clearing the streets. But, I always came back." Gregorio smiled, a small crack appeared in his unlined face. "Just as well, eh? If not my seven children and twenty grandchildren wouldn't have been born."

"You have a good family," Antonio murmured and, while they agreed, I collected the empty glasses, went to the bar where the barman silently replaced the drinks. When I returned Gregorio was lighting a fresh cigar. Antonio said, "Tell him about Jesús Cancio."

"Did you know him?" I asked

"We were together in the same prison for a time. I remember, he was cold. I lent him my overcoat. But he was not well. He was almost blind. He shouldn't have been there. He was never in the army. It was for his writings he was put in jail. For things he wrote for the Popular Front. But he was a wonderful man with a great sense of humour. He said life was like a chicken from Galicia. Too short and full of shit."

We all laughed and the conversation drifted away from war. For a time the old man had permitted me to see the heartlessness, the generosity, the helplessness that occurs between men in conflict. For a time he reminded me of my father, who fought in two wars and would say little of either. He had a handful of medals to pin on his chest, and a dent the size of a dinner plate in his leg shrapnel had left him with. He acknowledged that without it he might have died, might have fought on to be killed. Like Gregorio's fellow-prisoner's deafness, it could have saved his life. On each of the medals his name was spelt differently, on each his military number was correct. An officer and a gentleman he might have been, but by a number he was identified.

"You've not talked about your poetry," Antonio said. "You're the Troubadour of Cantabria, remember?"

"Of course, they gave me that honour when I was eighty. A few years ago."

"Recite some of your poetry."

Gregorio smiled, picked up his glass, found it empty. I refilled it and he was ready to begin. He lifted his head, his neck cords stretched against the collar of his shirt, and spoke his verses in a voice that was low and gentle, that held none of the earlier scorn. I caught the sense of what he was saying, images rather than words, as talked of trees and mountain tops, great waves in the sea, linking couplets that glorified freedom, the pride of being a man. It was a simple and moving performance, polished by time, done frequently in this crowded bar between the shouts of card players, the babble from a television screen, where cats chased mice down crowded streets and Californian wine growers squabbled over profit and desire.

"Very good," I said, when he paused to sip his *Jota Bey*. "You make wonderful pictures."

He nodded, pleased, and continued. I bought another round of drinks and felt the wine begin to brighten the dull and misty afternoon. It was almost dark, outside the shapes of the swings and seesaws had softened in the gloom. Gregorio recited a little longer, then began to talk to Antonio of people they knew, speaking only of the present, nothing of the past. Again I was reminded of my father, another small nuggetty man seated with his whisky. I'd never understood why he rushed off to war, not once but twice. Nor had I asked him about it. I wonder what he might have said if I'd faced him across a table and persisted as I'd done today. Perhaps he'd have told me more. Perhaps he'd have merely smiled and recounted how the iodine had stung when he finally reached a first-aid station, how sharp that pain had been.

◆ ◆ ◆

Later we drove home, the head-lamps cutting through the dark, scything the fine rain mountain people call *chiri miri*, an almost-invisible drizzle. We travelled through cloud down to Comillas, where the lights from the town sparkled like a chandelier.

"He talked a lot," said Antonio.

"Even though he didn't want to."

"The war was bad in this part of Spain. All along the north. I was a child, but I remember how people tried to hide from it. They wanted it to be over."

"I can imagine."

"I wonder if anyone can who wasn't there?"

I've never been in a war, although I've seen the aftermath of one. The first time I came to Europe I hitchhiked to Berlin. I travelled from New Zealand by ship, cocooned for a month in a community of antipodeans heading to what many called Home, the Old Country, the Old Dart, some to visit an aunt in Glasgow, others an uncle in Kent. We were accompanied by a collection of New-Australians, New-New Zealanders returning to the towns they'd immigrated from, going back to see Mutti and Papi, Mamá or Papá.

When the boat docked in Genoa, in the company of a long-legged girl named Susan, I left the ship and hitchhiked north, drawn by Berlin, a city that had touched my corner of the world. A cousin had died above it dropping bombs. My mother thought it one of the most beautiful cities in the world. When I arrived, Berlin was where East and West Europe met in those ununited days, where the Wall had been erected.

To get there, Susan and I travelled by thumb along many highways, staying in youth hostels and small hotels. Breathing new and heady air, we went through Italy and Switzerland to the West German border. But, from the moment a white open-topped Mercedes-Benz drew to a halt to offer us a lift to Berlin, the journey became unreal.

Hitchhiking was not difficult in Germany, even less so with a long-legged girl by your side, people were happy to pick us up. However, the grey-bearded smiling man who drew his Mercedes to a halt was not your average driver. He was in his fifties, with only one good arm. The other, an ugly but effective construction, had the bones separated and bound with flesh. With this giant fork thrust onto the steering wheel, he drove at considerable speed.

"The war, my arm was reconstructed then," he shouted in English, lifting his voice to reach us in the back. "Not bad, it is?"

"Very good," I replied.

"Wow," said Susan. "Does it hurt?"

"No," he said cheerfully. "So, you're going to Berlin?"

"Any problems about that?"

"None. Except that when we cross the border they'll time us. We have to reach the frontier outside Berlin within a certain hour."

"Why's that?"

"To show we've not stopped anywhere. All the land between here and Berlin is East German. No stopping's allowed."

As he swung into the border check point, armed soldiers approached the car. They carried machine guns, wore pistols, were dressed like no one I'd seen in my part of the world. They asked for passports, car papers, opened the boot, made us get out while they removed the seats. Mirrors were wheeled beneath the vehicle, flashlights explored the interior. Finally, with a glance at his watch, a guard waved us on.

"What'd I tell you," our host shouted. "They mean business here."

"Amazing," said Susan. "Is it always like that?"

"Sometimes it's worse. Once they took the panels from the inside of the car."

"Why? You a spy or something?"

"I'm a publisher." The grey-bearded man, whose name was Otto, changed gear. "They don't allow my books in the East, although they're published in Berlin. A madness, don't you think? Berlin is an island of madness in the East."

We laughed, Otto's enthusiasm was contagious. The car picked up speed along the autobahn, following an asphalt avenue between barbed-wire fences, pines that flickered past.

"Why are you going to Berlin?" he asked.

"I want to see the Wall," I replied. "It's hard to believe it exists."

"It exists all right. It cuts the city in half. And it's crazy. In some places it goes through buildings that have been blocked up. In others it looks as if it was made by amateurs. Elsewhere it is like a fortress. With soldiers and earthworks, everything."

"Where's the best place to see it?"

"At Dortmunder Platz. A place that was once in the heart of Berlin. Go there if you want to see the Wall. See what lunacy they've constructed." Otto shook his head in disbelief. "You can cross it, you know. Get through to the other side, but not at Dortmunder Platz. Checkpoint Charlie's the best. They have some good exhibitions there."

"Checkpoint Charlie? Just the sound of it gives me the creeps," said Susan. "What sort of exhibitions have they got?"

"Photographs, mostly. Of people who escaped. Some who didn't."

"That's even creepier."

Otto gave her an admiring glance. "What are you doing tomorrow?"

"Looking around, I suppose."

"I'll meet you in East Berlin, if you like. At thirteen hundred hours in the *Hungarisher* Restaurant in Karl Marx Platz. How's that sound?"

"Wonderful. What can we do there?"

"Have a drink. Then I'll drive you through East Berlin. That's the way to see it. Otherwise, you won't get very far."

"Goodie. This place easy to find?"

"Of course, just go through Checkpoint Charlie and turn right." Otto looked up as we approached an overhead bridge. On it two figures were staring down. He reached into a jacket pocket, produced a packet of ten Rothman's cigarettes. It was one of the many he carried. "Watch this," he shouted, tossing the packet out as we went under the bridge. The figures above scrambled down. "I do that to produce chaos." He laughed. "One of the ways I have of undermining the Communist system."

He drove into the centre of West Berlin, dropped us by the zoo, in front of the burnt and blackened ruin of a church kept to commemorate the city's destruction. Around us was a tinsel-town of new buildings and neon signs advertising lights and bustle.

"Tomorrow," said Otto. "In the eastern sector."

"Got that," replied Susan. "Hungarian restaurant in Karl Marx Whatsaname."

"At thirteen hundred hours."

We found the youth hostel. Susan decided to wash her hair. I set off for the Wall, walking through part of the city that was patched and papered over. New brickwork covered some old wounds, unredeemed buildings carried scars and shrapnel damage, bullet holes on broken facades. I walked steadily for hours, asking directions in the little German I'd learnt on the long voyage around the world. Finally I came to Dortmunder Platz, to the remains of the U-Bahn station that had once been the heart of Berlin.

The entrance to the Underground was choked with rubble, the blown litter of the city, papers dropped by those who'd come to see the Wall. Sun-bleached photographs, behind grubby glass, showed what life had been like before the war. Evening-hour scenes, where business men and late shoppers bustled to gain places on trains that were homeward bound.

No one else was there as I climbed a simple wooden structure, looked out into no-man's land. It was an April evening, late sunlight slanted across hard dry earth. On the far side of the dead zone were watch-towers where guards stared back. Huge bunker-architecture walls carried red and black slogans proclaiming peace, a worker's paradise. Between them and where I stood were rows of dragon's teeth, crossed structures of iron and concrete designed to prevent attack.

As I waited, impressed by the emptiness of the once bustling space, a silky grey creature bounced out, sat blinking in the sudden sun, wiping its whiskers with a paw.

"My God," I said aloud. "A rabbit."

I don't suppose it was that unusual, there were probably hundreds of small animals in the tunnels beneath Dortmunder Platz, pets that had escaped when houses came down and the Wall went up. But after a morning with one-handed Otto, the long walk through the shattered city, the sight of the rabbit was startling. To find one in the erstwhile centre seemed absurdly out of place. Rabbits were rural creatures where I came from, symbols of the countryside. One seen so unexpectedly was a sharp reminder of how fragile our hold is over anything we touch, how easily we can be replaced.

◆ ◆ ◆

The following day, when we arrived at the *Hungarisher* Restaurant in Karl Marx Platz, Otto was waiting in a large and almost-empty dining room. Few of the other tables were occupied, but in one corner huddled a small wedding group, the bride still wearing her gown. Before them a man in a burgundy coat was playing a violin. Sad gypsy songs filtered across the room.

"It's not fair," said Susan. "She looks terribly unhappy."

"Give them these," Otto said to a nearby waiter, holding out a packet of Rothmans with his forked arm. "Tell them I wish them well."

The wedding group waved and raised their glasses when they were given the cigarettes. A little later, Otto drove us through the broad avenues of East Berlin, across enormous squares where half-finished buildings stood solidly on every side. They seemed massive, those eastern structures, when compared to West Berlin's varnish, looked as if they would last forever, never be torn down or have wild creatures scampering through their dust.

"How was the old Revolutionary?" Virginia asked, when I returned from the bar where we'd left Gregorio "Did he tell you much?"

"He didn't really want to talk about the war."

"Was he very old?"

"About the same age as my father when he died."

"That's the whole point of what you're doing, isn't it?" She began making a cup of tea. "If they don't talk to you, or someone like you, they'll die with their memories. They're not going to write anything down."

"I suppose not. All the same, he made me feel like an intruder."

"Well, they don't have to tell you anything if they don't want to." She put mugs on the kitchen table, reached for a biscuit tin. "What did Antonio have to say?"

"He was great. I'd never have got anywhere if it hadn't been for him."

"He's a nice man." Virginia poured tea, sat opposite, looked at me with big eyes. "Now, there's something we've got to talk about."

"What's that?"

"You've, ah, never been baptised, have you?"

"I had my bar mitzvah when I was thirteen, but only to placate my grandfather."

"You know I was baptised a Catholic?"

"What are you getting at? Does Kitty want to be confirmed?"

"Well…" Virginia tried to restrain a smile. "Would you mind?"

"Why should I?"

"You can be quite intolerant when it comes to religion."

"Only when it's bigoted."

"You should hear yourself sometimes." She pushed the biscuit tin in my direction. "Have a chocolate bikkie, they're delicious."

I took one. "I suppose we'd have to get Michael done too," I said.

"The same thought crossed my mind."

So, it was settled, though not without some personal concern. Religion has been responsible for so much misery, so much blood has been spilt in its name. Yet the basic rules we live by, the guidelines that hold our society on course, come down in the name of God. And man's hand, lifted to honour the Lord, has created some of the greatest treasures the world has ever seen.

These thoughts apart, as our children were growing up in a household where there was little bigotry, no pressure for or against any shape or colour or choice of god, where the right to have faith was as acceptable as the right to choose not to, it seemed reasonable they should be like others in the village. That Kitty, and Michael in his turn, should share a day of First Communion with Dolores and Inmaculada, with Jesús and José María. That seemed preferable to denying them the opportunity to explore the mysteries of a religious belief; and to help them understand what is meant when someone is called a Catholic. I hope they'll come to respect all religions and any who follow their paths. As Virginia does, who was baptised a Catholic, yet almost never goes to church. As I do, who was tossed between Protestant and Jew, and ended up believing in nothing at all.

Later, I walked up the hill to the Seminary in the misty embracing dark, to where the lights that flooded the building lifted its delicate red brickwork out of the invading night. I stared up at its majesty and thought of how it had come into being through one man's money and a host of faith. Its presence was undeniable, its cross a symbol of belief. Yet, a symbol that had caused men, who came to pray beneath it, to be shot when war rampaged through this part of Spain.

I breathed deeply, filled my lungs with cold clean air, and hoped that what we were doing for our children was right, that our decision would not shackle them with the dogmatic chains that have caused so much pain and hatred throughout the world, but would give them instead an insight as to how many others lived.

7

The Church's embracing arms

"We'll need godparents," said Virginia, a day or two later. "Anyone come to mind?"

"I suppose Antonio is as close a friend as I've got here."

"That means Chus too. She'll take her responsibilities seriously."

"That's for Kitty, I presume. We'll need a couple more if we're doing the children as a job lot." I caught her look, held up my hands in a gesture of peace. "I *am* taking it seriously, I promise. Who do you suggest for Mike?"

"Chary'd love to. And Rubén, I think he's old enough."

"Good choice," I said. "You ask Chary. I'll talk to Antonio."

When I spoke to our neighbour about being a godfather he was delighted. "That means you're really staying in Comillas?" he said with a smile.

"We are, and we'd like you to give us a hand."

"Of course I will." He settled his English cap firmly on his head. "And so will Chus."

Chary, when Virginia spoke to her, was just as ready to play her part.

Chary, a trim attractive woman with long blonde hair, had become one of Virginia's closest friends. Her father, another whose life the first Marquis of Comillas manipulated from beyond the grave, was a merchant sailor who'd gone off to sea on one the marquis' ships. Chary's husband had also been a mariner, until he drowned soon after their son, Rubén, was born.

When she learnt of his disappearance, in a storm off the Mediterranean coast, Chary drove across the width of Spain, refusing to accept that the man she loved wasn't stranded on some beach alive, awaiting her arrival.

"How could I have done anything else," she told Virginia. "He'd always gone and then come back. I know it was illogical, but it was what my heart told me to do."

"It was very brave of you to go alone."

"I had to see the water that'd taken him. It was the only way I could accept the truth. When I got there I talked to people, others who'd lost the ones they loved. I stood on the beach for a long time, looking at the water. Finally, I accepted the reality and came back home."

"What then?"

"I went to bed." Chary coiled her long blonde hair, pulled it closer, examined the ends. "For a week I went to bed and held Rubén, then decided to live again. There were things I had to do. Rubén had his life before him. So did I. That's why I refused to be a widow. Now, I'm someone living on their own, bringing up their son. Not a widow, dressed in black, only remembering what life was like."

Soon after her return, Chary rented a small shop beside the school, where she sold pens, pads and pencils, all the necessities of classroom life. Plus a kaleidoscopic range of lollipops, chewing gum, sherbet suckers, liquorice and marzipan, making sure that all around her life was a full and delicious mix, showing everyone it was still sweet. Later she opened a charmingly decorated café, where many of her old customers come to drink hot chocolate, sip coffee, gossip and play cards.

When Virginia asked her to be Michael's godmother she agreed immediately. Rubén, at the time of the baptism, a teenager who looked like his mother's younger brother, also happily accepted his role.

"I think up," I heard Virginia say one afternoon. "Or over one ear?"

"I want two long curls at the back," Kitty replied firmly.

"What about the dress?" Chary asked. "You know how important that is. Some of those dresses have been used for generations. Beautifully embroidered, they're works of art."

"Rosalía said she'd lend us a dress."

"Rosalía?" Chary frowned, possessively. "Whose dress would that be?"

"Her niece's. It was used some years ago."

"We'll have to examine it." Chary spread Kitty's hair. "Sometimes they get stained."

"We're talking First Communion, I suppose," I said, entering the conversation. "Shouldn't we get the baptism done first?"

"Everything's under control." Virginia smiled a soft mother's smile. "Don't worry about a thing. I've spoken to Padre Ignacio. The baptism will be Sunday week. After that he'll come up to the house to give Kitty her instruction."

"Instruction, I remember it well. The first school I went to was a convent. What was it? *Who made me? God made me.*"

"You've never told me that."

"Haven't thought of it for years."

"When's her saint's day?" Chary asked, interrupting a conversation that had escaped into English. In Spain saint's days are as important as birthdays, quite often they're when the party is held. "Do you know?"

"No," replied Virginia. "Now, what have we decided about the hair?"

"Two long curls at the back," insisted Kitty. "I want to look my best."

On the day of the baptism we were a mixed group before the font. Our ages ranged from Michael's four to Antonio's seventy and, as it turned out, we *were* a job lot. A pair of twins, babes in arms, was included. They cried when the water touched their heads, causing Mike to giggle.

"Shhh," whispered Virginia, a trace of moisture in her eye. "Don't laugh."

Kitty forced the smile from her lips, looked as grown up as she was able.

As we waited our turn, I glanced around the church, the huge space the villagers had built with their own hands. Behind the altar was a giant cross, designed in the form of twin tree trunks laid one over the other. High above, round stained-glass windows let in rays of coloured light. The Stations of the Cross were simple three-dimensional tablets of Christ's journey. Brightly coloured, they stood out like children's toys. Four towering stone pillars supported the domed ceiling. From behind the congregation came the sound of the choir, their voices lifted in harmony. I caught sight of the baker, his throat open to the Lord.

"Rather nice," I whispered, a crack in my voice. "We're part of it now, I suppose."

"Yes," said Virginia, her smile close to breaking. "We are."

◆　　◆　　◆

Some months later we were in the church again, this time for Kitty's First Communion, an even more enveloping event. Accompanied by school friends dressed in billowing white, small boys in suits and formal ties, each turned out as if they were the dream every parent longed for, Kitty made her commitment to all who came to share the day.

Virginia's father, Peter Whalley, a man not known for parochial attendance even in the church he called his own, flew in from Majorca to be by Kitty's side. At first he seemed uncomfortable amidst the bustling congregation, the free flowing felicitations, but when Kitty took her place beside the microphone and her little voice came out, his creased face broke into a gentle smile, his shoulders eased. He turned and nodded at Virginia. She reached out and took his hand.

"I pray that there are no more wars that children have to go to," Kitty told the overflowing assembly, her small face serious and unashamedly proud. "I pray that there is peace."

The congregation murmured its approval.

When we emerged with the other parents, the aunts and uncles, the grandmothers who could not contain their tears, we felt the ties that bound the townsfolk reach out once again. There was Cuadri, beaming broadly. Eladio, the Book, smiled and raised a hand. The viscount Santiago nodded sympathetically before lighting a cigarette, and other neighbours, shopkeepers, the trades' people we dealt with all shared their joy with us.

"Your daughter was so lovely," someone said in English. "Quite delightful, I must congratulate you both."

We turned to see a small upright woman, whose age would have been difficult to judge. She wore a tweed skirt, a twin set, a necklace of pearls. On her feet were well-polished court shoes. She could have been in Bond Street, or Henley on a rowing afternoon.

"Thank you," replied Virginia. "She did her little bit quite well."

"Perfectly. She speaks Spanish like a native."

"Well, she was born in Majorca. Michael too."

"You do remember me, I hope." The woman's eyes crinkled at the corners. "We met last August at Pepuco's, your neighbour."

"Of course," I replied, grateful for the reminder. "You're Beatriz."

"How is Pepuco, by the way," asked Virginia.

"As well as ever. I expect they'll be in Comillas soon."

Pepuco, a tall architect with John Lennon glasses, came every summer with his family to a house just down the road. Our children played together. On occasion, in the early sun, he would sit and talk, or merely sit, appreciating life's beauty. Zen was a state of mind Pepuco sought constantly, an emotional calm he often achieved while raking the gravel on his drive, forming neat parallel lines, putting everything in order.

"And Isobel?" continued Virginia, referring to Pepuco's wife. "How's she?"

"Coping as well as ever," replied Beatriz with a laugh. "How she manages with all those children I'll never know. Thank God, I had only two."

Beatriz was a countess, part of the flow that brought aristocrats to the town following the king's visit in 1881, to create a social layer now ingrained in the community. Down through time noble families had built or bought, on one occasion moving in a house stone by numbered stone.

"When we met you said you were writing a book," Beatriz added. "How's it going?"

"It's coming along."

"Santiago tells me it's about Comillas. He said you'd talked to him."

"Yes. He was most helpful."

"Did he tell you the story of the church?"

"He said it was built by the people."

"Oh, there's lots more to it than that." Beatriz glanced around her, at the bustle, the children eager to be off. "Come up one afternoon. I'll tell you all about it. It's one of my favourite stories. It says so much about the people here. Their independence, you know."

"I'd like that."

"Good, give me a ring. You know where I live."

We smiled, nodded and parted then took Kitty home to the *fiesta* Virginia and Chary had worked for days to provide. Her friends were there, their long embroidered dresses safely put away as they waded into a vast array of cakes and pastries, buns and tarts, sponges and pies all filled with cream, decorated with brightly coloured icing.

"I feel a bit sick," said Kitty later. "But, I had a wonderful time."

◆ ◆ ◆

The following week I climbed a long curving drive to a house above the town, up past manicured gardens, shrubs recently pruned, to a forecourt overlooking a spread of clustered roofs. The countess, Beatriz, at a table in late afternoon shade, smiled and waved me toward a chair.

"You're be punctual," she said. "You English always are."

"They say it's to do with toilet training."

"Oh dear, I wonder what that means as far as we Spanish are concerned. We're customarily late." She reached for a coffee pot, poured me a cup. "Now, what was I was going to talk about? Please remind me. At my age things just flit across my mind. Was it the church or the war?"

"The church. But, do you remember the war?"

"Of course I do." She laughed. "There's no point in trying to flatter me. I'm almost eighty, way beyond that sort of thing."

"I wonder if we ever get beyond that sort of thing."

"Perhaps not, but you know what I mean."

"Tell me about both," I said. "The church and the war."

"Oh, the war." Beatriz shook her head sadly. "It touched us all, you know. This house was part of the war." She waved a hand at a heavy stone archway framing a cool dark interior, where a bowl of bright red geraniums stood on a wooden table. Beside it was a stand with walking sticks, some with silver handles, others with ivory. It was quiet and secluded, a world away from the deaths in Santander, from Gregorio waiting in the bull ring before being taken to jail. "The place was occupied by both sides," she continued. "The Reds, then the Germans from the Condor Legion. The Germans were better. They left it almost as they found it, didn't take a thing."

"You must have been extremely fortunate."

"We were. Shall I tell you why?"

"Please do."

"Well, when I was a child I had a series of German governesses. We were in Seville then, and my parents wanted me to grow up speaking as many languages as possible. I had governesses from different countries. Later they were English, but the first were German." Beatriz smiled softly, a smile that came from a lifetime of security, the certainty of who she was. "I spoke German better than Spanish then. It used to make my father furious."

"And now?"

"Oh, I suppose I could manage, given a little time." She sipped her coffee, so did I. It was strong and dark and delicious. "Anyway, I was about to say we were on our way here when war broke out. We were in France, actually. We did a lot of travelling then. And when I think of what it involved in those days, it's almost beyond belief. Do you know, I had an aunt who used to visit us from Paris. She'd travel for days on end. Sometimes by train, sometimes by coach, even on horseback. What a performance that must have been. Yet, you know, that same woman lived long enough to see the first man land on the moon." Beatriz laughed brightly. "On the television, of course. She didn't actually witness the event in person."

"I remember it well." I'd been on a bed-and-breakfast holiday in Ireland, where I watched the event at four in the morning. The woman who ran the house kindly left a glass of milk, a plate of biscuits to accompany me while I peered at black and white figures bouncing across a screen on a television below a crucifix outlined by glowing neon red. I recall thinking of the difference each lit space represented. "You aunt must have been very impressed."

"I suppose so, but that was one of the amazing things about her. She took everything in her stride. Anyway, what was I talking about? Oh dear, I tell you, once I begin the thoughts just flit across my mind."

"You were in France before war broke out."

"Ah, yes, and once we were there we had to stay. But, they didn't know about that here. The servants, I mean, who were expecting us. They'd put out everything, awaiting our arrival."

"When you say everything…?"

"The linen, the silver, some of the paintings. Things that were stored when we weren't here. And, of course, the family photographs." Beatriz leaned across and touched my arm. "That's what made the difference, the photographs. Snaps that had been taken wherever we'd lived. The servants always put them out to welcome us, to make the place feel like home."

I glanced back into the dim, wooded interior, past the bright geraniums to the portraits hanging on the walls. Severe men in frock-coats accompanied elegant women, their pretty lips curved into gentle smiles. Here and there my eye caught the glint of copper from old kitchen implements, bed-warmers long since left to cool.

"Of course, once the servants realised what was happening they took the valuable pieces away, and actually hid them in their own homes. They were afraid the Reds would steal them. Very brave of them, when you think of what was going on."

"Weren't they sympathetic to the Republican cause?"

"No, none of the servants around here were. Most of them had been with the same families for years. Their loyalty was decidedly with us. And they were very clever the way they kept the house open all through that first horrible year. It made everything seem better, somehow."

"They weren't tempted to take anything themselves," I asked. "They must have been short of food and, well, to sell something just to survive would have been understandable. After all, Cantabria was with the Republic."

"Not in its heart," Beatriz contradicted firmly, using the slightly admonishing tone she would with a wilful child. "This has always been a conservative part of Spain. We had no trouble that first year, none at all. Even though the Reds did take over the house."

"Were they here when Franco's troops arrived?"

"Absolutely. General Franco came so rapidly the Reds ran off leaving everything behind. Things like a trunk of linen they were going to steal. And the food they were eating on the table. I remember the servants talking about it. There were bowls of lentils, some bread and wine. All left behind when they ran away."

"Like the *Marie Celeste*."

"Exactly like the *Marie Celeste*. There are lots of things about Comillas that are like the *Marie Celeste*. It's a place of many mysteries."

"Then the Germans came?"

"That's right, that's what saved us."

"From what?"

"Well, you must know what it's like when an army comes through where another has been before them. They're flushed with victory. The town turns out to welcome them and, well, sometimes things get out of hand. Soldiers get drunk and become quite nasty. Terrible things can happen." Beatriz's lips formed a thin line of distaste. "That was one of the dreadful aspects about the war, the things that happened afterwards."

"Even in Comillas?"

"Precisely. Some people had many old scores to settle."

"But nothing happened here, in the house?"

"That's exactly what I was saying. A number of German officers were billeted here, and one of them recognised a girl in one of the photographs. She had been my German governess when we were in Seville. And, would you believe it, she'd also been his girlfriend." Beatriz leant back, gazing at me profoundly. "Now, isn't that amazing?"

"Yes, that is amazing."

"When he recognised her he took special care of everything. He even left a letter hoping that we'd send it on. We tried to, but we'd lost contact by then." Beatriz sighed, picked up a brass bell from the table, gave it a sharp ring. "I'm going to have another cup of coffee, fresh this time. Would you like one, or would you rather have something stronger?"

"Coffee will be fine, thanks."

"Very well." She spoke to the elderly maid who answered the call, then settled back in her chair. "Now," she added, with a little sigh. "I'd better tell you about the church before I wander off on another family tale."

"Family tales are fascinating."

"I think so too. But now, the church. Just look at it down there. You get an excellent view from here."

My eyes went to the grey stone spire. From where I sat it rose above red tiled roofs, stood boldly against the black-green chestnuts in the Corro. I could see two faces of the clock. Each showed a different hour.

"That's not the original spire," Beatriz explained. "The first was knocked down by the Reds. They also tore out the altar screen. Such a pity, it was a wonderful piece of work."

"What happened to it?"

"I'm not sure. You'd have to talk to Joaquín about that."

"Joaquín?"

"Oh, you must know him. Must have seen him tearing about on that motorcycle of his."

"Of course." I'd exchanged the time of day with Joaquín, known as Juaco, a big man with an open smile from another noble family, who rode a 1960's Harley Davidson, a flash of red lightning on its tank. "I'd like to get to know him better."

"That shouldn't be difficult. He's the friendliest person I know. He's chums with the gas man, the fishermen, the men who clean the streets. They were his boyhood companions and he always says hello. You'd like Joaquín, he's wonderful company and he knows so much. There's lots that he could tell you." She waved an admonishing finger. "Now, stop interrupting or I'll never get around to the story of the church."

The village church, the *Iglesia Parroquial de San Cristóbal*, was not Comillas' first, Beatriz told me. That had been the building, with its *Romanesque* arches and niches for the dead, now used as the cemetery. Built in the eleventh century, when the town was no more than a fishing village, the first church had served as a centre of worship for hundreds of years, bathed in sunshine much of the time, lashed by storms when the wind roared in from the west.

Its services, however, came to an end one morning when an administrator of the Duke of Infantando, the lord who held Comillas in his reign, rudely interrupted them. Entering with a swagger, the official found the pew he called his own occupied by a determined old lady who refused to budge.

"There are always old ladies, with wills of iron, in these stories," I said.

"We have our uses," Beatriz replied. "Now, please let me get on with this."

The administrator ordered the old lady to move in a voice that was heard throughout the church. Others rose in protest. Murmurs filled the ancient walls. The old lady remained adamant. The official became increasingly irate. Finally, in the midst of the hubbub, the mayor of Comillas rose to his feet and, in words that have rung down the ages, told the old lady she would have to go. It was a demand that changed the course of history.

"Authority siding with authority?" I asked.

Beatriz held up a warning hand, advising me to be patient.

What the mayor went on to say, she continued, was that the entire congregation would also leave, accompany the old lady out of the church, never to return. They would build their own place of worship where all would be equal before the Lord. There would be no pews reserved for administrators, no privileges for anyone. All would be free to sit where they wanted, wherever they wished to be.

"They did it, that's what's so wonderful." Beatriz's face lit with pleasure. "They actually built their church."

"It has that feeling. Big and open to all."

"That's what I love about San Cristóbal, I feel so welcome there. Mind you," she added. "I doubt if it would ever have happened if it had been the duke *himself* that morning. I think he'd have found somewhere else to sit, being the gentleman he was."

"I wonder."

"Oh, you know what minor officials are like. Forgive me for saying it, but especially here in Spain. They're given a little power, not born with it. Sometimes it goes to their heads."

"At least, in this case it had a good effect. The people built their church."

"They did. Even though it took them twenty-five years."

"Where did they pray in the meantime?"

"In that rather nice building the Town Council uses. That used to be called the *Capilla de San Juan*. It was a hospice for pilgrims on the way to Santiago. But that's another story. Now, let me tell you how the new church was built."

Beatriz went on to describe how practically everyone in Comillas lent a hand. Those who had carts with horses, oxen or cows, worked one day a week on the church. Every man who was able, laboured to build the temple. The fishermen, instead of toiling with stone and mortar, gave the earnings from a day's catch to help finance San Cristóbal.

"Even the school children were involved," Beatriz said. "After classes they did whatever they could. And when it came to putting the roof on they carried the tiles. Everyone took part. That's why it's so important. It really *is* the people's church, built with their very own hands." She turned to me, her eyes shining. "Isn't that a wonderful story. It just shows you what people can do."

"It certainly does."

"I'm very fond of everyone here, I really am. Even though they can be quite reserved."

"A lot of people agree with you there."

"You know, there are those who blame the first marquis for that. He gave them so much. Practically everything they wanted."

"I heard someone say he established one of the first welfare states."

"I wouldn't go as far as that, but he gave them a great deal." Beatriz glanced at her watch. "Now, I'm going to walk down to the church to pray a little. All this has made me want to visit it again. Would you care to join me?"

"I'd be delighted to walk down with you. But I doubt if I'll go inside."

"You're not religious? I would have thought, after seeing your daughter there the other day, that you might have been."

"I'm not sure if I believe in anything."

"You must believe in something," Beatriz said firmly. "In our hearts we all do."

"Perhaps," I replied. "Although I'm not quite sure what it is."

We walked down into the town, past hedges overgrown with early blackberry, the sky softening as the day began to fold. Outside the massive moss-clad walls of the church, we stared up at its weathered sandstone, patched with red brick to cover the damages of time.

"Isn't this where the first marquis' mother sold fish?" I indicated the buttressed wall. "Before anyone knew anything about him?"

"She did," replied Beatriz. "She was a relative of mine, you know. The first marquis' brother was my grandfather."

"I wasn't aware of that."

"Oh, you'll find we're all related in some way or another."

"That's what Viscount Santiago told me. He suggested that everything in Comillas was connected."

"I imagine it's like that in every small community."

"But not quite like this. The first marquis made this town. He was like a medieval lord, carving out a kingdom."

"He fascinates you, doesn't he?"

"Certainly for what he accomplished."

"Is that important?"

"I think what we do is much more important than what we are."

"Because it affects others?"

"And leaves something behind."

"Is that why you write?"

"I don't know." I looked into Beatriz's knowledgeable eyes. "Sometimes, I think it may be. Sometimes, I think it's just because I like doing it so much."

"Are you sure you wouldn't like to come inside and pray?"

"No, but thank you for the invitation. And for your time and your stories."

"Oh, I'm just an old woman remembering things. I don't suppose you'll use a word of it when it comes to writing your book."

"I will, I promise."

"We'll just have to see about that. Give my regards to your family," she added, before turning toward the church. "I've enjoyed this afternoon."

I stood a while longer outside the heavy dark wooden doors. Beatriz had gone into a world of new and old, where, some years ago, the priest added Simon and Garfunkel's *Bridge over Troubled Waters* to the hymns sung by the choir. Where simple craftsmanship had pieced together, with the tools at hand, a temple that stands in dedication to the townsfolk's God.

8

Outside looking In

Over the years people have brought a range of living creatures to our door. Fledglings fallen from their nests, kittens, often infested with mites and worms. Once a horse landed nose-first on the doorstep, its metal shoes having slipped on the road outside, causing its cartload of scythed-grass to drag the floundering animal almost into the house. For a few moments the horse struggled then lay still, eyes rolling, breathing like a furnace, waiting for what was next to come. Quickly, neighbours ran to the rescue. Finally, a number of us managed to undo the harness. The horse then struggled to its feet, only to be re-shackled and led away by its owner, its load intact.

Of all the damaged creatures that have been brought to us, we've had least success with birds. They perish readily, in spite of the care we give them, the books we consult, the advice we solicit. At least, we console ourselves, their last hours are spent in relative comfort instead of being tormented by our cats. The only real success we had was with Taxi. A blue pigeon I came across flapping bloodily in *La Fuente de los Tres Caños*, having been hit by a passing cab. Several locals were standing outside the Bar Filipinas, watching Taxi die. I picked him up, took him home and he survived. Having lost the sight of one eye, he spent some time in a cage getting used to the fact that the world had gone dark on one side. When we set him free, after flying in a semi-circle or two, he set off for *La Fuente* once again, where he lived out the rest of his days.

Marcello, the white haired painter we met at Pilarine's funeral, knocked at the door one day with Willie, then a four-day-old pup, eyes tightly closed. Brown and white, a mixture of hunting hound and mastiff, he's grown to become one of Comillas' best known dogs. When we walk down the road he's greeted by almost every passer-by, some of whom give me a nod, while others ignore me completely. But all have words for Willie.

"I hear him crying in the road," Marcello said, in English not unlike my Spanish. "So I bring him. You cure him, no?"

"You found him by the roadside?"

"In a box. He is put there. From car, you know." Marcello shrugged as it's fairly common to dump unwanted animals in other towns, then drive off rapidly while the abandoned creature sniffs out the new terrain. "It happen much. In the vacations when people go away."

"You don't want him?"

"What can I have with a dog? I live in a small *apartamento*."

"We've already got two dogs."

"What difference with a small one more?"

"He's not going to be small for long."

"Perhaps you look for him a home."

That, we agreed to do. Although, I must confess when we finally did find Willie a new master we couldn't bear to part with him. The would-be owner arrived late one night. We were already in bed, and lay very still listening to the bell, but made move to answer it.

"That's them," I said.

"Shh," replied Virginia. "If we're quiet they'll go away."

Virginia, as she always does, nursed Willie through his first frail weeks, sat up at night giving him bottles of warm milk. She chopped up chicken breasts, cooked them in olive oil, fed them to him piece by piece. She scrambled eggs with a little milk to see that he had a balanced diet. She got up at first light to make sure he'd survived the rigours of the dark.

Willie grew so fast that in a very short time he couldn't manage the cat-flap, had to resort to pushing his head through, barking at visitors from below. A not very dignified pose for so large and handsome a dog, although it had its effect. Many a beggar approaching the front door remained in the street calling for help rather than coming any closer. Many a gypsy asking for something to feed her starving children, the husband who is unemployed, her old mother who can no longer work, has had to leap back sharply as Willie's head emerged at toe-level, growling with a fierceness he didn't really intend. In spite of his protests we always give the callers something, help them as we've helped others who've come to our door.

◆ ◆ ◆

Willie's arrival overlapped Bienvenido's presence. The little black hound, who'd chased sheep in Majorca, lived for nineteen years. The third of our trio at the time was Lulu, a breed the Spanish call a *ratonera*, a rat-catcher. A wire-haired bitch, snow white unless she needed a bath, short-legged and looking as if she might be related to a pig. We first saw her one summer, on heat, in the Corro begging wistfully at tables, followed by every dog in town. We spoke to her and some of our sympathy reached out. Within a day or two she'd found her way to the house and, without any hesitation, leapt onto the seat beside us and settled in. She became what the Spanish call an *inquilino*, a lodger, right away.

The three dogs, once Willie was old enough to join the party, accompanied me on my morning runs until Bienvenido's jogging days were over. However, when it came time to leave the running life he did so with a resounding bang, there was never any thought of a whimper.

It happened one morning going up the hill to the Seminary, the red-brick building overlooking the town which used to be the Pontifical University. However, on that particular morning a local farmer had left four sheep grazing on the Seminary's rich green flanks. At first sniff Bienvenido's old grey muzzle lifted and he was off, Lulu and Willie with him.

"Stop," I shouted pathetically. "Don't."

I should have saved my breath. The sheep scattered downhill, Bienvenido in hot pursuit, Willie close behind, running, stopping, looking back to ask why we hadn't thought of this exciting game earlier. Lulu scampered after them as fast as her pig-like legs could carry her.

"Stop," I yelled again. "I'll murder the lot of you."

That cry had no more effect than the first. The sheep ran on, paused when they came to a cottage at the base of the hill, pushed their noses against a low wall, the sole protection between themselves and the barking dogs, then leapt into the garden and ran straight into the house.

Oh God, I thought. What now?

I waited, expecting the worst, but no human head appeared. No windows opened. No one came angrily to the door. I managed to catch Willie and Lulu, who'd remained on my side of the wall, tie them up then looked for Bienvenido. He'd disappeared into the cottage after the sheep. Only frantic barking gave me any idea of his whereabouts.

I had no choice but to go inside, make my apologies to the owner and try not to sound insane. I went into an untidy kitchen to find one of the sheep beneath a table cowering from my old grey-muzzled dog. I got hold of Bienvenido, put him on a chain, was about to knock his head off when he developed a pathetic limp. He took one step, his back legs collapsed and he stared up at me with mournful eyes. I carted him outside and returned for the sheep, expecting, at any moment, to hear outraged cries, to find the householder thundering down the stairs.

Fortunately, no one appeared during the frantic ten minutes I spent chasing sheep in narrow cramped rooms, catching them, carrying them over the threshold, putting them down on their side of the Seminary wall. The last of the herd had found shelter in a bath. It skittered and slipped, defecated before I could grab the terrified animal and take it outside. I rushed back, found a roll of toilet paper, hurriedly cleaned the bath then ran away, the dogs firmly on their leashes.

My God, I swore. Never again.

It was never again as far as Bienvenido was concerned. He never set paw on Seminary turf after that. He was taken to the beach to get whatever exercise he needed, although this became less frequent as time went by. His limp developed and, quite soon, he began to accompany the ninety-three year old neighbour on their mutual shuffle down the road for a combined piddling by the rubbish bins on the corner. In the end, sadly, he was put to sleep.

The Seminary, the Pontifical University of Comillas, where the old dog had his final fling, had lain unused for more than twenty years when we first came to Comillas. A few ageing priests, who were necessary to maintain possession, was all the life within. While they were present the building and the glory it contained, remained in the hands of the Church. Almost empty, slowly mouldering, it lay outside public reach, falling into dark decay, gazing across the countryside like the marquis on his statue.

My first exploration of the interior was with Elena, a bright-eyed girl who became a guide when the doors were finally opened to the public. But that came later, after Pepuco, our neighbour who raked the gravel on his garden path with thoughts of internal clarity, had walked me around the exterior describing the magic within. One afternoon, pushing his John Lennon glasses firmly into place, he suggested we take a stroll up to where one could see for miles.

"Look," he said, when we'd climbed the winding road. "Isn't that a perfect view?"

Below us the town lay in its fold in the hills. All around, noble houses stood on their pinnacles. In a hollow, surrounded by chestnuts, the Palacio de Sobrellano and the Capilla Panteón were fragile gothic structures, pale and golden in the hazy sun.

"Sometimes I look for walks I haven't taken before," Pepuco murmured. "So I can see Comillas from a different point of view. To appreciate its beauty. When you see it from a new angle it's like for the very first time."

We came to the Seminary's massive bronze door. This was the work, Pepuco explained, of the Catalan maestro, Lluis Domènech who, when designing the final stages of the building displayed an attractive sense of humour. Martorell, the architect responsible for the marquis' palace and the Capilla Panteón, had planned the main building, but it was Domènech who added the whimsy that gave the Seminary its charm. Among his contributions was the bronze entrance, a door of Virtues and Vices, where maidens stood above their opposing peccadilloes. Each virtuous figure was Grecian-robed, each pious head surrounded by a simple halo, each pair of feet delicately suppressed the vice below.

"Look at her." Pepuco pointed at a figure in high relief. "She's Generosity. Her hands are empty, she's given everything away. Beneath her is a magpie. The bird that takes whatever it can. In this case, it's got a stolen brooch in its beak."

"That's rather nice." I reached out, as hundreds had before me, and touched the brooch. The metal shone where fingers had rubbed. "It's lovely work."

"Let me explain the others."

Pepuco's fingers traced the figure next in line, Chastity, who stood with her knees together above a crouching monkey, a lustful gleam in its wicked eye. Beside Chastity, the half-turned form of Patience had her hands tied behind her back, her expression calm. She was prepared to wait forever. Beneath lay a coiled serpent, its eager tongue about to spring from parted lips, it's eyes, perhaps, on an apple. Then came Diligence, busy at an anvil, hammer raised above her head. Under her feet a dormouse slept, idling away the hours. Alongside Diligence, Charity presented her open hands, palms empty, all worldly goods given away. Her vice was a chameleon, an ever-changing symbol of self-interest, ready take another's colour if needs be. Last in the line was Temperance, sober, steadfast and demure, holding a loaf of bread, a flask of water. Below her snuffled a prick-eared pig, looking for whatever could be consumed.

"Very clever, no?" Pepuco murmured.

"It's brilliant. But you said there were seven virtues."

"That's the best part." Pepuco stepped back a pace. "Examine the entire door."

I gazed up at the elaborate bronze, the loops and coils of intertwined flower, the exquisitely detailed leaf and bud, the gothic pillars framing the virtuous figures and their vices. The ornateness of the structure, as intricate as embroidery, as arrogant as a medal on a chest, was a stamp of unashamed vanity in the simple red brick wall.

"Impressive, no?" asked Pepuco. "But would you call it humble?"

"Not for a moment."

"Look at the top. Where the angels are on their knees. One on the left. One on the right. What's written there?"

"*Humilidad?* Humility."

"And the vice below? Obviously, the door."

We smiled at the arrogance, the vanity cascading below the kneeling angels, one holding a prayer book, the other a lily. With it the architect had ridiculed all those too wedded to their own creations, too much involved in what they did.

"Domènech was another Catalan. So was Joan Miró. And Salvador Dali. They had a great sense of humour and enormous talent. There's much more inside, but unfortunately we can't see it now." Pepuco pursed his lips regretfully. "I remember when the Seminario closed. When the noviciates were gone, I thought the town had died. It was so quiet. There were no bells from up here. No students in the streets. It was very, very sad."

"Doesn't it ever open?"

"In the summer they have English classes here. During July and August. Children come, stay a week or two. They study English in the morning. In the afternoon they go to the beach."

"A lovely place for a summer camp."

"It is. Sometimes, I come and sit under the pines and look at the sea. The birds fly and the crickets sing in the grass. I lose myself, it's very peaceful here." Pepuco moved on. "Come, we'll go around the back. There's great beauty to be seen everywhere here."

He led me around the side of the building where rows of glazed tiles, bearing the words *Ave María*, shone in the softening light. The grounds held the remains of ornate gardens although, on that afternoon, they were only tangles of unkempt grasses, cactus run to seed, rambling flowering shrubbery, where bramble was taking control.

"It's nothing like it was," Pepuco said. "I appreciate it still, but I regret what it used to be."

"The place was given to the Church by the marquis, wasn't it?"

"Well, yes and no."

He told me, as we walked past palm trees growing out of shaggy lawns, how Antonio López y López had intended to build a school of higher education to the town. Then he discovered that a seminary in Galicia was to move, so he proposed it be re-established in Comillas.

"The Church was very reluctant," Pepuco said. "They didn't think Comillas was suitable. They thought it too remote."

"What persuaded them?"

"The marquis pointed out that Comillas was really very famous. The king had been here. There was electric lighting in the streets. Many of the aristocracy were building houses here."

"That persuaded them?"

"Well, as I said, yes and no." Pepuco smiled. "In the end he said he'd pay."

"That usually works."

"It did, but the marquis didn't see the Seminary. He died before it was begun. His son, Don Claudio, the second Marquis of Comillas took over. He might have become a priest himself if his older brother hadn't died. He was extremely religious. Never had any children. It's said he took a vow of chastity, but nobody knows for sure."

"His wife must have known."

"Well, the expression on her marble statue, in the Capilla Panteón, is certainly quite melancholy." Pepuco said gently. "The second marquis was known as *El Santo*. They say he was once seen in two places at the same time."

"That's considered to be pretty holy."

Pepuco smiled and we walked on, went past a worn football field, where a group of local lads was kicking a ball and shouting. Beyond, its rusty iron roof letting in the sky, was all that remained of a pelota court, left to decay when the Pontifical University of Comillas moved to Madrid. As we gazed at the ruin a large barn owl swooped from the roof and flew away.

"There," said Pepuco, his eyes shining behind his glasses. "Isn't that a nice surprise?"

"Where small creatures find refuge is always surprising," I said, and saw again the grey rabbit bounce out into the sun under the Berlin Wall. "It's quite amazing."

"It certainly is." Pepuco glanced at his watch. "Now, I suggest we have a *corbata*. I suppose you know what I mean?"

"They're a sort of pastry, aren't they?"

"In the form of a bow tie, that's how they get their name."

"I've never tried them."

"Then it's time you did. Come, let's go to Unquera. They make the best there."

We walked away from the splendid building, left behind the other surprises it contained. Pepuco collected his car and drove west through La Rabia, where a wheel-lock dam controlled the level of an estuary. There, black and white swans, ducks, coots, a dozen other species swam and waded in what had become a wild fowl park. In the distance a crane stood motionless on one leg, with little regard for our passing.

"Have you heard how that place began?" Pepuco asked. "About the swan with a broken wing that came to stay?"

"No."

"What about the English House?" He indicated a sprawling bungalow, half-hidden in the trees on the far side of the water. "Where an English mining engineer came to live with a man who turned out to be a woman?"

"Not that either."

"You've a lot to learn." Pepuco drove on, past plane trees, tall and stately with their peeling bark. "You'd better talk to Juaco."

"The man with the Harley Davidson?"

"Ask him about the English House. And the Yellow Bird. He knows all about Comillas."

We came to the main highway, went into the next harbour-town, San Vicente de la Barquera, which lies on the far side of tidal marshlands. In the afternoon glow the water, catching the slanting light, gave back a spread of softly shimmering colour that beamed up as we came down the hill. Behind the town the Picos de Europa, their black-slab peaks holding the last of the winter's snow, rose in majestic backdrop.

"Beautiful, no?" said Pepuco softly "Another nice thing to remember."

"Something to rely on, to put aside for a rainy day?"

Pepuco nodded as he drove slowly through the town, past the fishing boats lined along the quay. San Vicente is one of the biggest fishing ports on the northern coast, he told me, and lamented how flat-fronted apartment buildings made it look like so many Mediterranean resorts.

"That's what's good about Comillas," I said. "There are still lots of old buildings."

"Unfortunately that's changing now. Although we do have many. Did you know the first marquis was responsible for that? They say he kept the trains away from Comillas. He was afraid they'd spoil the town."

"He was able to do that?"

"*Bueno*, it was his railway-line."

We drove on to Unquera, past a long string of buildings, stacks of timber, piles of fragrant pine, went into one of the half-dozen cafes selling the *corbatas* the town is famous for, ate delicate honey and cinnamon flavoured pastries that dissolved in the mouth. Pepuco took his with hot chocolate, I had black coffee with mine. We ate a plateful each, talked a little more, considered our good fortune to be living in Comillas, and shared a richly flavoured moment that each of us could put aside for a future rainy day.

Not only have lost kittens, abandoned puppies and fallen fledglings found their way to our door, quite often mushrooms are bought as gifts, or something to be identified as edible or not. Many of the townsfolk have seen us in the autumn gathering field mushrooms, heavy spongy cep, golden chanterelle, blood-red and purple russula, craggy morels or fresh puff-balls, to accept that we know something about the local crop. Especially when they see us walking through the Corro a day or two later, still in reasonable health.

For our part, we're just as surprised by the locals limited appreciation of the wealth the meadows and pine-groves provide. Some will eat field mushrooms, others brick-caps, delicate, long stemmed fungi that grow on tree trunks, but their prize pick are orange milk-caps that come up under pines. Comillanos are conservative in their taste and smile doubtfully when we pounce on a shaggy ink-cap, whose black and evil-looking liquid makes them wrinkle their noses in disgust.

My interest in fungi goes back a long way, but the high point was the plateful of magic mushrooms I ate in the islands of Fiji. They took me on a tour of wonder, distorted sensations, flights of fancy that were out of this world. At the time, I was working as a geologist in a small gold mining town, married to my first wife, Pamela. Our daughter, Sarah, was five then. She's now a well-known New Zealand potter.

Late one Sunday afternoon we collected a basketful of what appeared to be field mushrooms, even though their colour was darker than usual. This, I attributed to a day beneath the tropical sun. Pamela fried them in butter with black pepper, didn't fancy a taste, so I ate the lot. They were delicious. Half an hour later I discovered they weren't as innocent as they appeared.

When I picked up the remains of my pre-dinner drink to empty it, I saw a beam of light leap from my throat. A tinkling sound filled the air. I looked around to find the room was changing shape. I called Pamela, attempted to describe what was happening, but failed. Between one word and the next my mind became so crammed with images I lost track of what I wanted to say.

"It's the mushrooms," she said. "Thank God, I didn't have any."

"It's…well, it's quite nice, although…it's very busy."

"Do you feel all right?"

"Fine. It's…just…I'm about three feet off the ground."

Pamela called the doctor.

I wandered outside and listened to the sound of the constantly roaring mill, where rock was crushed, gold separated from the ore. I could see through the walls of the building, watch the men as they serviced their thundering machines in the fiery glow of the furnaces, feel the light that shone on their sweating brown backs.

Pamela reappeared and asked if I was getting any better.

I wanted to say I was, but could no longer make much sense. Very patiently, she told me the doctor suggested I drink a glass of salty water in an attempt to vomit. I listened and nodded vaguely. Pamela said she'd prepare the emetic. However, when I tried to drink the mix, I couldn't bear to swallow it. Everything in the mushroom world was too magical to relinquish. For long moments I stood before the lavatory, glass in hand, then poured the contents into the bowl.

Pamela gave the doctor a second call.

I went out again into the warm embracing night. An ambulance was on its way to take me to the nearest hospital, twenty miles to the west, where they'd pump my stomach out. All the while, Pamela handled my condition well, gave little sign of the concern she felt. I, on the other hand, was enchanted by what lay ahead. The mushrooms led me gently, without any of the fear I was to experience, years later, when I walked on Hampstead Heath after eating hashish.

With headlights blazing, white paint shining, the ambulance arrived. Someone opened the back door, but I refused to enter and lie down. I wanted to share the ride up front with the Fijian driver, a man named Moses, who in my condition had skin as white as snow. He was very polite, and all through the winding journey addressed me a *tauraga*, chief. I think he felt it better to placate the madman he was racing through the night. Each time I spoke he drove a little faster, crouched more determinedly over the wheel, eyes fixed on the road.

We flew to the hospital, almost literally as far as I was concerned. I sat back, my hands behind my head, and my arms turned into giant wings. I soared along, swooping around each curve, gliding past native huts with thatched roofs and earthen floors, where dark figures stood silhouette in doorways watching us go by. I could taste the food they were cooking.

At the hospital Moses gratefully handed me over to the medical staff. "Come along," the doctor said cheerfully. "We'll have that out of you in no time."

"It's necessary, I suppose?"

"I think it might be a good idea. I've no idea how much you ate."

He led me to a surgery, placed me face down on a table, fed a rubber tube down my throat. "This won't hurt," he assured me. "We'll just wash it out."

I tried to speak but the tube got in the way. I moved it around my mouth, bit into the yielding surface and it immediately became a rubber bone. I was a puppy, chewing. I growled and showed my teeth.

"What's the matter?" the doctor asked. "Hurting, is it?"

I shook my head.

"Don't bite on it, then. That'll only take longer."

I growled again and tried to bark.

"Ah," he said, with sudden understanding. "Turned into a dog, have we?"

I nodded.

"Well, there's a good boy. Don't bite boney. That's the chap."

I stopped biting, wanted to wag my tail.

"Good. Just a little further and we'll be there." He smiled, fitted a glass funnel to the end of the tube, and reached for a jug. "Now we'll just pour this in. You'll be sick. But, don't worry, we'll wash it all away."

I looked up with worried eyes.

"Just to get your tummy nice and clean." He poured the contents of the jug into the funnel. "There now. When I pull boney out you'll be sick."

I was vastly sick, vomited the black mushroom-mix into a bowl held impassively by a Fijian nurse. She took the magic away, then came back and wiped my face.

"How do you feel?" the doctor enquired.

I thought about my reply for so long, he asked the question again.

"Well," I told him, finally. "I feel very well indeed."

"Then I suggest you get some sleep. I've given you a tranquilliser."

"I think I'd rather stay up and enjoy this. That's if you don't mind."

"Of course. Though it's getting rather late."

"Do you have any books on mushrooms?" My mind was slowing, some of the fantasy was beginning to fade. "Perhaps I could identify what I ate."

"There's an encyclopaedia in my office. Let's take a look at that."

I spent until five in the morning looking at colour plates, carried away less frequently, but at times just as far by the images before my eyes. There was a moment when I distinctly remember being a dog again, sniffing through wet autumn woods with a French farmer, scratching for truffles. By then, the doctor had long since gone to bed.

That night I failed to identify the mushrooms although later, in correspondence with R. Gordon Wasson, the American banker who'd written a great deal about what fungi can do, concluded they were a species of Stropharia, well known for their hallucinogenic effect. But, perhaps, they were best identified by the Fijians themselves who call all mushrooms *viu-ni-tevoro*, the Devil's parasol, presumably because they cover a field of magic dreams.

"How did you get on with Pepuco?" Virginia asked on my return from Unquera. "Is the Seminary as interesting as it sounds?"

"Quite as interesting. Then, afterwards, we went to Unquera for *corbatas*. I suppose you know what I'm talking about?"

"Of course, we girls know about things like that. Kitty and I indulge from time to time. Delicious, aren't they?" She smiled artfully. "How's the book coming along?"

"It's the most difficult thing I've ever tried to write. It's not like *Mexico*. The publishers knew what they wanted there. I thought this might be the same, but it's not."

"Why not?"

"Every time I start something it reminds me of something else."

"Perhaps you're going about it the wrong way. Just a simple history might be enough. About what Comillas is like today, and how it got to be that way."

"That's what I thought I was doing. But it's taken on a life of it's own."

"You'll get it done. You always do."

I went upstairs, made notes about the afternoon, tried to put together a picture of Pepuco and the Seminary resting splendidly on the hill, the emptiness inside, the grounds that were turning into a wilderness. I saw the owl swoop, with slow demanding grace from the ruined pelota court, saw the rabbit by the Berlin Wall. Before I knew it I was somewhere else, in another place, another country, carried by association, taken by whim. And there wasn't a magic mushroom in sight.

After a while I gave up, collected Virginia and we went down to the Corro to sit outside the Covadonga. Eladio, the Book, went past. He waved and smiled.

"I must talk to him again," I said. "About that book he lent me. The one they call a libel, written by the Marquis of Comillas' brother-in-law."

"What did you think of it?"

"I found it fascinating. It's the other side of the story. Rather bitter, but understandably so. There were thirty years of hatred between the two. The brother-in-law claims the marquis took the family fortune. Then, made much of his money from slavery. I must ask Eladio about it."

"Do that, he seems quite happy to talk. Fancy sharing a plate of *rabas*?" Virginia asked, referring to sliced squid, dipped in batter and deep-fried, delicious with a squeeze of lemon, a crust of bread. "Go especially well with your wine. Or would you prefer another *corbata*?"

"*Rabas* would be fine."

The *rabas* were delicious, the flesh succulent, the batter crisp. We were thinking of ordering another ration when I caught sight of Juaco on the far side of the Corro, sitting with a group of friends outside the Samovy. As I watched, he stood to say good-bye.

"I'm going to grab him," I said. "According to Pepuco he knows more about Comillas than anyone else. Maybe he'll help me get something done. Mind waiting a minute?"

"Not at all." Virginia glanced away, and her eyes lit up. "Well, look at that. Here's Kitty and Mike. I'm sure they wouldn't mind sharing a *corbata* or two."

"Save me one. I shouldn't be long with Juaco."

I wasn't, the friendly man with the Harley Davidson said he'd be happy to take me wherever I wanted to go.

9

A Sport of Kings

The morning Juaco arrived on his ancient Harley Davidson, red lightning on the fuel tank, I was standing on the upstairs balcony listening to a pair of neighbours complaining about our moggies, emphasising their remarks in terms of ladies' genitals.

"*Qué coño*," protested one. "The English cats have dug up my garden."

"Mine too. *Coño*, they get into the house."

The word they used was commonplace, means anything from *gosh* to our word for the female organ beginning with the same letter. Uttered in anger or surprise, admiration, joy or even disgust *coño* leaps from the lips of women you might suspect didn't even know it existed. It's heard on radio and television and, like *cagar*, to defecate, together with its companion *mierda*, shit, is part of every child's vocabulary. Even greater mileage is given to *cojones*, balls, which covers a whole range of astonishment, indignation, bravery, impertinence or being utterly fed up. *Más negro que los cojones de un grillo* means blacker than the balls of a cricket, just about as black as things can get. However, none of this is surprising in a freely-speaking country where there's an annual prize for erotic literature known as the *Sonrisa Vertical*, the Vertical Smile, a not too subtle reference to the same item of female anatomy our neighbours were using to express their outrage at the cats.

"Hi," Juaco called when he arrived. He spoke English with an American accent, talked with great enthusiasm about everything. "Coming down?"

"Be right down." I leant over the balcony. The neighbours looked up sharply, then turned away. "Where are we off to this morning?"

"Oyambre," he replied.

"That's the big beach with a ruin at one end and a monument at the other," I said, when I joined him "The monument's for the Yellow Bird."

"That's it, the *Pajaro Amarillo*. It's in memory of the first European flight across the Atlantic. Only the second in the world. The plane came down on the beach. At the other end, that ruin used to be a golf club. Very fashionable in it's day. Come on, I'll take you on the bike if you like."

"Great. I used to have a Honda Three Hundred. Nothing like yours, though."

"What happened to it?"

"I sold it in Mexico. It still had English air in the tyres."

"Why'd you sell it?"

"I didn't want any more trouble. I got stopped by a motorcycle-cop who bit me, as the Mexicans say, for forty dollars. Once was enough."

"The old *mordida*. What'd you done?"

"Got unlucky. It was midday. He was looking for lunch money, so he pulled me over and told me the papers were false."

"Were they?"

"Yes, but they were good ones. Anyway, he was going to take me to the *delegación*. He said I'd lose the bike. So, in the end, we did a deal."

"A forty-dollar deal?"

"When I paid him. He gave me a big salute. And when I asked how to make sure I'd have no more problems with the papers, he smiled and said, *Señor*, just leave forty dollars with them all the time. If anyone asks, hand them over. I guarantee, no more problems."

"That's the system there, I guess." Juaco laughed. "Mind you, it can be pretty bad here. You know what happened to a former president of Cantabria, I suppose?"

"He got six years for embezzlement?"

"Something like that. He beat the jail sentence, but it'll be a while before he can stand again. That's what makes the world go round. Both here and Mexico."

"At least I didn't spend my first night in jail when I came to Spain."

"You did in Mexico? I'll be damned. Where?"

"Matamoros. On the Texas border."

"I know the place. Across from Brownsville. Not a great town."

"Especially in jail."

"I guess not." Juaco handed me a helmet. "Hop on, let's go over the hill. From the top you get a wonderful view of the beach."

He kick-started the bike and we set off, up around the corner we call Fishermen's Bend, where rusted cranes, that haul up the weed harvested from the sea, stand like relics on a builder's site. We roared along a back road, beneath the stately Seminario, its windows shining in the morning sun. It looked like a space ship coming in to land. We went on between long rolling hills, the sea crashing in beside us, spun through eucalyptus planted by local government to be cut down and pulped for paper. The breeze of our passing brought up the silver undersides of their leaves.

"You comfortable?" Juaco shouted.

"I'm fine."

We came out behind the hilltop hamlet of Trasvía, where Chary lived; where, like a golden scarf along the shore, the sands of Oyambre stretched far away.

"Beautiful, isn't it?" said Juaco. "One of the best beaches in this part of the world."

"We love it. In winter we walk the dogs and collect firewood."

"It's a good place to surf. Even though, we lose a tourist or two every summer. Mainly when they've had a damned good lunch."

"There aren't many buildings here."

"It's protected park land. The Queen came to Comillas a few years back when the deal was signed. That made the local farmers madder than hell."

"Why?"

"They're caught in the middle. As it's a park, they can't sell their land for holiday homes. As farmers, their milk production's been cut by the Common Market."

"What can they do about it?"

"Well, you know what local politics are like." Juaco grinned broadly. "A bit of give and take. Some of the land will be sold for houses. Most will remain protected. For a while, at least. Come on, let's go down to the beach."

We rode the Harley down to the ruins of the golf club at the near end of Oyambre, where crumbling brick, rotting timber and broken tile surrounded a massive structure that formed the core of the building.

"That's an old whale tower," Juaco said. "The club house was built around it. They had them all along the coast?"

"I've heard the Cantabrians were great whalers. These days we feel sorry for the whales, but they must have been brave men."

"They had fantastic courage. Towers like this were signal posts. When they saw a whale they lit a fire. Then ran down to their boats."

We got off the bike. Juaco led the way toward the ruin, climbed through a barbed wire fence to scatter a dozen sheep.

"The whales they went after were called *right* whales," he said, as we approached the tower. "Know how they got that name?"

"Haven't the faintest idea."

"They were right in every way. They swam slowly, you could catch them in a rowboat. That's all the hunters had, in those days. Rowboats with eight men crews. Six on the oars, a tiller man and someone at the prow with a harpoon. Thrown by hand, so he had to be good."

The whales were also right, Juaco went on to say, because they floated when they were caught and could be towed back to shore. Right, because the blubber they carried was rendered down to oil and used to light the lamps of Spain. Their skins were as good as leather, and the bones taken from their jaws could be carved like ivory. Even the thin slats of baleen they carried in their mouths to filter out plankton, krill, the tiny prawns they fed on, was used in the fashion business. Its firm elastic strips held ladies' waists in shape

"There's a rock in the port at Comillas called the Whale Stone," Juaco added. "You must have seen it. A flat outcrop next to the road."

"Below the fishermen's sheds?"

"That's it. They towed their catch in there, cut them up and rendered them down. They had special shoes with claws, so they didn't slip while they were working on the carcass. By God, that must have been a sight. I bet they had a *fiesta* each time one was caught." Juaco tapped the moss-encrusted tower "That's what this was for. To get things going when a whale was seen. Come round to the front."

We made our way through bushes to face the spread of Oyambre. On either side the sands reached out like golden arms. Out at sea, the water was smooth blue glass.

"I suppose whaling's how the Cantabrian sailors developed the talent they used at Seville," I said. "When they sailed up the river and broke the chain the Moors put there."

"Who told you that?"

"Eladio, he was explaining the Cantabrian shield."

"*Eladio el Libro*. He's a good person to talk to. He and the man they call *El Rey*. Between them they've more books about this part of the world than all the libraries put together. Have you spoken to *El Rey* yet?"

"Not yet."

"You'd better, he's getting on." Juaco peered through a wrecked golf-club window at peeling panels, shards of concrete on ruptured floors, scattered bricks that had tumbled from the walls. "By God, when I think what this place used to be like. The king came here, you know. I've got photos of him standing right where I am now."

"That would have been...?"

"Alfonso the Thirteenth. Son of the king who visited the Marquis of Comillas. The son his father never saw. The last king we had in Spain before the one we've got now." He turned from the broken room. "Funny how the royal family kept in touch with Comillas. Alfonso's younger daughter, the present king's aunt, came here every summer until she died, a year or two ago. She had an apartment above the Corro."

"I met her once. My only contact with royalty."

"Really, where was that?"

"At Rosalia's, we were having coffee. She ordered *churros*. Mike started talking to her. She offered him one."

"She was a very lovely lady."

"Yes." I recalled her sitting in a yellow plastic chair, simply but elegantly dressed, not a hair out of place. "She said I looked like Van Gogh. And laughed when I told I still had both my ears. Would she have come here too?"

"As a child, I guess. They used to race along the sand in boat-like things with wheels. *Aeroplage*, they called them. Bicycle wheels and big sails. When the tide was out they'd be off, hell-for-leather along the shore. I've got photos of an aunt of mine in an *aeroplage*. If you ever want any pictures for your book, just ask."

"I'll take you up on that." I looked over undulating scrubland, where the ancient fairways once witnessed the sport of a king. "Was Alfonso the Thirteenth much of a golfer?"

"I don't know. His friends would have been, though. This place was the first in the country. Some of the best professionals in Spain worked here in the summer months. And the clubhouse had a great restaurant. That's probably why the king came here. It's said he liked his food." Juaco paused thoughtfully. "It wasn't long after that he left the country. Never came back. Some say he went to avoid the war. Others think his going only made things worse."

"History books don't rate him too highly."

"The sad thing is, Alfonso the Thirteenth didn't have much luck in life. He never saw his father. On his wedding day he was almost killed by an anarchist's bomb. If it hadn't caught on the power cables, he and his bride would've been blown to bits. She was your Queen Victoria's granddaughter, by the way. He didn't have much luck with his children either. Not on the male side. His first son gave up his right to the throne by marrying a *Cubana*, a Cuban woman, then killed himself in a car crash without leaving any kids. His second son was deaf, *Jaime el Mudo*, and nobody thought it was much of an idea to have a deaf king. So he gave up his right to the title. In the end the third boy, Juan, became heir to the throne, then got pushed aside by Franco."

"You feel for him, don't you?"

"I guess I do. My father knew him well."

"How long was he king?"

"About thirty years. A long while, with not too much to show for it. He never had it easy, you know. For a lot of the time half the country was against him. They wanted a republic. And that's what they got when he went to Rome."

"He never came back?"

"Only what was left of him. A few years ago his remains were returned to be buried."

"It's a shame what this place's become. Like the Seminary over there."

"That might be restored, from what I've heard," Juaco said, his eye on the majesty on the distant hill. "This place too, you never know." He lifted a hand to shade his eyes, his face touched by regret, and turned to stare at the wreckage of the golf club, the broken walls, the greenery, the sunken roof. Only the whale-tower remained intact above the ruin. "Come on, let's get back. I was going to take you to the monument at the far of the beach, but we'll save it for another day."

"The one for the Yellow Bird?"

"Yes, that's a great story. The way the French aircraft got off course. They were headed for Le Bourget, you know, but came down here." He smiled wryly. "Come on, glass of wine at La Rabia's what I need now." He began walking back to the Harley Davidson. "I've talked too much. The damned golf club's taken too much time."

"It's not all lost," I said. "Severiano Ballesteros, one of the best golfers in the world, is from this part of Spain."

"You're right, he's a Santanderino, keeping the tradition alive. And this place isn't dead yet. They're talking of opening a nine-holer here. I hope so. Now, let's get that drink."

He kicked the motorcycle into life, we were off again, and his expectation was to come true. Within a year a small course was opened at Oyambre. Later, Ballesteros himself inaugurated a large and expensive complex he'd designed at La Revilla, a few miles away. The swish of clubs and the click of golf balls are still very much alive in Cantabria.

"I'm being passed from hand to hand," I said to Virginia, as we sat in the garden with an evening drink. "What began with Cuadri has taken off."

"You mean he unblocked more than the loo?"

"Seems like it, Juaco introduced me to an old chap who's also interesting. Cypriano, he runs the hotel at La Rabia. We went in for a glass of wine and a *tapa* of anchovies."

"Where did the wine come from?"

"The Penedés."

"It's very good there."

"You know a lot for a person who doesn't drink."

"I should. I'm always buying it for you."

"Very true." I reached for my glass. "Cypriano is someone else the Marquis of Comillas controlled from beyond the grave. He spent most of his life on one of the old man's ships, working behind the bar. Perhaps that's why he runs one now."

"What did he talk about?"

"The wild-fowl park."

"Oh, it's lovely there. They've got some wonderful birds. I take the children down quite often." Virginia sipped her Diet Pepsi. "How did you get on with Juaco?"

"He's great company. Gets completely involved in what he's talking about. His mother played golf on the old course there. Probably with the king."

"He's a marquis himself, you know."

"Beatriz told me that when she was talking about the Germans who were in her house during the war. But, I can't remember what he's marquis of. I'm hopeless with people's surnames and titles. You, on the other hand, remember everything about everyone."

"I grew up in a house where the occasional baroness or viscount popped in. Some of them were relatives. I had to remember or get told off."

"Your father said there's a Whalley signature on the death warrant of Charles the First. That's worth remembering."

"That was an Edward Whalley. I think he was Cromwell's cousin."

"We come from different worlds."

"Makes it interesting though, doesn't it?"

A few days later I went back to see *Eladio el Libro*, having slowly made my way through the *libelo* he'd lent me, the bitter biography of the Marquis of Comillas by his brother-in-law. When I arrived the gentle man was sitting in his book-lined room, a pot of coffee, a plate of little sponge cakes on a low table. He rested his feet, shoes unlaced, beside the coffee, smiling easily.

"So," he said. "Now you're familiar with the dark picture of the marquis."

"How much do you think is true?"

"Well, there are two sides to every coin, and every person."

"I was surprised it was ever published. Considering the power the marquis had."

"It came out a few years after his death. His son tried to stop it, I believe. But, as always, a few copies escaped. That's why I have a photocopy only."

"It's pretty critical, especially when it talks about the way the marquis began. His brother-in-law claims he virtually stole his father-in-law's fortune. That's a very different story from the complementary versions."

"The complementary versions?" Eladio smiled. "Your Spanish is improving."

"Thank you, reading this has helped." I tapped the book. "What surprised me is that the brother-in-law openly calls the marquis a pirate, a swindler. Is there any way of finding out exactly how he made his money?"

"Perhaps if you went to Cuba. But, as I said, history belongs to those who write it."

"Are there no records here?"

"None. I've enquired at the *Ayuntamiento*, in the mayor's office. They say all records went to Santander. I asked in Santander, but they tell me everything was destroyed in the great fire in nineteen forty-two, when so much of the city was burnt. There may be something somewhere, who knows? But, tell me, why is it important? Does it matter how the marquis made his fortune?"

"It might make him easier to understand."

"It's very difficult to understand a man as driven as he was. If you listen to his friends they will tell you one thing, his enemies another." Eladio poured two cups of steaming coffee, offered the sponge cakes. "Take a *sobao*. They go well with coffee at this time of day." He glanced out into the late November afternoon, at the shadows giving new shape to the walls of the church. On the far side of the Corro the chestnut trees had lost their leaves. "Did you know his statue was pulled down during the war?"

"The one with him staring out to sea?"

"That's what we have today. Made of stone. The original was bronze." Eladio dipped a *sobao* into his coffee, chewed it thoughtfully. "On the original statue there were Negro slaves. The sides had shields with rampant lions. During the war the metal was ripped off and taken away."

"Who did that?"

"The Reds, of course. Republicans. Socialists. Communists. They went by many names. The same people who took the bells from one of the towers in the

Seminario. Those who pulled the spire off the church. Whoever did it, Reds were given the blame."

"What happened to the statue of the marquis?"

"No one knows. The bronze was taken away. Some say the metal was used to make cannons to fight the good fight. Others believe it went to a junkyard. Whatever happened, the marquis, the slaves and the rampant lions, all met the same fate. In the end there was no difference between them." Eladio smiled widely. "That's true democracy, isn't it?"

"All in the same melting pot?" I returned his smile. "What about the church tower? What happened to that?"

"The stones from the tower were used to build a house."

"Where?

"A little out of town. *La Casa Sagrada*. So you see, what does it matter how the marquis made his fortune? What's important is what he gave to Comillas. What we have today."

"Most people can accept that, but not his brother-in-law. He accused him of being a slave trader." I drank a little coffee. "Do you think the marquis built so much here to recompense? To make up for what he'd done somewhere else?"

"Not for a moment. He wanted to make Comillas appropriate to what he'd become. He changed the town to show the world what he'd achieved." Eladio shrugged. "My life was also controlled by the man. And, today, my nephews criticise me for it."

"Why?"

"I spent my life in the tobacco industry. Another of his ventures. My nephews say I sold cancer. The brother-in-law says the marquis sold human flesh. *Bueno*, that was the business of his day. Selling tobacco was mine."

"Not quite the same."

"Not at all the same. However, I'm not speaking about what was right, but about what was legal. Today it is legal to sell armaments. Mines you can leave in the ground to blow off children's feet. That's not right either. But it's *legal*. Selling slaves in Cuba wasn't illegal until eighteen eighty. So anyone in that trade, at that time, was merely being commercial."

"That's difficult to accept."

"I don't accept it either." Eladio spread his eloquent hands. "But that's not the point. All we can do now is live, as best we can, with what we have."

"You don't want to change anything?"

"I'd like to change a great deal in the world, but *I* don't have the means. Nor does anyone these days. Neither kings nor queens, prime ministers or presidents.

Not even the Pope. It's not like it was when the marquis was able to do what he liked. We live in different times, and sometimes I wonder if that's worse or better." He stretched and stood, went to a side table, picked up two small glasses and a bottle. "*Bueno*, we've talked enough of serious things. Let's take a *chupito* of this excellent brandy. It is soft, just right after coffee." He poured a little into each glass, handed me one, held his up to the light. It glowed. "Now it's your turn to talk. What have you discovered in Comillas?"

"That has nothing to do with the marquis?"

"Not a word. Tell me something I've never heard before."

"Difficult."

"Come on, you've been talking to all sorts of people. Some of whom I'd never meet even if I spent another lifetime here."

He was right. For so small a town the social layers are distinct. Townsfolk pass daily in the street, each knowing who the other is, yet barely exchanging a word or a nod. Some sit on summer mornings, taking coffee at the Samovy, without thinking of walking twenty steps to Rosalia's. There are those who go only to Oyambre, never to Comillas' beach and, once established on their selected spot, are reluctant to move to any other section of the sand.

Certain neighbours are in each other's houses two or three times a day. Others can't bring themselves to enter the house next door. We've invited friends to our small Christmas parties who, with looks of genuine embarrassment, have refused for fear of being out of place among the Juacos, the Pepucos or their bank manager. They'll complain bitterly if something goes wrong with their account, yet can't face the same person over a glass of wine or a piece of Christmas cake.

"Come on," urged Eladio. "You must've discovered something about Comillas I've never heard of."

"How about *Felipe de las Placas*?" I asked, and saw Eladio smile warmly, shake his head. "He knows every number-plate in town? He might be, what's the Spanish term, lacking a summer, but he knows everyone who owns a car. Not by their names, but by their number plates."

"That says where his eyes are when he walks. Who told you about him?"

"One of Virginia's friends."

"Has she met this Felipe?"

"Yes, and when she was introduced, he said, 'Ah, you are S nineteen ninety-six, AF. The dark green Ford Fiesta.'"

Eladio smiled widely.

"Now, it appears there was a man who borrowed a car and drove to Madrid. He parked it, went into a bar, drank a little too much, and when he came out there were two cars exactly the same. Both had S-plates. Both were from Santander."

"Was he seeing double?"

"No, what he saw was real. There *were* two identical cars. However, he was sober enough to telephone Comillas, contact Felipe and ask which car he'd borrowed. Felipe knew immediately, he didn't have to ask him twice."

"Very good." Eladio poured more brandy into my glass. "I've never heard that one before. It's surprising how much you *never* learn. We live in little worlds, you know. Except you, who is discovering Comillas."

"Perhaps that's what I'll call my book."

"*Discovering Comillas?*"

"That's what happened. We knew nothing before we came here."

"When you've written it, and it's translated into Spanish." Eladio gave me a kindly smile. "Because, even though your Spanish is improving, you must write in English, then have it translated. When that's done, give it to me and I'll read it if you like."

"I'd welcome that."

"I'll treat it as my own, help to make it as I'd want it to be."

"That's very kind of you."

"Not at all, perhaps I'll discover even more about this town."

I had a further brandy with Eladio then left his book-lined room, his view of the chestnuts shadowed in the late and changing afternoon. I walked the long way home, over the hill between the town and the sea, through the park where the statue of the marquis stared from his masthead out to sea. His body might lie in the Capilla-Panteón, the miniature cathedral below, but his image, one hand in his frock coat, Napoleon-style, towers above the town.

Antonio, our neighbour, who sailed in the marquis' ships for more than thirty years, at the time the largest fleet of steamships in the world, told me that when the vessels passed the statue they blew their sirens in acknowledgement of the local lad to whom they owed their being.

I went home and, as I sat before a fire of driftwood from that same unending sea, the telephone rang. It was the London publisher, who'd commissioned the book on Mexico, asking if I'd do another about Australia.

"I'd love to," I replied. "Although it's a while since I was there."

"I'm sure you can bring yourself up to date."

"I'll come to London to do that."

"The only thing is, time's rather short."

"That's all right. I'm on my way."

I went to London, spent days in the reading room of Australia House, obtained help from the cheerful librarians there, and once again the half-formed thoughts for my book about Comillas were pushed aside. But, at least, it now had a title.

"I'll do it one day," I said to Virginia, when I phoned from London. "In fact I've got a few more ideas, working on this."

"I'm sure you will," she replied. "Come back soon. We miss you."

10

The Builder's Follies

Soon after my return, on a fine rich autumn day, Cuadri was back, not in the bathroom but the kitchen, studying Virginia's sketch of how she wanted her workplace altered.

"*Bueno*," he said, turning the drawing the right way up. "No problem with this."

"I want a bigger bench," Virginia said. "This kitchen was made for a dwarf. I have to get on hands and knees to do the washing up."

"Well...." Cuadri caught my eye, shrugged to show how women were. "We'll tear everything out and start again." He was back on favourite territory, ripping things apart. "All this." He waved a hand at the working surface, an uneven mixture of low sinks, roll-in gas cooker, brickwork where a wood-burning stove had been, a wooden structure I'd made to take the bottled gas. "Then, we do it again, from new."

"The way I've drawn it," insisted Virginia.

"Of course." Cuadri's eyes went to the sketch again. "What's this?"

"An electric stove. With a vitro-ceramic surface. In an old-fashioned style."

"What taste." There was admiration in Cuadri's voice. "Will you get it?"

"We'll get it. What we'd like from you is a price for the work."

"*Bueno*." Cuadri looked at me for confirmation. "What about the sink?"

"You can get the sink."

"The taps?"

"The taps also."

"I have a very good sink. And taps. I bought them for my mother, but we didn't use them."

Virginia gave me a dubious glance. "Why not?" she asked.

"They didn't fit. Not in the corner where she wanted it."

"Like the angel on the cemetery?"

"Not exactly the same." Cuadri gave a short barking laugh. "The taps are modern."

"So's the angel, it's timeless." Virginia pointed at her sketch. "Now this, the bench, I want it in marble."

"Very pretty. Easy to keep clean."

"We'd like you to get that too."

"No problem."

"Underneath." Virginia's fingers traced the row of doors she'd carefully drawn. "These are cupboards. Can you do those too?"

"I have an excellent carpenter."

"Good. When the price is agreed you can start."

Again Cuadri's eyes came to me seeking approval. I smiled, gesturing that as far as I was concerned everything was fine. He nodded once, then limped around the kitchen, measuring everything in sight.

A week later his men were at work. They arrived on a day when mists filled the surrounding countryside, pockets of cloud lay deep in the hollows around the town. Comillas, in its shelter of hills, was packed in cotton wool. Out of the haze a truck swirled up, came to a rattling halt, scattering cats in all directions, some of whom didn't return until the work was over, the sound of hammering had ceased.

"Is Cuadri here?" asked a rangy youth with a gold rings in his ears. He turned out to be Jesús, one of the master builder's hands. "Or do we wait?"

"You might have to wait a while," I replied. "He said he was coming two days ago. But, there's been no sign of him yet."

"He's coming," Jesús replied cheerfully. "I've talked to him. He's coming." He turned to his co-worker, a huge crouching man who held his head at a curious angle, had several missing front teeth. "Manuel," he called. "We'll wait."

Manuel nodded and climbed back into the truck

After a while Cuadri drove up, began shouting instructions from the driver's seat. Shovels, picks and two-kilo hammers were unloaded from the truck. Jesús and Manuel carried them into the kitchen, from which everything we thought valuable had been removed.

"We'll take all this out," Cuadri said, limping into the room, waving a hand at the uneven working surface. "The sink?" He turned to me. "What do we do with that?"

"You can give it to some old lady, if you like."

"You don't want it for fishes in the garden?"

"No, all we've got are tadpoles. They won't be round for long."

"Jesús might like it. He's building a house."

"He is welcome to it."

"*Bueno*," said Cuadri. "Let's begin."

They did, with a density of dust that made Virginia reach for her asthma inhaler, shouts and continual cursing that drove us eventually to Rosalia's where we sat drinking coffee and reading the morning paper, which every bar and café provides. However, before leaving, Virginia had to tape-up a gash on Jesús' forehead that left blood running down to his chin.

"You must be more careful," she told him. "There are bits of brick flying in all directions. What's more, the air's full of dust."

"That is bad?"

"*Fatál*. Especially for people like me who are asthmatic."

"I'm asthmatic too," Jesús said, lighting another cigarette.

"Then you shouldn't be doing work like this. Not without a mask."

"A mask?" Jesús shrugged. "Well, Cuadri..."

"If he won't get you one, get one yourself."

"*Bueno*." Jesús glanced at Manuel, who smiled as he tore down another piece of wall with a crash. "Perhaps, I will."

"I don't know why you use Cuadri," Virginia said later. "He comes in like gangbusters and he's not very nice to his men."

"Gangbusters?"

"You know what I mean. There must be other *contratistas*, as they call them."

"I talked to one once. He said he'd give me a price, shook my hand and I haven't seen him since. Anyway, I like Cuadri. He's got some good ideas and I don't suppose he treats his workers any worse than anyone else. What's more there's an emotional bond between us."

"What emotional bond?"

"He covered me with shit."

"Good God," said Virginia disgustedly. "I don't think I'll ever understand men."

After two days of crashing, levelling and wheeling rubble into a pile near the front door, Antonio, our neighbour, pushed his nose into the mess. "*Reformas*," he said, his English cap as firmly on his head as a contractor's helmet. "What are you doing?"

"Replacing a section of the kitchen," I told him. "I hope they're not making too much dust."

"It's not bad." Antonio shrugged. "Chus has to clean the front steps twice a day, but she's used to that. It won't be for long, will it?"

"They've done most of it." I looked at the sky, a little watery sun was peeping through. "I wonder if we could go octopus fishing? That'd get us away from this."

"Not any more. Now it's a *fooking*," Antonio said sadly. "The Guardia, they've made it a *fooking*. You need a special licence."

"Can we get one?"

"They're only for professional fishermen. Those who go out in boats."

"But they don't go where we fish for *pulpo*."

"They don't. That's what's absurd about it. They don't fish by the rocks, and we're prohibited. *Pulpos* are shellfish, even though they don't have a shell."

"That's true enough. But, couldn't we risk it?"

"A friend of mine did that. Now he's got to pay a fine. Three Guardia hid in the grass, watching him for ten minutes. He thought they were boys playing truant, and nearly asked them why they weren't at school. But, when he caught a *pulpo*, they ran out and took it away."

"Didn't they have anything better to do?"

"He asked them that. They said they were only doing their job."

"I suppose they were. Isn't there anything that can be done?"

"There's talk of manifestations. Letters will be written. I don't think it'll make much difference." Antonio shrugged, a gesture without hope. "But, for us, it's a *fooking*."

Some weeks later a demonstration was held in front of the local Guardia Civil. A few token octopus were caught and displayed. Sea urchins, also on the prohibited list, whose eggs in April are rich and tasty, were strewn around by a group of sun-baked fisherman, grinning self-consciously for the camera. But, as Antonio predicted, nothing changed. Now the Guardia can be seen, when tides are low, on cliff-tops scanning the coastline. Looking through their binoculars for townsfolk following a tradition that for generations has given men hours of pleasure and, in times of hardship, food for meagre tables.

The Guardia caught me on one occasion with two *pulpos*, and were quite pleasant about the transaction. They relieved me of the smaller, and I was duly fined. Since then octopus fishing has become a game of a different sort. I feel, furtively searching for the eight-legged delicacies, one eye on the cliff-tops, the other on the prey, that I should be wearing a poacher's jacket with pockets big enough to hide octopus.

"Anyway, let's get out of here," Antonio said, as there was further crashing in the kitchen and more brick dust swirled into the already-laden air. "Let's go and look at the Capricho. It's a building that always makes me smile."

"They're working there also, aren't they?"

"Yes, it'll soon open as a restaurant," Antonio said, as Jesús swing a metal hammer and the house shook. "Their *reformas* are almost over. You'll be happy to see a finished job."

"I'm glad it's being done up. It was a wreck the first time we saw it."

"It was rotting. In a dreadful state for one of our treasures." Antonio smiled. "You know, when it's opened it'll be unique. There can't be any other Gaudí that's been restored with Japanese money, then turned into a restaurant selling Spanish food."

"You're right. Let me get Virginia, she'll want to see what they've done."

We set off beneath a watery sun, leaving Cuadri's men up to their ears in wet cement, the dust and rubble of their making. It felt good to be walking away.

When we first arrived in Comillas, the Capricho de Gaudí was in sad decay. The same Emilio, who gave us a private tour of the marquis' palace, had shown us around the neglected structure. The whimsical building, its colours soiled, its rounded walls near collapse, was losing its beauty. Sunflower tiles were falling off the walls, the rolling ironwork was rusting. Water stains marked the once glowing facade, splintered timbers held broken glass in twisted window frames, and a sheet of mildewed pink plastic covered the sunken roof.

"Who owns this now?" I'd asked Emilio.

"Someone in Torrelavega," the squat man replied. "He doesn't care what happens. Look at it. It's a shame. A shame to us all."

"When was it built.?"

"The Capricho de Gaudí was built between eighteen eighty-three and eighty-five." Emilio went straight into one of his well-practised monologues. He was, after all, keeper of the keys. "It was built for Don Máximo Díaz de Quijano, a relative of the Marquis of Comillas. But was paid for by the marquis. The architect was Antonio Gaudí y Coronet, who was very famous for buildings, especially in Barcelona."

"He's now famous all over the world."

"Yes, Gaudí is very famous," Emilio went on smoothly. "Here, his design was supervised by Cristóbal Cascante y Colom. Cascante, another architect from Catalunia, was a friend of Gaudí's. It was Cascante who designed the statue for the

Marquis of Comillas. Cristóbal Cascante y Colom, like Antonio Gaudí y Cornet, was a very illustrious architect."

"Who was this Díaz de Quijano? The man the Capricho was built for?"

"Don Máximo Díaz de Quijano was brother-in-law to Antonio López y López, the first Marquis of Comillas. He was poet and a lover of the arts." Emilio's eyes flickered toward Virginia. "He was a man with very delicate tastes, if you know what I mean?"

"Of course," Virginia replied. "But, will anything be done about this? The state it's in is deplorable."

"Who knows. We hope, but there are no plans."

Plans, however, must have existed. Quite soon after that work began with money from the Japanese, a circumstance that caused many heads to shake in disapproval, in spite of the fact the Capricho was fast moving beyond repair. They were afraid that a local treasure was passing into foreign hands. But, gradually, as work progressed, and a restored Capricho began to rise from the fallen timbers of the old, the protests died. It was clear that without outside help Gaudí's jewel would have remained a home for rats, a feeding ground for termites.

By the early 1990s, the sunken roof had been rebuilt, rotted woodwork replaced. New handmade tiles, bright with sunflowers, were inlaid to match those that had broken off, cracked or simply been stolen. Marble floors were re-done completely. Decayed balustrades and wall surfaces were repaired with something very close to the original stone. The Capricho began to glisten again, to shine with its former glory, which is what Antonio, Virginia and I found when we walked around the almost-finished building.

"It's lovely," Virginia said, her eyes alight. "How different from the first time we saw it."

"This work's very good." Antonio nodded approvingly. "You know, I've lived in Comillas all my life, but I don't come here often. They say it's for tourists, but really it's for us all."

We walked around the colourful confection that looked like a rounded sponge with rich fillings oozing out. The sponge gave a curve to the Capricho's corners; the fillings were layers of sunflower tiles binding the length of the structure. Red-tiled roofs sloped up to chimneys in the shape of cup cakes, and all around were balconies and overhangs, wrought-iron balustrades stretching like musical scores. Above, rose a Moorish tower, a green, white and vermilion onion-top, reaching toward the sky. Held by slender, almost invisible columns, it seemed to dance in the air. The building was indeed a *Capricho*, an architectural folly, designed to make everyone smile.

"What a shame Gaudí can't see it now," said Virginia. "It looks so good."

"He never came to Comillas," I said.

"He's here now," said Antonio. "Come, I'll introduce you." He led us to one side of the building where the bronze figure of a small bearded man, wearing a suit and tie, sat gazing up at his building, a look of quiet pride on his face. "Señor Gaudí," Antonio added quietly. "I would like you to meet my English friends."

"How wonderful." Virginia laughed. "Who thought of putting him there?"

"I don't know. Perhaps the Japanese."

"Well, bless them if they did."

◆   ◆   ◆

The architecture of Antonio Gaudí y Cornet, now the most famous of the Catalan *modernistas*, was not fully appreciated in his time. Some of his creations were scathingly referred to as hornet's nests, stone quarries, slices of paté. Undismayed, the architect continued his work, and though part of an international group that reached for the glories of the past in an attempt to counter the ruthless effect of the Industrial Revolution, he remained isolated.

Many of the group became celebrities, but not Antonio Gaudí. He was less flamboyant than fellow workers who reached for the rebirth of medieval arts and crafts, for a past when mass-production and capitalism didn't have the same embracing power. He wasn't as out-spoken as the socialist William Morris. His sexual preferences weren't talked about as John Ruskin's were. Nor was he known for the laudanum, and other drugs, that destroyed Dante Gabriel Rosetti. Instead, he became increasingly religious, finally to reside in the *Sagrada Familia*, his cathedral in Barcelona. There is talk today of making him a saint.

However, almost from the beginning Gaudí's talents were appreciated by the wealthy and discerning Güells, a family of Catalan industrialists, who recognised the young architect's talent when Eusebio Güell, the first Conde de Güell, saw a glove-stand Gaudí designed for the Paris Exhibition of 1878. The two men became fast friends and, later, Gaudí was to build the family an imaginative mansion, the Palau Güell, in Barcelona. In another project for Güell, who became not only his companion but his benefactor, he added touches of fantasy to extensive gardens, known today as Park Güell, where a spectacular maze of bright ceramics, hand-carved stone spirals, cross the rolling landscape in a feast of colour and design.

In Comillas, the association with Gaudí came through Isabel López Bru, second daughter of the Marquis of Comillas, the only one of his four children to bear any heirs. She married Eusebio Güell, and through him brought the talent of the Catalan genius to Cantabrian soil.

Gaudí's first project in Comillas was a kiosk, a summerhouse for the first visit of Alfonso XII, in 1881. His craftsmanship can also be seen in the pews and the priest's chairs in the Capilla-Panteón, and in the twin thrones where the second marquis and his lady sat to receive guests in the grand salon of the Palacio de Sobrellano. But it is the Capricho that captured everyone's imagination, that brings many tourists to the town. By this Gaudí is as fondly recalled in Comillas as he is in his native Barcelona. Though, even there, at the time of his death in 1926, when hit by a tramcar while crossing a street, nobody recognised the shabbily dressed stranger as the city's famous architect. It was a while before anyone identified the man who gave Barcelona so much splendour. As he lay hurt in the street, a taxi driver refused to touch the figure he thought was a tramp. Kinder passers-by finally took him to a hospital where he died a few days later.

The most famous of Gaudí's creations, the *Templo de la Sagrada Familia*, begun in 1884 and unfinished when he died, today remains incomplete. It dominates Barcelona's skyline with its open-work of spires and rising columns, towers that curve out of line, undulating roofs and an amazing blend of colour and light. There are those who believe it will remain unfinished, as a continuing monument to the man whose mind it came from, a mind that never lost its faith.

As we said good-bye to the statue of Gaudí a little rain began to fall, but even that failed to take the glow from the lovely confection the man with the pointed beard had created in Comillas.

"Let's go to a bar," Antonio suggested. "Take a little *caldo*."

"Sounds like a good idea," agreed Virginia. "I could do with something warm."

We went to a long bar, with scrubbed wooden tables, run by Alberto, a grey-haired man who laughed when he poured drinks, joked as he took money, never waited for a reply. With a grubby tea towel over his shoulder, pale arms never still, he was on constant patrol.

"*Caldos?*" he said loudly. "A day for *caldos*. You need a little fire inside. Here you are," he added a moment later, returning from the kitchen with three cups of steaming chicken broth, reaching for a bottle of brandy. "A little *chupito*? To give more warmth?"

Antonio and I agreed. Virginia shook her head. Alberto winked, implying that certain ladies didn't need any warming up. We leaned against the bar and sipped our soup. The owner went back into the kitchen, returned with fine slices of *sal-*

chichón, a salami sausage made from pork, black peppercorns, and a plate of crusty bread.

"Take some," he said cheerfully. "To keep the *caldo* company."

We spent a pleasant hour sitting in the dark and welcoming bar, greeting those who came and went, some of whom we had never seen before. Almost all said hello as they entered, good-bye as they left. There was a warmth in the wood-lined hostelry that had nothing to do with the *caldo* or the brandy, but lay in the heart of the smiling man who took great pleasure in seeing his customers content, enjoying what he had to offer, sharing time with them beneath his roof.

A week later, work in the kitchen complete, the mess cleared, the pile of rubble by the front door taken away, I sat with the gnome-like builder sharing a glass of wine. The rest of his slash-and-recover crew were working elsewhere, pulling an old stable apart.

Jesús, his face showing only a thin pink scar, had by then put our old sink in the house he was building. Manuel, his head held at the same curious angle, the missing front teeth unreplaced, was eagerly breaking down other walls. In their own way they endured, unscathed by their boss's bullying, ready for more. Only the carpenter, who produced such fine, well-crafted work, failed to survive. After installing his excellent cupboards, he retired from the construction business. I see him often in his new occupation, cleaning the streets, whistling as he sweeps up leaves and plastic bags, an altogether different man.

"The kitchen came out well," I said to Cuadri. "It's quite surprising what you did with Virginia's sketch."

"*Gracias*. There was a little mess. But it's all right now."

"There was also a lot of shouting."

"Sometimes I have to raise my voice to make myself understood." He twirled the glass in his fingers. "You went to see the Capricho when it got too bad, no?"

"I'm glad I did. They've done a wonderful job there."

"Quite good. Some of the detail, well, you know." He looked up, quizzically "You've heard about the kitchen, I suppose?"

"As it's now a restaurant, I imagine there's a first-class one."

"Of course, but I'm talking about the original building."

"What happened?"

"*Bueno*, this man the Capricho was built for, Máximo Díaz de Quijano, the marquis' brother-in-law, was a man who lived in another world. He had some talent as an artist, but wasn't very interested in everyday things." Cuadri moved his shoulders eloquently. "You see, in those days the nobility had people to do things for them. Administrators, *mayordomos*, officials like that. Sometimes the administrators became very rich. Richer than those they worked for."

"It happens all over the world."

"Perhaps. Anyway, when Don Máximo was told the Capricho was complete, he came to Comillas. Arriving at night, he was enchanted by what he saw. Under the moonlight the building looked like a dream. He told his *mayordomo* to wake him early the next morning so he could have breakfast in the tower and watch the sun come up. It's very beautiful, some mornings, when it comes up over Miradorio. The point that's opposite the port."

I nodded.

"It is big and round. Like an orange in the sky. I can see it from where I live."

"Don Máximo wanted to see it too?"

"Yes, that's exactly what he wanted. Breakfast on the tower, watching the sunrise. But, it didn't turn out that way."

"Wasn't the tower finished?"

"It was a little more basic than that. The next morning the *mayordomo* woke Don Máximo and took him to the tower." Cuadri's smile was benign. "And there he saw the sunrise, but didn't get his breakfast. It seems that Gaudí had been more interested in what was seen than what was eaten. He didn't include a kitchen in his plans for the Capricho."

"That's hard to believe."

"Perhaps it was the overseer." Cuadri shrugged. "You know what staff are like. All I can tell you is, according to the story, there was no kitchen in the Capricho when it was built. It's strange, but that's what I heard." He lifted his glass. "All the same, it's a rare building, no? Who could design something like that today?"

Another local feature, as rare as the Capricho, is to be found at Altamira, seventeen kilometres to the east. There, images of the beasts that once roamed the land come to life. A bison settles, as if struck by a spear, hind legs doubling beneath it, head sinking slowly in death. A deer races, stiff with fear, its tail outstretched, an eye rolling in terror of the hunter in pursuit. Bumps and elevations in the stone were carefully selected to give a three-dimensional effect to the prey Cro-Magnon man pursued.

The paintings were done during the last Ice Age, ten to fifteen thousand years ago, when small communities sheltered in the caves. The artists of the time used coloured earths, mixed with the fats of animals they'd caught. Red and black, shades of orange and brown dominate the paintings, often startling in their movements.

It was a latter-day hunter's dog that led modern man to the cave. Chasing a fox, the dog fell into a crevice. The owner, extricating the animal, discovered the entrance, partially blocked by stone. There was nothing unusual about a cave in Cantabria's Carboniferous landscape. Most of the province consists of limestone twisted by the forces that raised it from the sea. Subterranean waters, forming giant caverns, stalactites, stalagmites and shining sheets of salts, have eroded miles of rock. Speleology is a Cantabrian sport, followers come from all over the world to explore the honeycomb lying underground.

Nor is losing a dog rare in this part of the world. Quite recently, the front page of a local newspaper featured one that had fallen into a similar cave four years earlier, and had survived on rainwater and the carcasses of cattle dumped in the crevice. The mutt was rescued, taken home, given a badly needed bath and seemed little disturbed by its adventure.

However, back in the middle of the nineteenth century, the owner of Altamira, Don Marcelino de Sautuola, on hearing of the find decided to investigate further. He was one of those Victorian gentlemen with an interest in geology, palaeontology and other emerging sciences. At the Paris Exhibition of 1878 his curiosity in anthropology had been stimulated by drawings of stone and bone implements discovered in southwest France. Curiously enough, this was the same exhibition that Gaudí's glove-stand, admired by Eusebio Güell, was also on display.

"Everything's connected in Comillas," Viscount Santiago had said, blowing a long plume of cigarette smoke. "That's something you'll find if you keep asking your questions."

On entering the cave, after workmen had cleared away the fallen stone, Don Marcelino discovered seashells containing pigments, black, yellow and red. There were large animal bones that had been cracked open so the marrow could be removed, an obvious sign of human habitation. He also found stone artefacts, similar to those at the Paris Exhibition, and the remains of ancient fires where cavemen had cooked their meals.

But, it was his five-year-old daughter who made the real discovery. "Look, Papá," she shouted excitedly. "There are cows up there on the roof."

Lifting his lamp, Don Marcelino saw leaping figures, realised what they were, but failed to convince many others. No one in the scientific world was prepared to accept their authenticity. They were too skilled, too gifted to have been done by Cro-Magnon man. In the opinion of the authorities of the day, Cro-Magnon was little more than a shuffling creature with neither the talent nor the perception to create so fine an art.

In an effort to have his find accepted, Don Marcelino made a fatal mistake. He wrote a report of what he'd discovered and had it illustrated by a French painter living with him at the time. Once it was known that an artist was involved, the scientific world became convinced the entire project was a fraud, initiated by some country squire eager to make his name. Obviously, they concluded, the painter who had done the sketches for Don Marcelino's report had also been busy in the cave.

Nevertheless, many came to view the paintings. In 1881, while visiting Comillas, King Alfonso XII wrote his name on the ancient walls with soot from a miner's lamp. While his method was not far removed from that used by Cro-Magnon artists, his skill was far less distinguished.

Don Marcelino died a disillusioned man. It was not until the early twentieth century, after examining similar caves in the Dordogne, that several French anthropologists recognised the worth of Altamira, and humbly begged forgiveness from his daughter, then a woman of middle age. Even though years had passed since she first saw the prancing beasts, which must have seemed like heavenly creatures to her child's eyes, she was grateful that her father's work had finally been recognised and felt he would rest in peace.

Interestingly enough, the earliest of the Altamira painting were done in black and white. Colour, as in the movies, came later to the art. Modern technology has also been used to duplicate the original Altamira scenes. Digital photography, hours of painstaking work, have led to the opening of an exhibition hall, where the work has been accurately reproduced. The fear that too much exposure to tourist's breath, the furtive flashing of cameras, would damage the originals led to the construction of the duplicate, which many say they prefer as the temperature is warmer, the air less damp, and a well-appointed café serves them before and after the tour. I wonder what Cro-Magnon man might have thought of that.

These days, the few hunters I've encountered when walking the hills with the dogs, have been poor reflections of Cro-Magnon man and the battles he fought with bison and bear. Nor are they modern day versions of the Wizards of the North, who set out in their fragile craft to bring right whales to shore. They don't even seem to share the enjoyment of the octopus fishers, who used to spend an agreeable morning catching a *pulpo* or two, until the Guardia ended their pastime.

One sweltering day I came across a *cazador* crouched behind a bush, his eyes fixed on a puddle over which he had lain a skein of sticks heavily coated with glue. He was waiting for sparrows, nuthatches, goldfinches, any small bird thirsty enough to fly down for a drink. Once ensnared he'd leap out and stuff them into his sack. My dogs ploughed straight through the water, emerged looking like ineptly built scarecrows, twigs, grass and leaves sticking to their hides.

"Poor little creatures," I said to the hunter, busily rearranging his gooey trap. "Don't you feel sorry for them?"

"Why? There are tons. And they taste very good."

"But, they're so small."

"Then I have to get a lot, no?"

He was one of many who take millions of small birds, local or migratory, each year from Spanish skies. A few of the creatures are caged, most are eaten, but no image is ever painted on any wall, no record is kept of their passing. There is no Bird Stone, like the Whale Stone, to keep the memory of sparrow hunts alive. Images of small birds aren't left on the ceilings of local houses. No excited child in ten thousand years will ever discover winged and delicate creatures soaring high above their head.

I left the glue-stick hunter, went off with the dogs to sit on the coastline below the marquis' statue, trying to get my mind back to the book I was writing about the town.

11

New York, New York

"I must get on with *Descubriendo Comillas*," I said to Virginia, as we sat beside the fire that evening. "*Australia*'s finished."

"Just the story of the town, without you in it?"

"Something like that."

"Then get on with it," she encouraged. "I think…"

She was interrupted by a thump, and we glanced toward the window as Michael's voice came off the street. He and his friends were kicking a football against a neighbour's giant door. Kitty was upstairs studying for an exam. We were becoming accustomed to the children's Spanish habits, how hard they worked at school, how late they played in the evenings.

"About time he came in, isn't it?" I said.

"He won't be long. Anyway, his exams are over. His holidays start soon."

Apart from Easter and Christmas, school holidays come in a solid package that lasts from June to September in this part of the world. Nearly four months of uninterrupted vacation give children time to forget almost everything they've ever learnt. On top of that, there are numerous fiestas during the scholastic year, including the famous Spanish *puente*, the bridge that links almost every public holiday, falling on a Tuesday or a Thursday, to the nearest weekend for a four-day break. As a result, school children, particularly in the secondary stage, work as hard as university students to pass their exams. If they don't, they repeat the course the following year, in some cases an advantage, in others a bore

"They're certainly active this evening," I said, as Michael's football hit the door again "Just as well the neighbours aren't here."

"They wouldn't mind if they were. They're good people, and it's a solid door."

The door she referred to was part of a gateway with carved stone columns, an ivy-covered cross above, belonging to a house known as *La Casa del Inquisidor*, where black deeds are said to have been carried out in dim and distant days.

There have been a number of inquisitions in Spanish history, all designed to rid the country of Protestant, Muslim and Jew. The most virulent was carried out in 1480 by *Isabella la Católica*, renowned for her devotion to the Church. Then, persecution, torture and the seizure of property were surgically put into effect. *Autos de fe*, the public acts of faith, when the condemned were paraded through the streets wearing gowns daubed with images of the devil, were commonplace. In fear, many converted to Catholicism but, even so, were lucky if they escaped with their lives. Often, their worldly goods went to the twin-crowns of Isabella and Ferdinand. The most recent outbreak of the Inquisition was between 1824 and 1834. That was when the house, where Michael and his friends were playing football, was given its infamous name.

"I'm glad that's not my door," I grumbled as the ball thudded again.

"What's got into you this evening?" Virginia asked.

"It's this book." I stared at the dancing flames. "When it's done I'll have to find a Spanish publisher."

"I was talking to Luisina the other day. You know, the woman who has the bookshop. Her son's a printer on the other side of Cabezón de la Sal. He wants to publish something new on Comillas, but hasn't got a text. Why don't you try him?"

"That's a thought."

"You could even try getting another agent."

"I could," I replied. "The trouble is I don't make it easy for an agent. Every time I write something it's different. That makes me hard to sell."

"You could go to New York, and see what's happening there? You may even raise Betty Anne Clarke from the dead. She was your last agent."

"She disappeared without a trace."

"Go anyway? I don't mind."

"You'd probably be better off if I left you in peace. I'm a pain in the arse at the moment."

"It's not that," she said. "And you know it."

"Thank you," I said. "What would I do without you?"

I went to New York but failed to raise Betty Anne Clarke from the living or the dead. Nobody had any idea where she'd gone. When I rang her old apartment a woman answered in Spanish. She'd never heard of *Betti-Anna*. I went to ICM, the literary agency she'd worked for before starting her own, taking me with her. There, I spoke to a chain-smoking replacement in her old office. He barely recalled her name. She, who'd been so efficient with ICM behind her, had faded from publishing sight.

I was no more successful with my New York publisher. He was on holiday in Europe and his assistant was dying of AIDS. His condition was a secret, so I wasn't able to visit him even to say hello. I did, however, meet an editor who'd worked on two of my novels, someone I'd come to know by correspondence only, and found her company delightful. And I stayed, once again, in the Henry Hudson Hotel, the stone mountain on 57th Street, where the seedy atmosphere was just the same. In the elevator, hesitant characters still eyed each other cautiously. There were people of every colour on every floor. I was on the twenty-sixth with a view over the Hudson River and a glimpse of Central Park. Nor had New York altered, its wondrous vitality was intact. There's something about the city that lifts the heart.

On my first visit to New York, I stayed at the Henry Hudson Hotel because Leonard Cohen had once written a song there. That seemed reason enough for me, even though the Madison Avenue headquarters of the advertising agency I was working for was dubious. A secretary made sure on three separate occasions she had the name right before she booked me in. It was a hotel that didn't appear on their list for distinguished visitors. Not that I was distinguished. I was sent to the Big Apple in appreciation for a TV campaign I'd handled well. And partly to learn something from our American cousins. I did, but not on Madison Avenue.

I found New York a pleasure-dome of sights and sounds, where voices emerged from every corner, steam came out of the ground, and the smell of wood-smoke from the pretzel stands taunted the appetite. Street musicians were a constant carnival, their flutes and steel drums merging with the noise of the traffic. Cars with more batters and dents than any I'd ever seen roared past. The sky was filled with more planes than birds. There was Chinatown and Little Italy to discover, and Central Park where cops in pale blue helmets rode horses over the grass. And Harlem, with its mysterious call.

I am usually a loner on visits to unknown cities. New York was no exception. I found street life more fascinating than any gathering with cocktails and canapés. I sought run-down bars in the Bowery, where men with faces like pizzas asked for money because they needed a drink. Some said they hoped to make it down to Florida in the winter. If they didn't they might freeze to death. I ate breakfast in diners, where eggs were sunny-side up, where all-night cleaners hung over cups of coffee, their shoulders sloped with fatigue. And I went to Harlem on my own because no one else would go with me.

"Can I show you some part of the city you'd like to see?" a black fellow-producer asked one day. "You know, some place you might not get to."

"How about Harlem? I'd love to go there."

"Harlem? It's not very nice." He scratched his head uncertainly. In those days 125th Street and the alleyways beyond, were not as up-market as they've recently become, were far less visitor-friendly than today. "It can get rough, you know?"

"That's why I want to go."

"Okay," he agreed dubiously. "I'll call you after work."

He didn't. So, I went to Harlem on my own. I took some money, a notebook, a large shot of Jack Daniels and left the Henry Hudson Hotel. I hailed a yellow cab, one of the host of golden taxis that bloom in New York streets, and told the black driver where I wanted to go.

"Are you sure?"

I nodded.

"What the hell for?" he asked suspiciously. "You want to buy something?

"I want to go because it's there," I said, feeling over-wired. "The corner of Fifth and a Hundred and Twenty-Fifth. I'm told that's the place to start."

"I'll take you where you want to go. But, I won't do no waiting round."

On the corner of 125th I paid the driver, watched him turn and head downtown. He was in a hurry. I looked at the passing faces, the cool arrogance of some, others that glanced away, many children's who were smiling. There seemed nothing unusual about where I was. Having been born in Fiji, grown up surrounded by black faces, I felt safe and somehow insulated. I went into the nearest bar, ordered a beer and sat beside a woman with an Ella Fitzgerald voice, who was talking about the difficulty of finding a decent apartment in all those high-rise blocks. It was a very ordinary conversation.

Out in the street again I stared through the glass of a pawnshop window, heavily barred, at the bits and pieces of people's lives they'd put on hold. I went on through a wall of soul blasting from a music store, past the dismembered body of a car where someone was fishing for parts.

I nodded at a pair of cops, and murmured, "Good evening."

They murmured back, and looked me up and down.

I went into another bar, ordered another beer, took out my notebook and began scribbling when a loud voice interrupted me. "Hey, man, what's that you writing?"

I looked up to see a smiling black man, an orange hat pushed back on his head. He wore a snakeskin pattern shirt loosely over his jeans. "I asked you?" he persisted. "What you writing?"

"Nothing much." I returned his smile. "A few notes about Harlem."

"You *writing* about Harlem? You didn't come to buy nothing? No dope?"

"No, it's the first time I've been to New York. I'm just making a few notes."

"You a Brit, right?" He leant closer. "You a Brit. And you writing about Harlem."

"Right. I came to see it for myself."

"Man, I'll *show* you Harlem." He spread his arms wide, displayed a scar that ran across his stomach. "Man, I even been shot in Harlem." He patted the scar. "Thirty-eight. But, it's all right. Got hit by a friend. Now, don't you worry. You okay with me. Name's Phil Hill. And, man, I'm gonna show you Harlem."

"Thank you," I said. My eyes went to the bar, where the barman was watching, his big hands drying a glass. "You'll be okay with Phil," he said, answering my unspoken question. "He'll take care of you. You want a couple of beers before you go?"

"Why not?"

When we went into the street the crowd had grown. Groups of youths, women, old men, were active everywhere. We went into bars and drank cold beer, used washrooms that smelt so strongly of ammonia it brought tears to my eyes. Into joints where the music was low, others where the sound was blaring. We drank beside men in suits, in jeans, in leather. Beside gays and straights and everything in between. We walked in and out of traffic, the sounds, the lifting smells of flesh and fried foods, of gasoline and grass. With Phil Hill talking all the time about Harlem. His dream town, where the world lay at his feet.

"I live here, man. Got a family in a block round the corner. You like Harlem? You like what I'm showing you?" He watched me smile and nod. "You gotta like it here. Everything happen in Harlem. Man, this mother's the middle of the world."

"I can believe it."

"You hungry, man? You wanna grab something to eat?"

"No, thanks. I feel fine."

"You should do, man. You in Harlem. You sure you don't want no soul food? Collards, pig's foot? Grits? Chitterlings?" He laughed, put an arm around my shoulders. "Soul food, man. The stuff whitey throws away."

"No, really. Not right now."

"But you like Harlem, that a fact? Like what I'm showing you?"

"Right now, I love it."

"You better." He grinned, his big face close. "Hey, you want some pussy, man? That's what you looking for. I can tell. I'm gonna get you some pussy." He turned, pointed at a girl leaning against a shop front window. "Look at that, man. So sweet. I know her. You want pussy, Phil here's gonna get you pussy."

"No thanks, I'm really all right."

"Come on, man. Talk to her. Tell her you a Brit."

"Not right now, if that's okay."

"Okay, man. You don't want no pussy, how about another beer?"

We went into a quiet bar, sat in a booth listening to voices, the distant sound of blues. Phil looked up, stared a moment. "You shoot up, man?" he asked. "You know, you a user?"

I shook my head.

"Me neither. Nothing regular, man. But, you know, I'd kind of like to shoot up now. Just a little." He smiled, not as broadly. "Come on, what you say? It's that kind of night."

"I don't shoot up. I never have."

"Won't do no harm, man. Get some kicks."

"I feel high enough just being here."

"You don't use nothing? No dope?"

"A joint sometimes, that's all." I drank my beer. "But I don't think I want anything more. I couldn't stick a needle in my arm."

"Nothing to it." Phil leant closer, pushed his orange hat further back on his head. "But, if you want to, I know some places round here. You wanna see Harlem. You gonna write about Harlem. You gotta see it *all*, man. You gotta know what's going on in town."

"If you want to shoot up, okay. But not for me."

"Okay." Phil scratched his cheek, the bristles rattled. "It's, well, man, I don't like to say this. But, I'm a little short right now."

"What's it cost?"

"I can get a bag for ten bucks. That's cheap. I told you, man, I know Harlem. Only, I don't have no ten bucks right now."

"I'll shout you," I said. "That's the Brit way of saying, I'll pay."

"Shit, man. You don't want nothing?"

"No, just being here's a high for me."

"Okay, man. That's good." Phil drank his beer quickly, anxious to leave. "That's good, man. You Brits, well, that's okay."

Out in the street we moved on, went a little deeper underground. Phil walked quickly, looking from side to side. "I need a spike," he said abruptly. "Know what I mean? Need to talk to that brother over there." His eyes went across the road to a little man, neatly dressed, standing beside a dry cleaner's window. "He's the one."

We crossed, skipped around a yellow taxi. The little man stood very still, watching, moving his hands, playing with something he didn't look at. When we got closer I saw it was an old-fashioned cut-throat razor he was opening and shutting with a click. Under the streetlight its silver blade flashed, went dark, flashed bright again.

"Hi," said Phil. "This here's my friend. A Brit."

"I know," the little man said softly. "I seen him around."

"You take care of him now. He's okay."

"Okay." The little man snapped the razor shut. "What you want?"

"A spike, man. You gotta spike?"

The little man nodded, produced a needle. Phil took it, paid and said, "Okay, fine." We walked away. The little man said nothing more. The only time he'd stopped playing with the razor was when he reached for the needle, took the money.

"You coulda had your throat cut," Phil said. "You wasn't with me."

"You think so?"

"Happens all the time." Phil grinned, his mood was lifting. "But, you okay with me. I told you, I'm gonna look after you good."

"You're doing fine, so far."

"Thank you, man. Now, you got that ten dollars with you?"

I gave him the money. He led me around a corner into an apartment building, where all but one of the downstairs lights were out, and the reek of urine invaded the hallway.

"Wait here, man," Phil said, knocking on a wooden door. A voice answered, the door opened, he went inside. A moment later he returned, a small plastic bag between his fingers. "I got it," he said excitedly. "Hey, what you think of that?"

"Okay. If that's what you want."

"You want some?"

"No, you go ahead." I was part of what was happening, yet removed, a spectator fascinated by the voyeur that rests in us all. "It's okay, I don't mind. You do what you want."

"Okay." Phil sat on the stairs, reached into one of his socks. "I got the makings here," he muttered. "Needed a spike. I got the rest." He produced the top of a whisky bottle, a syringe, a book of matches. Then looked up, a touch of panic in his eyes. "Hey, I need some water, man. There water round here?"

I glanced at the stairwell, the dark corners where the stench came from. I shook my head. "There's nothing here," I said.

"Hey, man. I need it." He was on his feet again, banging on the wooden door, his voice louder now. "You got water in there?"

A dark hand came around the door holding a white polystyrene cup. Phil took it quickly, returned to the stairs. "Yes," he said, and began fixing what he needed.

He poured a little water into the whisky cap, shook and opened the bag, carefully tapped the white powder into the water, heated it with a match. When it was ready he fitted the needle to the syringe and filled it. His eyes came back to me. "You wearing a belt, man?" he asked.

"Yes."

"Give it to me."

He strapped it around his arm, raised a vein and slid the needle in. For a moment he worked the syringe, adding his blood to the liquid, a darkness in the orange light. His head went back, he remained, eyes closed. I drank what was left of the water in the white polystyrene cup.

"Man," he said a moment later. "Yes, man."

Soon, we were out into the streets again, on another round of colour and sound. The smell of cooking had grown richer. Phil was different, active in a slower mode. A dreamer had replaced the brash scar-bellied man. He was as busy, as friendly, as helpful, but he walked and talked as if life was softer now. In a bar, we sat drinking beer slowly, he tapped the table, eyes closed, listening to the music on his own.

"Hey, man," he said. "I'm up there."

"I can feel it too."

"You can? You didn't take nothing."

"I guess it's a contact high."

"Hey, you Brits." Phil laughed. "You piss me off, you know. You didn't take nothing and you get a high."

Then we were outside again, turning into a side street where three men were pulling a car apart. They had opened the door of a pale green Dodge with a straightened coat hanger. One was inside, going through the glove compartment. The other two were working on the boot.

"Hey," Phil shouted, fumbling in his pockets. "Gimme a piece of this, man. I got keys."

"Fuck off," a big man in a T-shirt said, his manner easy, his voice hard. "This here's our shit."

"I gotta key."

"Fuck off, I told you. You'll have all them cops around."

"I gotta key."

"Then find your own fucking car." As the boot opened with a crack, the big man moved closer to Phil. He was smiling, but Phil put away his keys. "That's it," the man added quietly. "This mother-fucker's ours."

Phil watched from the sidewalk, hands in pockets, looking sad. Then he shrugged, turned away. We continued through alleyways that were becoming emptier, past glances that were cooler, more distanced, more removed. We drank another beer, but it was beginning to lose its taste.

"How much you got left, man?" Phil asked as we stood on another corner, looking across another street. "You got any ten dollars with you?"

I counted my money. I was down to eight.

"Shit, man. What you done with it all?"

I laughed, having paid for almost everything.

"Not funny, man." Phil's mood was altering, the brightness was beginning to dim. "We don't got enough for a ten dollar bag."

"Well, it's getting late."

"No, man, we got all night."

"I'm afraid I haven't."

"Wait…" Phil began, then his expression altered. "Shit," he muttered, moving to the edge of the sidewalk. "Shit, man. I gotta pain." He began vomiting into the gutter.

"You all right?"

"I gotta pain."

"You'll be okay." I bent, rubbed the back of his neck, his shoulders as he vomited, treating him as my mother had treated me as a child. "You'll be okay, don't worry. You'll feel better if you get rid of it all."

After a while Phil stopped heaving, wiped his sweating face with his snakeskin shirt. He looked up, his eyes surprised. "What you do that for, man?"

"I thought it might help."

"Shit." He spat into the gutter, straightened himself and shook his head. "Shit, man. You just a fucking nigger." He grinned. "You know that. No one else woulda done like that. You fucking nigger Brit."

"I take that as a compliment."

"Son of a bitch, you right." He breathed deeply, looked at me again. "That eight dollars, man. What you going to use it for?"

"I'm going back downtown."

"Over there." He indicated a Chinese take-away half way down the block. "We could get something for my family. They gonna be waiting for me now."

"That sounds like a good idea."

"Yeah, gotta take something home."

We went into the take-away, into fat-heavy fried air. Phil Hill bought two bags of food, joking with the man behind the counter. He was back to where he'd been when I met him in the bar. The brash survivor with the scar on his stomach, the orange hat pushed back on his head, had returned to Harlem, the mother of his world.

I paid, leaving myself with enough change to catch a bus back to the Henry Hudson Hotel. Outside on the sidewalk we shook hands, promised to keep in touch. He gave me one crisp prawn from a brown paper bag and walked away, swaggering a little, his snakeskin shirt swinging loose. He turned once and waved. I never saw him again.

On the nearly empty bus going down Fifth Avenue I tried to accept what had happened, but couldn't quite believe it had occurred. Phil Hill had come out of nowhere, gone away with two bags of food. He'd strapped my belt around his arm and slid a needle in. He'd vomited in the gutter when he failed to ransack a car. And he'd called me a fucking nigger as a way of expressing his thanks. I wonder, in these days of political correctness, what else he might have said. Nothing could have come close to the honesty those words contained.

The following day the black producer apologised for letting me down, for not taking me to Harlem as arranged.

"It's okay," I said. "I went there anyway."

"You got balls," he said. "Going up there alone."

"That's all right," I told him. "I wasn't alone."

I have been to New York many times since, but not to Harlem, it could never be the same. When I returned in search of an agent, I looked up Comillas in the New York Public Library, but found little that was any help. And I ran through Central Park in the mornings, past cardboard shelters where black faces peered out bleary-eyed. None belonged to Phil Hill.

I bought Virginia a pair of earrings, shaped like tiny black hearts, in a pawn-shop near Times Square. I had a small necklace made for a her in that wonderful gold-and-silver jewellery market on West 47th Street, where Hasidic Jews, with black suits and white shirts, beards and side-locks, their heads never uncovered, go dutifully about their work. None reminded me of my grandfather.

"How you want it?" the jeweller, who sold me the necklace, asked. "Poils? Or no poils?"

"Poils," I said. "It wouldn't be New York without the poils."

"Yeah." He laughed. "New York's poils everywhere you go."

Two days later he produced the necklace. It had a neat gold nameplate with pearls on either side. Virginia was delighted.

"I took the children skiing while you were away," she said, when I returned. She had skied with her father since early childhood, was fast and agile on the snow. "Up to Brañavieja, in the Picos. We had a fantastic day."

"That was clever. How are they getting on?"

"Kitty's coming along nicely. Although, she sometimes gets out of control." Virginia gave a motherly smile. "But Mike's like a bullet. He tackles everything, head first."

"Well, you got back safely. What was the weather like?"

"Perfect, there wasn't a cloud in the sky."

12

Beauty within Crumbling Walls

"The Seminario's open to the public," I said to Virginia, looking up from the local paper. "A bank, the Caja Cantabria, has bought it."

"What's a bank doing with a seminary?"

"There's talk of turning it into a Spanish American cultural centre."

"I'd get up there quickly, if I were you. Before they close it down again."

That afternoon I climbed the S-shaped driveway to the old Pontifical University, walked between files of plane trees, their leaves turning golden brown, to where Pepuco had taken me the afternoon we saw the barn owl swoop out of the pelota shed. At the top, I stood before the huge double doors where the Virtues firmly suppressed their Vices. The green of tarnished bronze blended into the autumn day. The doors were open, and from the interior a girl with short-cropped hair and bright eyes appeared.

"Can I see inside?" I asked.

"If you wait a little," she said. "There's a group you can join."

"Is it possible to be my own group? I'd like to make some notes."

"Are you are writing something?"

"A book about Comillas," I explained. "And the Seminary's the only place I've not seen yet. It's been closed up to now."

"One moment," she said, disappeared, then returned with a smile. "The other guide will take the group. I'll show you around. I'm Elena."

"Thank you." I stepped through the huge bronze doors and stopped before a black lion set into the pale tiled floor. It stood on its hind legs, clawing the air, mouth open in a snarl. "What's that?" I asked. "Anything to do with the marquis?"

Elena glanced at me uncertainly.

"There were lions on his statue, you know, before the war."

"It has nothing to do with the marquis," Elena replied. "When the Pontifical University of Comillas was accepted by the Vatican, Leo the Thirteenth was on the papal throne. That's why we have this lion with thirteen claws. It represents the Pope."

"Was this done by the same architect who designed the doors?"

"Lluis Domènech i Montaner? Yes."

"He had a nice sense of humour."

"I'm glad you think so? Come, let me show you something else by the same architect. He had a very good sense of humour, as you'll see."

She led me past elaborate arches supported by slender pillars, whose crowns were clusters of thrusting leaf, buds lifting their heads, overlaying sprigs and blossoms, all the floral emblems the Catalan *modernismo* masters used time and time again. Nature was part of everything they created, their work bloomed at every turn.

"Look at this." Elena pointed to an unsupported arch, running from one side of the vestibule to the other. Above it a double marble staircase rose to the floor above. "This is Domènech's masterpiece. This is what they said he couldn't do."

"Why not?"

"Because the engineers told him it would collapse. That it wouldn't stay up without columns to support it." Elena's arm outlined the arch. "He was told its construction would be as difficult as mice putting a bell on the tail of a cat?" She lifted her eyebrows. "You understand me?"

"Yes, we have the same expression in English."

"Then you know how difficult they thought it was? So when it was done, and *didn't* fall down, do you know what Domènech did?"

"What?"

"Here, at this side, he put the mice." She moved to one end of the long bow-shaped structure, as simple as a rainbow reaching from shore to shore, and pointed to a sculpture tucked into the wall. It was of three scampering mice, tumbling over each other in glee. "Look, at them. See how happy they are?"

"They certainly are."

"And here." Elena went to the far end of the arch where an angry feline clawed at the beam above. "Here is the cat. *Bueno*, it is not a happy cat."

"It's furious."

"That's what Domènech wanted to do. To show the engineers how wrong they were."

"What a lovely idea. But, what about the bell? The cat's not wearing it."

"I was wondering if you would ask me that." Elena went to an archway behind us, indicated a small old-fashioned bell, sculptured above the head of an angel. "Here's one bell," she said, laughing. "And there's another on the other side.

Domènech made sure everyone understood exactly what he'd done. You like it, no?"

"I love it."

"Come," she said, relaxed now. "Look at this, above the stairs. It's a miracle."

We left the angry cat, the cheerful mice, and climbed the stairs, cut from pale grey marble, the shapes of fossils intact in the stone.

"Look up," she said. "See what I mean."

Above, like a giant crown, filling the space between one wall and the other was a sculpted ceiling of beams and bosses, triangles, squares and circles bearing floral designs. Descending, on columns and pedestals along the walls, was a zoological feast of birds and beasts, fish and fowl, of bizarre living creatures. There was a locust poised to leap, a grouper with fins extended as if in flight, a smaller fish in its mouth. Nearby was a rooster, claws extended like a hawk's, an elephant with a thrashing trunk, a monkey with a human face. The menagerie hung above me, waiting, ready to pounce, softened only by the tinted light coming in through stained-glass windows at either end.

"That's incredible, I said. "It's like something from Hieronymus Bosch."

"I'm told it's based on the Psalm one hundred and forty-eight," Elena replied. "And everyone who comes here says they've never seen anything like it."

"I can believe that." I stared at the ceiling; the figures seemed to move. Later, I consulted the Psalm Elena referred to. In verse 7 it says: *Praise the Lord from the earth, ye dragons, and all deeps.* In verse 10: *Beasts and all cattle, creeping things and flying fowl are enjoined to praise the Lord.* Those were the words that had given rise to the fantastic scene above the stairs. "What is next?" I asked. "Anything else as wonderful?"

"The most important feature is the church." Elena pointed to one side of the stairs. "It's beneath us. You see, this part of the Seminary's built like two boxes put together. In the middle, where they join, is where we are. On both sides are gardens inside the exterior walls." Her voice had become formal again. "And the church is in the middle. Let's go down and see it."

"Is there anything else up here?"

"There's the priest's church, I'll show you that if you like."

We left the splendid ceiling, where creeping things were enjoined to praise the Lord, went into the dimness of a long chapel that smelt of damp. At one end, above the altar, stood a figure of Christ, his heart in his hand. Higher still was a curved ceiling with what appeared to be brick arches in support, but a closer look showed where rainwater had washed the facade away, leaving stained plaster in its place.

"It's decaying," I said. "Can't it be repaired?"

"For many years there was little done," Elena said sadly. "When the Pontifical University of Comillas moved to Madrid, the Seminary was left almost empty."

"Nobody cared?"

"They said they didn't have any money. I know the local government did some work. Fixed the roof a bit." She pointed to the washed-away paintwork, the stains on the wall behind the altar. "But that wasn't enough. A lot of the building's falling down."

"Where?"

"In the back. There it's very bad."

"Show me."

She shook her head.

"Please?" I said. "I want to write about everything."

"Well," Elena hesitated, her eyes going to a small door, peaked at the top in a gothic arch. "I went through there once, when it was open."

I tried the door. "It is locked now," I said.

"There was a key."

I walked the length of the Jesuit's Chapel, past dark pews where devout heads once had murmured, moved the air in prayer. Near the Christ figure, was a similar door. In it was a key. I tried it, but the lock remained firm, rusted through lack of use. I took the key, went back to the first door, tried it and it opened.

"No," Elena said. "That's not for visitors."

"A quick look," I said, seeing interest in her eyes. "Come on, it won't take long."

"Well, I *would* like you to see everything." She smiled knowingly. "For your book, of course, but we must be quick."

I peered through the door into a corridor, its plain wooden floorboards twisted by dampness and time, at walls that were covered with spider-webs, at an aspect of the building that spoke eloquently of its emptiness. The Pontifical University of Comillas had been left for decades to the whim of the seasons, the creep of rot.

"Where are we now?" I asked.

"We're in the middle. Like I told you, where the boxes join." Elena pointed through a dirty window. "There's one of the gardens, inside the walls."

I peered through grime to see wild grasses everywhere, a cactus that had run to seed, its tall stem lifted like a wand. A crumbling-stone garden seat. Bright sunlight caught a far wall setting *Ave Maria* tiles alight.

"It reminds me of something I saw in Mexico," I said. "Palenque, an ancient city of the Maya. There was so much life in it, even though it had been abandoned centuries ago."

"There's not much life here now."

"No, but you can see what man has done. Where he's been." I stared through the dirt-encrusted window, almost saw the black-clad figure of a priest turn past the trunk of an upright pine, as I imagined I'd glimpsed a Maya warrior, spear in hand, jaguar-cloak swinging from his shoulders, walk through a temple door. "You can feel what's been lost."

"That's very true," Elena replied quietly. "Sometimes in the mornings, before any visitors arrive, it's like there were ghosts in the building."

"There probably are."

"You believe that?" She looked at me doubtfully. "Spirits from the past?"

"Memories, more likely. To remind us of what it was." I turned away from the window. "Come on, let's see what else there is."

Turning a corner we came to a flight of crumbling stairs held together by G-clamps, their metal jaws preventing the treads from falling apart. Some of the clamps were rusted, looked as if they had been there for years.

"We can't go up," said Elena. "It's dangerous."

"What's up there?"

"An entrance to one of the bell towers. I've seen photographs, but I've never been up."

"Come along, you may never get another chance."

"Well, if you insist, but what about the stairs?" There was a taste for adventure in her eyes. "Do you think they'll fall down?"

"If we keep close to the wall it'll be all right." I took a step or two, nothing moved, the clamps remained. "Come on."

We walked up to a balcony with a view of the overgrown garden, the wild grasses, the cactus gone to seed. Moving on, we found the entrance to the bell tower, a flight of slender steps, the lower part littered with rubble.

"Look at that," Elena said. "We can't get past."

"Someone has." I pointed to a wall where a cross had been scratched into raw cement. Beside it was written the word *Maria*. "Come on, let's climb over this and take a look. You can't turn back now."

Without any further hesitation, her dark uniform showing stains where it had rubbed against the stone, Elena followed me up the circular stairwell. After the first hurdle the steps were clear of timber, fallen brick. We came out a small square platform below a hanging bell and there, through supporting arches, saw the rolling green hills of Cantabria, miles of quiet blue sea, scenes of blessed tranquillity, spreading far and reaching wide.

"My God," said Elena, her voice hushed. "These are views to die for."

"You're right, they're magnificent."

The four arches of the bell-tower framed four separate panoramas. Behind, through blue-tinted mists, the black slabs of the Picos de Europa rose to the snow they bore. To the east, nestled the town of Comillas, calm in the slanting autumn sun. To the west, beyond the lapping coastline, ran the sickle of Oyambre, where the ruins of the golf club lay, and the Yellow Bird had come down to rest. Before us, the sea itself was soft and blue and splendid. They were views, as Elena said, to die for.

I looked up into shadowed darkness, where one bell hung. "Does it ever ring?" I asked.

"No, they have two Masses in the church below each year. One in July, one in August, for parents of the students who come to study English. But I've never heard the bell. It's the only one that's left. The other was taken during the war. It was melted down for cannons."

"Like the marquis and his slaves? They say the same about the bronze from the original statue. The war levelled everything, the master, the servants, the church."

"They had a bad time here. Many Jesuits were shot."

"I've heard that. Churches are often the first to suffer in a war." I looked out again at the perfect sea. It remained eternal, unaltered by the conflict that had raged above. "Thank you for letting me come up here. I feel privileged to have seen all this."

"Me too," Elena replied. "Now, let's go down to the church."

We went down the curving bell-tower steps, descended the clamped stairs, walked back along the corridor to the gothic-arched door. In a corner I saw a chest of drawers that hadn't caught my eye before. Once, like so much in this treasure house, it had been beautiful, but now the delicate woodwork was splitting, the lacquer had begun to peel.

"What a waste," I said. "And no one cares."

"There's so much here like that."

I pulled at the top drawer, it stuck, came open with a rush.

"Shit," said Elena. "That is a profanity. It was sacred once."

We stared at what appeared to have been a bishop's stole. The cloth was a rich, noble green, embroidered with tarnished gold. It was covered with rat droppings, faecal matter had eaten into the fabric. In one corner were the remains of a nest.

"It's disgusting," Elena said. "They should have more respect."

"The people who left it? Or the rats?"

Elena looked up quickly, then shrugged. "Come, you'll like the church," she said.

We returned to the priest's chapel, replaced the key, walked down the softly shimmering marble stairs beneath the watchful gaze of the winged dragons, the creeping things. We left the furious cat, the gleeful mice and went into the sacristy, where handsome dark-wood cupboards once held vestments. Now their polished doors were locked.

"There," Elena said, as we climbed a few steps to come out behind an altar. "What do you think of that?"

I stared, humbled by the majesty.

"It is a waste, no?" she added softly. "All this, so seldom used."

"It's shameful."

Although alone, we were whispering, the grandeur keeping our voices close. From the high arched roof of stars to the fine mosaic floor, where Matthew, Mark, Luke and John, lent their presence to the Lamb of God, the church was a thing of beauty, a glorious cathedral left to silence, the shuffling feet of rats. From the walls painted angels peered down, their haloes bright with hope, even though some of the tapestries bearing them were peeling from the walls. Light poured in through stained-glass windows, red, blue, green and the colour of gold. It fell on the rows of empty pews, brought the wooden altar-screen alive with tones of autumn, fruitful seasons. The altar, a giant slab of pale marble, shone in the coloured light. I could almost hear the murmuring of acolytes in prayer, calling for a crusade to renew their long-suffering faith. The church was superb, yet it was hollow, an instrument without a voice.

"When it was occupied, nineteen Masses could be said here," Elena whispered. "There are chapels along the walls. And more in the gallery."

"It must have burst with life."

"Not any more."

"What'll happen now it belongs to a bank?"

"I hope they preserve it," Elena replied quietly. "I pray for that."

We stood a moment longer, our eyes taking in the fading splendour, lovely in the softening afternoon light. I thought of a recent journey to Santiago de Compostela, a visit to the cathedral where the whole body of the church was so crowded, so overflowing that visitors, pilgrims, penitents, stood jostling in queues, impatient to get to the shrines they'd come to see. In the centre of the pushing, elbowing, unfriendly crowd a priest in a central chapel was pleading for a little quiet, a small degree of peace.

"I know we're to blame," he said. "You've come to see the wonders we have here. But, please, I'm trying to conduct a Mass."

Around me voices muttered, barked, hissed. "I was here first," someone said. "You weren't," another protested. "You pushed into the queue." "Me, no," came the reply. "I've been waiting for hours." "My God, this is so boring," another complained. "Why does it take so long?"

"Please," came the plea from the pulpit. "This is the House of God. Quiet, please. Try to be little calmer."

"Have you seen this?" Elena's voice said softly. "So the priests could sit, and no one would be any the wiser." She stood in the apse where, below the stained glass windows, a semi-circle of beautifully carved, high and hooded seats ranged behind the altar. They were as delicately designed as Gaudí's work in the Capilla-Panteón. "During the Mass, if they got tired, they just put up this seat." She folded out a hidden stool, which came up to tail-level. With a bit of juggling a tired man could rest. "It went under the gowns they wore. And no one knew. A good trick, no?"

"They probably needed a lot of support at the end of a hard day's teaching."

"There's more to see, at the public entrance to the church." She walked briskly down the nave, past the chapels with their patron saints, the triptychs of sacred scenes, below the fretwork of the organ, her footsteps echoing as she clipped along. She stopped by a pair of open doors. "Look, as an Englishman would you expect to find this here?"

I peered at a wonderfully agile scene of Saint George killing a dragon, set in high relief on bronze that had turned dark green. On one door the knight was about to strike. On the other the reptile faced death.

"Saint George, patron saint of England," I said. "What's he doing here?"

"*San Jorge*," corrected Elena. "The patron saint of Cataluña. That is why he's here. The spirit of Christianity fighting the Devil in disguise."

"It's about time he came back. There are a lot of dragons to be put down here."

Elena smiled. "Shall we write to *San Jorge*?"

"Let's send him a postcard. One of those pretty ones with the gates of the Seminario on it. Then he'll know exactly where to find us."

We laughed quietly and walked out of the empty church, away from the slow decay, the dark woodwork, its burnished autumn tones, the empty marble altar, the painted tapestries peeling from the walls. Once out in the late afternoon sun I thanked Elena and said good-bye. But not for long. Later, I introduced her to Virginia and she became a friend.

When I spoke to Antonio, our neighbour, about the Seminary he nodded sadly and tugged at his English cap. "I remember when I could hear the choir. It came right down to the town. Especially on Sundays and the *fiestas,* you know. It was very beautiful."

"It must have made a great difference when they left."

"It was a blow to Comillas. I don't think the town has ever recovered." Antonio shrugged. "There are tourists now, but it's not the same."

"Why did the Seminary move to Madrid?"

"Some change in the Church. Something the Pope made them do. But, I can't think why they'd want to go from here."

"Neither can I."

I later discovered that the Pontifical University of Comillas had been transferred to Madrid as a result of a decision, taken at the Second Vatican Council in the early 1960s, to move the Church into the modern world. By 1966 the Seminary had closed down, only a few elderly priests remained in order to maintain possession under the agreement signed by the first Marquis of Comillas, the man who had fought so hard and paid so much to bring the institution to the town.

The Pontifical University moved away, bearing the name but not the majesty. In Madrid it no longer overlooks the Cantabrian sea, the Picos de Europa, the little village where kings bathed and nobles built, and the whole community became enchanted with its architectural beauty.

"Of course, there might have been another reason why the Seminario moved away," Antonio added wryly. "I've heard that the students used to visit the ladies of the town. At night, wearing ordinary clothes. They say that's one of the reasons they were taken from here."

"That'd be even easier in Madrid."

"But, no one would know who they were. No one could say anything about them." Antonio smiled. "It was a loss to many when they went."

"What will happen now it's owned by a bank?"

"You'd better talk to the mayor about that."

I found the mayor in the *Ayuntamiento,* the Municipal Building, an impressive double-storied edifice with three curving Romanesque arches, facing a cobbled square. It has its own illustrious history, was used as a church while the townsfolk built San Cristóbal. It has been a pilgrim's rest on the way to Santiago de Compostela, where the bones of Saint James, brother of Saint John, are said to lie. Apparently, his body was discovered when a field lit up with stars and led the searchers to the saint's remains. The place quickly became known as *campo de estrellas*, reduced to *Compostela* as time went by.

In the council chamber, where I spoke to the mayor, five sons of Comillas, who became archbishops as far afield as Peru and Mexico, are honoured with colourful shields. It's remarkable that so small a community, even before the marquis put his stamp on it, should have produced five international archbishops. In the Media, Comillas is often referred to as the Town of the Archbishops. Comillanos have more than one reason to believe that God is on their side.

The chamber itself is ornate, with crowns and shields on dark-stained walls. There is a semi-circle of chairs that look as if they might have been destined for a medieval castle.

"Very impressive, isn't it?" the mayor said, as he showed me around. "It's just been renovated."

"They've done an excellent job."

"Sit down." The mayor eased into the largest chair, behind an old well-polished table. Over him hung a copy of Dali's Christ, arms extended, head down. Below, on raging seas, a fishing boat struggled to survive. The painting was another version of *El Cristo del Amparo*, Christ the Protector, celebrated each year when Comillas' summer fiesta shakes the town. "Now, it's the Seminario you want to talk about, is that correct?"

"I wanted to know what's going to happen. You see, I am writing a book, and I'd like to get the details right."

"Of course." The mayor beamed, he was a plumpish man, who smiled easily, used his hands to speak. "There are great plans for the Seminario, you know. It is now in the hands of the Fundación Comillas. The King and Queen of Spain are honorary presidents. Many intellectuals are involved. From Spain and South America. Great authors wish to take part."

"What will be done, exactly?"

"*Bueno.*" The mayor's hands spread, encompassing everything. "The plans are at a very early stage. We don't know what eventually will happen. But we hope for greater cultural exchange between Latin America and Spain. An interchange of scientific and intellectual ideas between all Spanish-speaking countries."

"That sounds very ambitious." I made a note. "Does anyone have any idea of what all this is going to cost?"

"*Pouf.*" The mayor's hands spread even wider. "The cost could be enormous. The building, itself, is not in very good condition."

"I know. I've seen it."

"Then you'll understand we could be talking about millions of dollars. First we have to assess what needs to be done. And how long it'll take. I'm working very closely with the bank, the Caja Cantabria. But, of course, it's a complex project."

"Do you have any idea when they'll begin work. And if they're going to preserve the treasures there? That marvellous stair-head, for example?"

"Absolutely, I insist on it. They're treasures of the nation. As you must know, we have many in Comillas. I will make sure they are all preserved."

"When you speak of intellectuals from Latin America and Spain. Is there anyone well-known?"

"Of course." The mayor leant over the polished table, his face alight. "Have you heard of Carlos Fuentes? Or Gabriel García Márquez?"

I nodded. Carlos Fuentes' *The Death of Artemio Cruz* is probably the best novel ever written about Mexico. And García Márquez, apart from winning the Nobel Prize for Literature, altered the course of modern writing. Their backing could mean the difference between failure and success.

"Both of these illustrious men have given support to the Fundación Comillas. Carlos Fuentes is due here soon to take part in discussions about the project. And García Márquez has sent messages of support." The mayor smiled proudly. "Today people talk about them and Comillas in the same breath."

"That's very good news." I scribbled a little. "And you say, at this stage, no one has any idea what all this might cost? Or where the money would come from?"

"Well, it could come from industry, businesses that might like to donate. Some countries in South America, perhaps Asia and the Middle East, are interested in investing. We're working on that aspect at the moment. It is a great amount but we believe it will be achieved." He stood, not prepared to say anything more. "Now, let me show you the shields on the walls. Some have interesting histories."

We walked around the council chamber looking at the newly decorated walls, at versions of the official emblem of Cantabria, at galleons in full and thunderous sail, racing toward the chain the Moors erected to bring about the liberation of Seville. There were other heraldic devices bearing knights in cloaks and breastplates. Some of the Moorish tower standing alone, others surrounded by trees representing the great gifts of land made to Cantabrians in Andalucia, the first of the *jándalos*, who travelled south seeking fame and fortune. The *indianos*, those who voyaged further, the greatest of whom was Antonio López y López, first marquis of the town.

"It'd be nice if the marquis' efforts were maintained," I said to the mayor, by the door of the council chamber, as we parted. "He gave so much to Comillas."

"He did. And that's why I'm determined to preserve what we have. To keep what the marquis bequeathed us. It's our duty to preserve these treasures."

"So that his legacy lives on?"

"Of course. So that out children know what we're talking about when we speak of history, the beauty of our town."

"Let's hope that you succeed."

"We will. I'm sure."

There were further meetings between the mayor, the director of the Fundación Comillas and various well-known politicians, writers, lawyers and members of UNESCO. Some of whom visited the town, spoke to the Press, appeared on TV, were wined and dined extensively in an effort to inch the project forward.

The high point of possibility was the presentation of the scheme to UNESCO, in Paris, where it was welcomed as a decisive step toward bringing the cultures of Latin America and the European Community closer. Nevertheless, for a while, the project drifted aimlessly, and the splendid building, its treasures mouldering, was closed to the public once again.

Now, however, new life seems to have been breathed into the Seminary's old lungs. A change of regional government and a new administrator in Comillas, a mayoress even more determined to see the dream fulfilled, have re-presented the project on the basis of the old Pontifical University being opened as an international centre of *Castellaño*, the Spanish language. This time the central government in Madrid has become involved and promised money. Reconstruction of the splendid building is scheduled to begin in 2006. So, some expectation remains for the re-birth of Comillas and its crumbling hallowed halls. Let's hope so, and that those in power are not obliged to seek help from the Japanese. After all, it was their cash and initiative that saved Gaudí's Capricho from ruin and decay, that brought back to life one of the most joyful structures in the town, a place where all can sit, like Gaudí, in contemplative quiet.

13

Fiestas, Fiestas, Fiestas

But the quiet life Comillas enjoys most of the year is shattered when the fiestas arrive. There are two principal events, one in summer the other in winter, each with its effect on the Town of the Archbishops.

The summer fiesta begins on July 16 with a commemoration of *el Cristo del Amparo*, Christ the Protector, saviour of those in trouble on the waters of the world. His image is borne through Comillas in a procession headed by the priest. The convoy, solemn and impressive, winds down from the church to the sea, where the Christ figure is taken on a ritual voyage accompanied by the mayor, the people of the town.

I once asked Eladio the Book why Christ was honoured and not the Virgin, as in many other parts of Spain.

"In the church there's a stained glass window showing Christ in a boat," he told me. "It reflects the name the fishermen gave to their guild when they formed it in the fifteenth century. The *Cofradía del Santo Cristo*, to honour Jesus who calmed the waters. And, there's an old tale of fishermen who were saved, at the height of a storm, when the seas suddenly became still."

"Do you think it is true?"

"Who knows," Eladio replied. "In cases like this there's always something." He smiled gently. "There's often talk of miracles in this part of the world."

Until quite recently the *Fiestas del Cristo del Amparo* were relatively formal. Couples danced sedately, younger members of the community walked together holding hands, bought sweets and cakes and ices, took part in fair-ground activities in the port, where ducks were thrown into the water and those who caught the struggling creature took it home. There were greasy poles to climb; and local dancers, *Los Picayos de Comillas*, wearing white shirts, long white trousers, wide sashes of red or green, performed to trumpet and drum.

Today, while most of those activities remain, a racier style has taken over. Visitors, tourists, fiesta-hounds pour in to drink and dance, shout, sing and fall over. Vendors of all shapes and sizes come to the erstwhile fishing village to do business with any willing to buy. Stalls are set up, merry-go-rounds erected, shooting galleries opened. The normal population of around three thousand explodes to twenty thousand or more. Bars, shops and restaurants, that have remained closed for most of the year, open up. Houses fill as townsfolk take in lodgers, rent out rooms.

On the nights of the big events, bar and restaurants close their doors. Wooden planks are erected on the footpath as makeshift counters. Barrels of beer are rolled out, mountains of polystyrene cups stacked high. Hand-written signs go up announcing *cachis* of beer or *calimocho*. A *cachi* is a litre. *Calimocho* is a brew of wine and Coca Cola. The rate at which the stuff is sold drives bartenders into a sweat. Many drinkers, however, don't get their *calimocho* from wooden-breasted bars, but purchase the ingredients in supermarkets. They buy cooking wine, Coca Cola and two-litre plastic flasks of drinking water. The water goes down the drain. The flask is filled with wine and Coke. Thus armed, youths of all ages lurch through the night

Most fiesta evenings, two bands play in the Corro. The first begins about 9.00 pm, when few dance but many come to examine the stalls, give their children a turn on the roundabouts. The second rock band starts up at midnight, continues until dawn.

On the morning after the night before, roisterers can be seen lying beneath the chestnuts in the grounds around the marquis' palace, stretched out on Comillas' beach, regardless of the beating sun, asleep in their cars with feet hanging out the windows.

There have been times when we've avoided the fiestas by going further afield. On other nights we've joined in.

"We should go down," Virginia said one evening. "And see what's happening."

"Yes, let's," the children chorused. "I want a ride on the *cadenas*," said Mike, the roundabouts where wooden horses swung on chains. "I'd like to meet my friends," added Kitty more decorously. "Elena and Chrissy said they'd be there."

"Where?"

"In the Corro. I'll find them walking round."

"You'd be lucky to find King Kong on a night like this," I said. "If you go anywhere you go with us. Is that understood?"

"Of course, Daddy," Kitty replied sweetly. She was becoming surprisingly wise. "We must stick together."

"Will we be in time to see the *cabezudos*?" asked Mike, referring to the huge papier-mâché heads worn by classmates who, heavily disguised, paraded through the town hitting their friends with brooms. "That's quite early."

"All right," I agreed. "We'll take a look at things, then go to Chary's."

We made out rounds then went to *Café Rosel*, as Chary's bar is called. As we arrived more fireworks exploded in the fading summer sky. Dogs howled in further terror, slinking away. But even Chary's gentle interior had been closed-off by a bar erected on the footpath. Metal beer barrels stood ready, plastic cups beside them.

"*Hola*," Chary said effusively, kissing everyone. "Oh, I'm such a kisser. I'd even kiss the bum of a gypsy."

"I'm surprised you have this," Virginia said, staring at the makeshift bar.

"There's no other remedy." Chary smiled apologetically. "Last year, it took two days to unblock the toilets. We have to do this or they'll break all the nice things we've got inside."

"Can't you keep the drunks out?"

"They're everywhere. Like whoring flies." Chary poured us drinks. "Whoring sons-of-bitches flies. What else can I do?"

"Nothing, I suppose." I picked up my beer. "*Salud*."

We drifted away from Chary's, who waved cheerfully as she filled another *cachi* with a dreadful mix, to find ourselves in the Plaza de la Fuente de los Tres Caños, where the first water supply came into the town. The only water in sight that night was dripping from the fountain's taps into rubbish-filled pools below. The three maidens, their hands normally lifted in gratitude, seemed to be pleading for peace. There were no grandmothers watching over little ones. Their seats were occupied by young men, most carried a two-litre plastic jar of *calimocho*.

"I'm going down to look at the bracelets," Virginia said. "In that corner where the nice Argentinean has a stall. It's quieter there. You coming?"

I shook my head. The fiesta was beginning to take hold. "That chap over there. I think I'll buy him a drink." I indicated a man with a broken nose, leaning against a raw-wood bar.

"Daddy?" Kitty's voice was critical. "He's one of the drug addicts."

"He's always been fine with me."

"You said we'd stick together."

"We are. I'm just sticking here, that's all."

"Come along," Virginia murmured patiently, taking Kitty and Michael by the hand. "Go and have your drink, then we're all going to the fireworks *together*," she told me, firmly. "Make no mistake about that."

"I'll be right here."

"Just be sure you are."

I talked to the man with the broken nose, known as Lolin. He had a bruise on the side of his face, which he told me was the result of a car crash with an uncle a few nights ago. They'd been to Cabezón de la Sal, some fifteen kilometres inland, drinking with a pair of local ladies. He added that his aunt knew nothing about the ladies in Cabezón.

"She'll know about them now."

"I don't think so. Not now that her husband doesn't see so good."

The uncle had killed two horses belonging to a gypsy, and lost the sight of an eye.

"Was he drunk?"

"*Bueno*, he had taken a few cuba libres."

"Was the gypsy hurt?"

"Not a fingernail. Those gypsies, they're a protected race." Lolin banged the wooden bar in protest. "They get everything. The council gives them flats, but they don't live in them. They take out the bathroom fittings, even the *water*, to sell. Then, they go back to their miserable huts. But my uncle will have to pay for the gypsies' horses. Bad horses, not worth shit. And his van, *coño*, what can he do about that?"

"Wasn't it insured?"

"Insurance? To cover a van would cost a kidney. No, he has the compulsory insurance, that's all. Enough for the gypsies' horses. For his van he'll have to do something else?"

"What else?"

"Find a friend who says he ran into it. Then the insurance'll pay." Lolin almost emptied his glass, left the token drop. "*Bueno*, it was an accident, no?"

Around us the crowd thickened; voices shouted above the clamour of the band. Then Virginia was beside me, displaying an enamel bracelet with crescents of mother-of-pearl, surrounded by azure circles.

"That's lovely." I said. "Did it cost a kidney?"

"Not quite. He always gives me a good price." She glanced at Lolin. "What have you been talking about?"

"He's been telling me about his uncle. He lost an eye."

"I heard about that. It's his wife I feel sorry for." She smiled sweetly at Lolin. "They're bastards, you know. The way they treat their women."

"I didn't think she knew."

"They always know. That's the trouble."

"Señora." Lolin made a small bow. "I wish you very happy fiestas. *Buenos noches.*"

"*Buenos noches,*" Virginia turned to me. "Now it's time for the fireworks. Let's go to the Estatua. That's where they set them off."

We walked up the hill, through the Corro San Pedro, where I'd talked to Viscount Santiago about a book that now had shape. Whether it would show Comillanos how their town should be portrayed, as the viscount crisply suggested, remained to be seen, but at least it was progressing.

"Up here," said Michael. "I want to stand on the wall."

"Let's not get too close," said Kitty. "Sometimes the sticks fall back. Inmaculada got hit on the head last year."

We found a clear space on a grassy bank, waited among whispers of excitement, a sense of growing expectation, our eyes on the statue of the first Marquis of Comillas, the centre of the scene. Suddenly the crowd roared as the first heraldic bang exploded in the sky with sufficient force to rattle windows and trigger car-alarms.

"*Mira, que bonito,*" a grandfather said to the little girl perched on his hip. "Look, how beautiful."

His words were apt. Rockets, shedding gold and silver, red, orange, blue and green raced upward, burst with thunderous bangs, rained down showers of colour. A host of twirling Catherine wheels, spilling violet sparkles, made eerie whistling noises as they danced in circles. Sheets of stars boomed above our heads, drifted softly across the velvet dark, mixed into the nets of whitish smoke, the vapour trails of previous explosions, to form patterns of delicate design, as full of life as Virginia's Argentinean bracelet, as finely wrought as her new York necklace complete with pearls. Crowns, coronets, galaxies of lifting, drifting stars drew pictures across the dark, until a final desperate thunderclap, more deafening than all the rest, told us the performance was over and, for a while, our ears could rest in peace.

"That was terrific," Kitty said. "Really very, very good."

"I liked the *cohetes,*" said Michael, the Spanish word for rockets. "The ones that sang before they went off."

"I liked them too," Kitty agreed. "They were cool."

"Wonderful, wasn't it." Virginia turned to me. "You enjoyed it, didn't you?"

"I did," I admitted. "Due to the beer or the company, I'm not sure."

"A bit of both, I suspect. What do you want to do now?"

"Have a drink. What else?"

"We could go home."

"Probably a good idea, though there's a lot going." I looked at the crowd, streaming away from the marquis' statue. Some, clutching kegs of *calimocho*, were descending toward the Corro, where a fresh rock band was tuning up. Other groups were winding down to the beach, the lighted bars and cafés, the stretches of uncluttered sand. "Even if there's no running of the bulls."

Virginia frowned. "What a curious remark."

"In Pamplona that's what it's all about."

"Nothing in the world would get me to another bull-fight."

"I was only making a joke."

"About bull-fights? Not very funny."

"It was probably brought to mind by an article I read recently. In the Art and Culture section of the paper. Though, whether they're art or culture's hard to say. Anyway, someone was complaining because the bulls didn't want to fight."

"Of course they don't, the poor creatures. They're terrified. They come out piddling with fear." Virginia looked away, tight lines about her mouth. "It's not really something to make a joke about. It's not very funny at all."

She was right, of course, as she usually is, and spoke from bitter experience.

We'd gone to a Mexican bull-ring to see *novilleros*, young inexperienced fighters, prancing arrogantly in their suits of lights before attempting to slaughter frightened bulls beneath our ring-side seats. It was an ugly scene of incompetence and brutality, unattractive enough to disgust a lifetime *aficionado*. Virginia remained as long as she was able, left with tears in her eyes. I stayed on a while, hoping to see some of the spectacle the clash can provide, but what was happening that afternoon was a far cry from the skilled performance I'd witnessed the first time I went to Spain, when El Cordobés had the crowd in Alicante on its feet, myself among them, cheering wildly, caught by his daring, the respect he showed for the bull.

In Majorca we were persuaded, one final time, to go to a *corrida*, but the memory of Mexico lingered on, and no one on that steamy afternoon had the magic of El Cordobés. Since then our sympathy has remained with the animals. We'd like to see them left among the clover and the daisies, their lives uninterrupted by men in fancy dress. Curious, what hunters wear when they're after other creatures. Foxhunters in scarlet jackets, duck-shooters in uniforms, trophy-hunters in safari-camouflage, bullfighters in shining suits, all seem to need appropriate decoration before going out to kill.

It's unlikely, however, that our wish for the bulls will be fulfilled. There's too much money in the game, too much profit. Bull ranches are subsidised by the European Community and, in spite of growing opposition, the sport is part of show business, grist for the media mills. Young bullfighters, barely in their twenties, are treated like pop-stars, given fame and fortune before their wisdom teeth. Fight-promoters, to help safeguard their investments, indulge in devious practices to ensure the bull is rendered less capable before it enters the ring.

The *afeitado*, the *shaving*, the cutting back of the horns has become almost commonplace. This is most often done with a hacksaw, which severs the central nerve. The shortened horn is then filed down to leave a blunter, less dangerous point. But the damaged nerve remains painful, must be like chewing on a broken tooth. The last-minute swipe of Vaseline over the bull's eyeballs is another way of handicapping the creature. It would be difficult enough to see what was happening, chased out of a dark tunnel into an arena filled with light, without Vaseline hampering vision, adding to the terror. Unfortunately, with these and other tricks of the trade, the money and the publicity, bull fighting seems destined to continue for many years to come.

As we walked down the hill from the Estatua, the smell of gunpowder in the air, my eye caught the gnome-like figure of Cuadri at a bar near the church. "I think I'll have a drink with the master builder," I said to Virginia. "Be the decent thing to do."

"Why not? You have an emotional bond."

"Can I go to the *tiros*?" asked Michael, referring to the shooting gallery, where he'd won so many hand-woven bracelets his flesh was barely visible below the elbow. "If Daddy's going to have another drink, can I?"

"You go to the *tiros*," Virginia said firmly. "Be back in ten minutes. Kitty and I will buy some nuts. Daddy will have his drink." She gave us all a steady look. "Then we're going home. Is that understood?"

We nodded, I turned to the approaching Cuadri, limping slightly. "*Buenas fiestas*," he said, shaking my hand. "We have a *copa*?"

"What a nice idea."

"Good fiestas, no?" he said cheerfully as we went to a rough-plank bar, where he beckoned the youth, wearing a black top hat, serving drinks. "Brandy? That all right with you?"

"Yes," I replied. "You busy at the moment?"

"*Pouf.*" He nodded contentedly. "Comillas is popular again. After years of sleeping we've got a boom. New flats being built everywhere, you've noticed that?"

"It'd be hard to avoid."

"And the prices? *Zas.*" Cuadri made a skyward movement with his hand. "Like rockets. Your house, what's it worth now? Three times, four times, what you paid for it?"

"It's lucky we came when we did." I picked up my brandy, served, out of respect for the contractor, in a glass not a plastic cup. "I don't think I could afford it now."

"Many can." Cuadri held out a hand, rubbed his fingertips together. "There's a lot of black money coming out. It's going into houses, flats, cars. The Euro has done that. Now they're spending their money as fast as they can, so as not to reveal how much they've got."

"Very good for contractors like yourself."

"*Bueno*, money is nothing." Cuadri finished his brandy, watched the barman pour more. "Money's only money. It's what you do with it that matters."

"I suppose that's true enough." I yawned suddenly. "Sorry, too much fiestas."

"Tomorrow you'll take a siesta, no?"

"I always take a siesta."

"What siestas do the English take? Normal, or the *siesta de los borregos?*"

"*Siesta de los borregos?*" I laughed. The siesta of the lambs. "When's that?"

"Before you eat. That's a good time, no?"

"Any time's good. Without a siesta I doubt if I'd survive."

We chatted a few moments more, then Virginia was back offering a mixture of cashews, walnuts and pistachios. Soon we said good-night to Cuadri, began to wander home, finally arrived at our solid front door to hear the dogs barking a noisy welcome.

In winter, the fiestas are more dignified. They begin at Christmas, not traditionally a time of gift giving in Spain, although becoming increasingly so, and culminate on the eve of January 5, when the *cabalgata*, a mounted procession, leads the Three Kings, Gaspar, Melchor and Balthasar, down from the Seminary to the *Belén*, the Nativity Scene in the town. The weather is cold, the air frosty, townsfolk are dressed in coats, scarves, gloves and hats. All bars are both open and closed. Open to welcome everyone in, closed against the chill.

"Kitty has been chosen as an angel," Virginia said one year. "In the Nativity Scene in the Ayuntamiento. She's very excited about that."

"I thought she wanted to gallop down from the Seminary."
"She does, but she'd prefer to be an angel."
"A hard choice to make."
"She can ride in the *cabalgata* next year. But, being an angel's rather special. I only hope she'll be warm enough. They have to wear those thin white gowns."
"I didn't think angels felt the cold."
Virginia gave me a critical look, but kept her comment to herself.

Vehicles of every sort, decorated to resemble rural cabins, take part in the Nativity parade. Accompanying them are calves, lambs, goats, chickens, ducks and roosters. In trucks, tractors, ox-carts, horse-drawn wagons, the old, the young, the in-between are dressed to reflect country ways. They clutch livestock, carry candles and lanterns, wave burning torches trailing pillars of smoke as the caravan descends, like a travelling farmyard, from the Seminary to the town. With it are others dressed as Moors or Christians swinging make-believe swords, fighting battles of ages past.

Moor and Christian imagery is an essential part of the parade. While two of the Three Kings are white, Balthasar is black, echoing Moorish times. He is never, however, a genuine brother, as Phil Hill who escorted me through Harlem might have said, but a local lad with make-up.

In Comillas the Three Kings make their way to the plaza beside the church, where the Nativity Scene, awaits them beneath the Municipal Building. Most of the townsfolk are there. Necks crane as an ox, a cow or an ass moves uneasily on straw laid over the cobblestones. Voices lift as Mary holds her baby close, while Joseph keeps an eye on the animals, and the angels try to remain as still as they can in the chilly night air. When the *cabalgata* finally draws up, a hidden voice questions the youngsters as to whether they've been good or bad, asking who'll be rewarded, who'll be threatened with a gift of coal.

"Me, me, me," cry the little voices. "I've been good."
"Have you obeyed your parents?"
"Yes, yes," they chorus, with a few uncertain frowns. "All the time."
"Gone to school? Done your homework?"
"Of course."
"Gone to Mass?"

The plaza roars in response. There's no doubt about that. By now, the Three Kings have climbed onto a large open-backed truck, crammed with gift-wrapped boxes, packets and parcels. Names are read out, small hands reach up, cries of delight, squeals of joy are heard throughout the plaza as presents are given away.

When the truck is empty the fireworks begin. With a blaze of penetrating light, Roman candles fill the air with acrid smoke, drive out the terrified pigeons that have sought sanctuary in the church. The Three Kings move to a walkway beside the main door. Children mill past, shake their hands, receive vast quantities of sweets. While from the *Belén*, shivering now, their breaths pluming the winter air, the angels and the Holy Family watch events draw to a close. No one staggers past on such an occasion, clutching a flask of *calimocho*, singing a ribald song. All return home to warm hearths, hot food and more gifts that need unwrapping.

"*Felicidades*," the townsfolk say as they shake hands or kiss, wishing each other happiness for fiestas yet to come. "*Felices fiestas*."

One other fiesta celebrated in Comillas is Carnival, which takes place at the start of Lent, before the period of self-denial that precedes the Crucifixion. The nights of Carnival can be mild or freezing, but never warm and summery as they are in carnival-land itself, Brazil. The weather, however, doesn't dissuade many Comillanos, or those in other parts of Spain, from wearing their *disfraz*, their fancy dress, and competing for prizes as the best group, act, or would-be pop idol.

In the hunt for fancy dress, clothes are pulled out of cupboards, local shopwindows are filled with hideous masks. Grotesque apes, beasts that range from vampires to several versions of Frankenstein's monster, witch-like women, men who look as if they've been run over by a bus, are on sale. On the night of Carnival these creatures walk the streets. Half the fun is guessing who you're talking to, who's hitting you with their witch's broom, who's giving you a vampire kiss.

To end these festivities, all through Spain, a paper mâché sardine or *besugo*, a red sea bream, is burnt or buried. As the legend has it, the original *besugo* kidnapped a mermaid he was infatuated with. For his crime he was condemned by Neptune to never see his darling again. The poor fish died of love, but every Carnival is resurrected, only to be penalised once more

◆ ◆ ◆

In a warm bar, at a recent Carnival, I saw Juaco, whisky in hand. There was no sign of the Harley Davidson, the red lighting on its side. He called out a friendly greeting then, closing his eyes in mock shame, patted his forehead.

"You don't have to tell me," he said. "I haven't done it, yet."

"What's that?"

"Taken you back to Oyambre. Told you the story of the Yellow Bird." He shrugged apologetically. "How's the book coming along, by the way?"

"It's taking shape," I said. "But I'd like to include the Yellow Bird. And, wasn't there something about an English House?"

"There was. We'll do it all tomorrow. If that's okay with you."

"Fine," I replied. "I look forward to it."

14

The Yellow Bird

As promised, Juaco roared up on his Harley Davidson, wearing heavy gloves, jacket, a helmet. "Come along," he shouted, as I emerged from the house. "It's a lovely day." The sky was almost clear, a skein of wraith-like cloud hung below the golden sun, yet the air was crisp with cold. "You ready for Oyambre?"

"Let's go in our van," I suggested. "We can take the dogs."

"Fine with me." He locked his bike. "Be much warmer, I can tell you."

We drove down the stretch of highway from Comillas to La Rabia, through a long avenue past the football field, between lines of giant plane trees. Just before we came to La Rabia, and the still waters of the wildfowl haven, Juaco touched my arm.

"Pull over here," he said. "That's the English House. It belongs to an old friend of mine, but there's no one at home at the moment. Come on, we'll take a look."

"Does it have a formal name?"

"Yes, *La Casa de Gerramolino*. But, as an English architect designed it, that's how it got to be called what it is," Juaco explained, as we walked around a two-storied house with wide windows, broad eaves, and walls of stone. Wooden balconies gave a sense of lightness to the building and, from the sloping red-tiled roof, dormer windows peered out. It was a house as settled in its trees as a villa in the Lake District, a stockbroker's dwelling beside the Thames. "Look at the windows," Juaco said. "They're different to anything else round here. The English want to let the light in. We do our best to keep it out."

"Was it built for an Englishman?"

"A man called Pontifax. He worked in the calamine mines near Cobreces. You know the place I'm talking about?"

"The open-cut workings. What do they call them? *Los Pozos Azules*, the Blue Pools? I had a look at them once. Calamine, that's lead-zinc if I remember rightly. Must have copper in it too. The pools are a bluey green."

"The mines were pretty famous in their day. The Romans worked them, and much later the French. You won't believe this, but the ore was so damned important to the French they kept a consul here. Seems hard to believe, but there actually was a French consul in Comillas. Boats used to come into the harbour, load up and sail away." Juaco walked past the house, looked out across the wildfowl park. White swans approached, expecting food. "As I said, this Pontifax was a mining engineer. He had a wife in Liverpool, but spent most of his time in Comillas. He travelled home, now and then, and on one significant occasion met a young lady in distress in Paris."

"Sounds like a familiar story."

"I guess it is. Anyway, Pontifax gave her a helping hand." Juaco's laugh rolled across the water, stopped the swans. "More than just a hand, if you know what I mean. The upshot was, they decided to come and live in Comillas. In the town, before this house was built."

"While his wife was still in Liverpool?"

"That worried Pontifax a bit. Most Comillanos knew he had a lady back home."

"Were they offended?"

"You bet they were. The locals could be very moral when it suited them."

Juaco went on to tell me how Pontifax and the young lady decided that the best way to avoid gossip was to pretend she was his male secretary. She cut her hair short, wore no make-up, dressed in a simple suit and settled in Comillas. They lived a quiet life, but tongues soon began to wag.

"They thought, well you know what I mean." Juaco let his wrist drop in an unmistakable gesture. "The word *gay* hadn't gotten into the Spanish language then. They were *maricones*."

"Why should that have worried them?"

"It didn't. Until her stomach began to swell." Juaco shook his head in sympathy. "They didn't have the pill in those days either."

In the end, the gossips had their way, the couple was forced out of town. Pontifax, as many good and watchful souls had suspected, was not only an English Protestant but a philanderer as well. A corrupter of young women, even if they looked like men, who had the audacity to live in public with his paramour. He had no sense of shame. The tenancy, in the town house he occupied, was terminated and he had to move on. Which he did, a kilometre and a half down the road to the lakefront at La Rabia, where huge willow trees grow by the water, and herons hunt the shore.

"Was that far enough?"

"More than enough in those days," replied Juaco. "La Rabia was another village. He bought a piece of land. A friend of his designed the house, and he became a man of property. A country squire. That was quite different, of course, from hiring a place in Comillas."

The child was born, a daughter. The mother let her hair grow into long red locks. She became a famous figure on the landscape, galloping her horse up the avenue to Comillas, her bright hair flowing behind her, her black cape swirling in the wind.

"My aunt described her to me like that," Juaco told me. "I think she secretly admired her for being a rebel of her age."

"So, they lived happily ever after?"

"Well, no, it didn't turn out quite like that."

Some years later, Pontifax drowned crossing a ford on horseback at the height of a storm. The horse stumbled, the rider was flung into the torrent, and it was the end of the mining engineer's dream. The young woman, who had been taken under his wing when alone in Paris, now found herself once more in distress, and with a young daughter to look after.

"What happened then?"

"Ah." Juaco raised a significant finger. "Here the tale takes a real Victorian turn. She wasn't very wise. And she didn't have any family here. That's what's so important in a place like this. A family you can count on. She had no one to advise her, no one to tell her what to do."

For a while the woman mourned, then a young man from Comillas came down the road to comfort her, to lessen her distress. She responded, and once again was taken beneath another's wing. A less benevolent wing, it appears, because before very long she was persuaded to sell the house and travel to Barcelona with her daughter and the new man in her ill-starred life.

"He took her money and left." Juaco picked up a handful of small stones, tossed them into the water. Rings ran out toward the swans; they paused uncertainly. "He left her and the little girl. Went off with another woman."

"Anyone know what happened to the mother?"

"She returned to England, I believe. I guess she had family there. The daughter came back here once, I remember my aunt talking about it. She still had a Comillano accent. You know, where *vino*, sounds like *vinoo*. And a small cup of coffee becomes a *cafesitoo*. But, I don't know what happened to the mother. Damned sad, when you think about it."

"As you say, a Victorian tale."

"It sure is. Well, come on, let's get to Oyambre and I'll tell you about the Yellow Bird." Juaco grinned. "You'll like that story, it's got a happy ending."

We walked back to the car where the dogs were becoming restless, they could smell the sea and a stretch of sand. We left the house among its chestnuts and magnolias, with its memories bright and sombre, standing on the wildfowl shore, where swans waited to be fed.

"*El Pájaro Amarillo*, the Yellow Bird, that's what the plane was called," Juaco said as he strode along the broad sands of Oyambre. The tide was low, seagulls waited in flocks until the dogs sent them skyward, where they wheeled and protested, to land grumbling further along the shore. "It took off from Old Orchard, in the United States, in nineteen twenty-nine."

"Two years after Lindbergh?"

"That's it. Only the second plane to fly the Atlantic. Amazing to think it came down here on Oyambre. They were damned lucky the tide was out. Otherwise they'd have all been killed."

"They weren't heading here?"

"They set off for Paris. Le Bourget, where Lindbergh went. When they came down they thought they were in Ireland. Boy, were they in for a surprise."

"What went wrong?"

The aircraft and its crew were French, Juaco told me as we walked the beach. The *Pájaro Amarillo* was a yellow, single-engined monoplane which took off in a blaze of glory hoping to emulate Charles Lindbergh's famous *The Spirit of St Louis*. All went well until an American stowaway was discovered aboard.

"The stowaway, a guy called Schreiber, was a journalist out to make his name," Juaco explained. "He made all the difference between success and failure."

"How?"

"His weight was the problem. They had to get rid of two hundred litres of gasoline to compensate for his kilos."

"That wouldn't have made him too popular."

"It didn't. In fact, they made him sign a contract guaranteeing the crew fifty percent of whatever he made out of writing about the flight. My guess is, they threatened to toss him overboard if he refused. Anyway, when they got rid of the gas, they realised they weren't going to make it to Paris. There were other problems too. They ran into a storm."

The storm damaged the aircraft. The magneto began functioning irregularly, radio contact was lost. The pilots changed direction, thinking they were heading for the Azores, but to their dismay, mile after mile, no land appeared. After twenty-seven hours of non-stop flying, with fuel low and no real idea where they were, they came to the Cantabrian coast, saw the long stretch of Oyambre, reconnoitred the sand, and then brought the aircraft down safely.

"I tell you, it scared hell out of those up there." Juaco pointed to the tiny village of Güera, a line of white-walled houses on a hill. "There's an old lady who lives in your barrio. She hid beneath her bed."

"I don't suppose she'd seen a plane before."

"Most of them hadn't even heard of one. And when this giant came out of the sky, some of them never recovered. Amazing, when you think of it. The second flight across the Atlantic, the first with a European crew, actually landed on this piece of sand." He shook his head in awe. "Made Oyambre famous for a while. Got Comillas into the headlines."

The flight of the Yellow Bird was front-page news all over the world, especially in Paris, where the plane had been given up as lost. In Comillas, the French flyers and their American stowaway were tremendously well received. Thousands of people swarmed to the beach to stare at, touch, to be photographed with the enormous creature that had flown from the other side of the Atlantic, a distance beyond the imagination of most who came to view. For three days the plane stood above the waterline while the radio was repaired, the magneto put back into working order.

"Know who did that?" Juaco asked, and watched me shake my head. "An ex-neighbour of yours. A mechanic, newly appointed. Hispano-Suiza had just opened an agency here. The engine of the Yellow Bird was Hispano-Suiza. They couldn't have landed at a better place. There was an expert ready and waiting."

"Who was that?"

"I don't think you ever met him. But, you knew his wife. I saw you at her funeral."

"Pilarine?"

"That's right. The guy who fixed the plane used to live next door to you."

"Curious," I said. "When I talked to Viscount Santiago, he said everything was connected here. Everything was linked."

"That's the sort of thing Santi would say." Juaco laughed. "But he's right, you know. Comillas, when you come to think about it, is full of amazing stuff. Anyway, this is what they put up to celebrate the event." We had reached a whitish slab of stone, set on a concrete block now eroded by the waves that roll constantly in. It seemed an inappropriate symbol to something as glorious as the second flight over the Atlantic Ocean. "It doesn't look like too much now, but it made a splash in its day."

We climbed onto the concrete base to peer at a barely legible message inscribed in memory of the Yellow Bird. Few of the words could be read, time and the sun, the constant erosion of wind-blown sand had nearly obliterated the text. Above the names of the pilots, the aircraft and the date were the sculptured shapes of two half-worlds, with the flight-path of the aircraft in between.

"The pilots came back when this was inaugurated," Juaco said. "Several government ministers turned up. The bishop of Santander was here also. It was quite an event. They put on an aerobatics display with a couple of squadrons. One French, the other Spanish." He laughed. "It had to be cancelled half-way through. The spectators got into a panic. Ran around like headless chickens. Thought it was the end of the world. I tell you, it took them a long time to get used to flying machines around here."

"Did the stowaway come back for the celebration?" I looked at the inscription, the friable stone. "After all, he was responsible for the plane landing on Oyambre."

"I never heard any more about him." Juaco climbed down, stood staring at the monument. "It's a damned shame what's happened to this. It should be taken care of."

"Shows what Mother Nature can do when she gets to work." I touched the sandstone, it crumbled between my fingers. "This stuff's pretty soft. One day the monument will be isolated. The tide coming up around it."

"Then it'll sink." Juaco began walking back along the beach. "Like that fishing boat at Comillas. You ever seen that? The ribs show when the sand gets washed away."

"I've often wondered what that was."

"A French lobster boat. Sank there years ago."

"Makes you think what else is under the sand."

"The history of the whole damned place. But, I guess, we'll never find out exactly what," he said as we walked back along the great curve of beach. Ahead, on the crest of the hill, stood the handsome outline of the Seminario, appearing too solid to be touched by time, yet beneath the skin decay was nibbling at its ageing heart. "You must have got a lot of stuff together by now."

"For the book?" I nodded. "Almost a manuscript."

"Talked to El Rey yet? The old guy with who lives up the hill?"

"He's a bit of a recluse, I understand."

"Depends on his mood. Sometimes he greets you, sometimes he doesn't. He has days we call *malas pulgas*, bad fleas. When he's irritated, you know. But, he's okay and really helpful. Like Eladio, anything you want to know, he's got a book on it."

"I'll get in touch."

"Do that, give him a call." Juaco glanced at his watch, quickened his pace. "It's time we had a drink. Come on, let's get to La Rabia and watch the birds being fed. I tell you, that's a sight. They come from miles around."

From a bank overlooking the wildfowl park we watched an iron-haired man, with a thin lined face, row about the inlet, leaving corn on floating feed-stalls. He grinned happily as brown and green-crested mallards, redheaded pochards, a range of coloured creatures closed in around him. Black and white swans beat the water eagerly as they approached. And all about, the coots and the divers came nearer. Only the herons stood apart, observing the frenzy with disdain.

"He's great, isn't he," Juaco said. "Gives his life to the birds nowadays."

"Someone else I should talk to?"

"You should talk to everyone. But, that could take years."

"It could. In the meantime, I'll get in touch with El Rey."

"Do that. He's got an amazing collection in that little house of his."

When I got home, Michael was standing by the front door holding his nose, eyes streaming. "Willie's just done a big toad on the mat inside. I tried to clean it up. But it's making me sick," he managed to splutter.

"It's a turd, not a toad," corrected Kitty, as she emerged.

"Looks like a toad."

"Don't be disgusting." Kitty sighed impatiently. "At least he's stopped saying gomit when someone's sick."

"It's all right, I'll take care of it," I said, as Virginia arrived with a cloth. "You shouldn't be doing any bending."

A week or so earlier she'd discovered a lump in her groin. The local doctor confirmed our suspicions. It was a hernia and, although it would have been possible to wait, the decision was taken to operate before it became any larger. In a week she'd go into hospital. In the meantime she had to move as little as possible, not lift anything heavy or get down on hands and knees.

"I worry about my ladies," Virginia said, when the decision was made, referring to the loyal band who attended her aerobics classes. "I'll have to put them on hold."

"Give them exercises to do at home."

"I've thought of that, but they won't get much done without me."

"When you're back you can give classes sitting down."

"I'll have to, for a bit."

"What's best while you're in hospital?" I asked. "Should I stay here with the children?"

"Yes, and don't worry. I won't be alone. Chary's coming with me."

Going into hospital in Spain is quite unlike anything we'd experienced in the lands we knew. This first came to our notice when Kitty was born. Virginia's room in the clinic was furnished with twin beds. One for her, the other for someone else to see to her minor needs, particularly through the night. Night staff, in general, is thin on the ground. Medications are given, those in need are regularly checked, temperatures and blood pressures are taken, but the companion who shares the patient's room attends to personal requirements. Going into hospital can become a family affair.

All very well if you have a large family. A little more difficult if you are the only English unit in a Cantabrian town. Unless, of course, you have friends like Chary, Renée or Elena who are prepared to drop everything to be by your bedside.

"You're like my family," Chary said, when I tried express our appreciation. "Don't thank me. There's no reason for that."

"There is as far as I am concerned."

"*Pouf*, you English…"

"Nevertheless…"

"*Nada más*." She put her fingers over my lips. "If you have any problems with Kitty and Mikey ring my mother. She'll come straight away."

We were fortunate to have such friends. After two nights, when Chary had other matters to attend to, Elena moved in and took over. We were also well served by our medical insurance, and found local specialists to be very good, in some cases outstanding. In public wards however, under Social Security's financially strained system, matters can be grim. From time to time the whole tottering structure comes close to collapse. A smiling red-haired friend of Virginia's had to give birth without an anaesthetic.

The day for Virginia's operation was in bright September. Appropriately enough the Virginia creeper along our high back wall had turned its lovely red-vermilion, hung in gorgeous layers as we drove away from the house. From the eucalyptus and linden trees around the Seminario, the pines and chestnuts in the grounds of the marquis' palace, came the flutter of crows, the occasional boom of pigeons. Sparrows chattered in the air. Delicate orange and black butterflies spun in the end-of-summer sky. The hedgerows were heavy with blackberries.

"It's lovely," Virginia said quietly. "It's the best month of the year. I love the beach in September. In the mornings when I walk there with Amapola there's hardly anyone else." She paused. "It's ridiculous, isn't it? You go into hospital feeling pretty good. They reduce you to a wreck, then tell you you're getting better."

◆ ◆ ◆

The following day we all went in to see her, propped up in bed. "Last night was pretty bad," she said weakly. "Thank God, Chary was here."

"This place is *fatal*. The noises from the street. Those students *gilipollas*, shouting." Chary said, picking up the conversation, using the Spanish version of *silly pricks*. "The noise was like a whore-house."

"It's good you were here."

"Now, I'm going to have a coffee." She held out her hands to Kitty and Mike. "I'll take them with me. You're on duty for a while."

"Thank you." I turned back to Virginia. "What'd the doctor say?"

"He was here this morning and said everything would be all right." She smiled. "But they always say that, don't they?"

"Why shouldn't he be telling you the truth?"

"I only hope he did. I don't want to go through this again." She moved, and smiled wanly. "Are you all right? Not too much to do on your own?"

"No, I'm fine. I've got a date with El Rey tomorrow."

"They say he's amazing."

"That depends on the state of his fleas."

15

Magic Castles

When I first made contact with El Rey, the man Juaco said had wonderful a collection of Comillas' bric-a-brac, his voice sounded cautious over the line. However, after I told him I was writing a book he relented, and said he'd be pleased to see me. His cottage was in a back-lane on a twisting hill, a cobblestone passageway where stone-walled houses spilled geraniums in cascades of pink, orange and red over dark-brown wooden balconies.

When I knocked on his iron-bound front door, it was opened immediately by a small chubby man, wearing a red and white striped jacket, who smiled and warmly shook my hand. "Come in, come in," he said, a halo of soft white hair floating as he moved his head. "Consider this to be your house. You're very welcome here."

"I should have spoken to you sooner," I said, as he ushered me into his sitting room. "They say you know a great deal about Comillas."

"Oh, not me." He smiled modestly. "I really don't know anything at all."

"They also say that if you don't have the answer you know where to find it. You've got books on everything."

"That is true," he replied. "I have seven thousand books, which I intend to leave to the town when I die. I've spent a lifetime working with books. So, when I move on to the next world, I'd like to think they'll be appreciated here."

"I am sure they will," I replied, glad I'd caught him on a day of good fleas. "What did you do with books?"

"I restored them. Very old manuscripts especially. I was a type of doctor, you know. A doctor of book diseases."

"When I was a geologist in Fiji they called me a rock doctor."

"Is that so?" El Rey replied, unimpressed. "Books are much more important."

"That's one of the reasons I gave up rocks."

"*Bueno.*" He eased himself into a comfortable armchair, and pointed to a couch where I squatted amongst old newspapers. "What is it you wanted to know?"

"I'd like to talk to you about the town," I said, my eyes going around the walls with their vast array of pottery, ceramics, implements of iron, brass and copper; assemblages of jugs, vases, metal-bound bottles, swords, shields and fighting masks. "And I'd like you to tell me about yourself. You have some wonderful things."

"If you want to know about the town, I suggest you consult a book." His soft smile returned. "But if you'd like to see my house, I'd be happy to show it to you."

"I'd love to see your house."

"Then, come with me." We stood and began a tour through a piggy-bank of precious pieces he'd gathered throughout a lifetime. "There are three floors. I'll show you all of them."

El Rey's house was a museum, a parade of unexpected treasures, a collection unlike any other in the town. On almost every wall, interwoven with figurines, beautifully dressed Japanese dolls, were paintings, drawings, charcoal sketches of Comillas, the Picos, the rock-bound coast, and the man himself.

"Done by my students," he explained. "When I taught in Barcelona."

"They're very good."

"There were many who were talented. Their work keeps my memories alive."

He smiled and looked around him, at the enchanting display of his life. Anything that was delicate, richly crafted or finely made, that he had been able to get hold of, lay within his nest. Each piece was presented like a jewel.

"This is wonderful," I said. "You live in a museum."

"Not really." He shook his head, his soft hair floated. "Just a simple house with a few things I've collected. I have been lucky in my life."

"You have so much of Comillas." My eyes went to an original sunflower from Gaudí's Capricho, a pair of glazed *Ave María* tiles from the walls of the Seminario, a fragment of interwoven floral sculpture that had once been part of the marquis' palace. There was a small finely mounted chip of blue-veined marble that could have come from one of the sculptures, cut by the hands of a Catalan master, in the Chapel Mausoleum. "Everything that's beautiful in the town, you have a piece of it here."

"Just little souvenirs." El Rey glanced toward the door, as if afraid of being overheard. "But, please, don't talk about these things of mine. There are many who are jealous."

"You must have been collecting for years."

"All my life. Beautiful things are our measure. They make us what we are." El Rey's face lit up. "It delights me that you're interested. Come, I will show you more."

He led me from room to room, through three immaculate floors of his memento-filled house. There were beams with lines of oil lamps in polished bronze, silver and brass. El Rey stooped as he walked beneath them in a gesture of respect. On a gleaming mahogany table stood a turn-of-the century gramophone, its huge brass speaker gleaming, its wind-up box brightly polished. It was a living His Master's Voice, all that was missing was the dog. There was a wall whose every inch seemed filled with clocks of all shapes and sizes, differing faces and numerals, hands that moved steadily in the apparently timeless air. Most worked, those that did were accurate. Their clicking, the soft metallic sounds they made, measured our temporary passing.

"What amazing clocks."

"Of course, they're beautiful. Like us, they're never still."

El Rey moved into a bedroom. "These bed-heads are interesting," he said. "They're old Portuguese cattle yokes. Nicely made, no?"

"They're superb."

"It *is* fine work." He touched the wood, ran his fingers lovingly over dark red cedar, crafted in a pattern of vines, spreading leaves, clusters of grapes adorning a yoke that must have been used on special occasions to show the bound beasts at their best. "It would have taken a long time to create something as lovely as this."

"Have you lived in Portugal?"

"I've lived in many places." El Rey closed his eyes, as if seeing distant lands. "In many parts of the world. But, really, I'm just a simple Comillano." He turned again, left the bedroom, climbed another flight of stairs. "Look at this," he said, switching on a light. "This is my best room. My *sala de estar*. Although, I don't spend as much time here as I should. I sit downstairs too often. In front of the television."

"We all do that."

"It's a vice. You see, I live alone these days. My wife died some years ago. I find companionship in television. Someone talking in the room."

"I'm sorry to hear about your wife."

"She had great talent as a book-restorer." El Rey walked toward a tall, glass-fronted bookcase, filled with leather bindings stacked row upon careful row. "I taught her myself. She was a student of mine in Barcelona, when I lectured at *Bellas Artes*."

"About books?"

"Restoring them, bringing them back to life. As I told you, I was a book doctor. Books get ill. They become infected. If you don't cure them they die."

"You're talking about mildew, things like that."

"It might be mildew. It might be more."

El Rey opened a door of the bookcase and reached inside. As he did so he became more animated, his voice lifted as he told me how inks become oxidised, how acid in the air can attack certain papers, what is needed to be done to restore a volume's health. He smiled fondly as described the work of re-gluing, of replacing sections too far gone with Japanese paper. He spoke of re-sewing bindings with silken thread, of ironing pages as carefully as if they were delicate garments. He frowned when he told me how to wash pages in alkaline solutions when human hands, not entirely clean, had touched them; when bookworms or other insects had died and the rot had spread. He lifted a careful finger as he said mild bleaches could be used to restore a page, but extreme care was needed. He shook his head in severe rebuke when he spoke of manuscripts that had come from churches, old monasteries, even government archives where they'd been left too long unattended, permitted to decay.

"They weren't loved," he said sadly. "As they should have been. Sometimes they were lost. There was nothing that could be done to save them."

"How disappointing."

"A tragedy, nothing less." El Rey paused a moment, then took a beautiful volume from the bookcase. It had a soft leather binding, silk end-papers. "Look at this," he said proudly. "Restored by my wife. As I said, she had a marvellous gift."

I opened the book and stared. It was a copy of *Opus Super Quatoz Evangelia* by Saint Thomas Aquinas, in Latin, dated 1493. "My God," I whispered. "I've never touched a book as old as this before."

"It is quite old, and the work is beautiful. She had wonderful ability."

"Do you realise that Christopher Columbus could have held this in his hand. When he returned from the Americas, he could have picked it up. I find that amazing. I'm here, talking to you, holding a book he might have read."

"Yes, that is very interesting." El Rey took out more volumes. "There are others, but not quite so old. All are first editions. Some from the seventeenth century."

"You're going to give all these to Comillas?"

"Only if they are properly cared for. I have a friend who will catalogue them. He'll see they are adequately cared for. Whether I'm alive or not."

"I hope so. They're treasures."

"They are small possessions that are important to me." His head moved, the soft hair flowed. "I have many memories in this house of mine. Especially the books."

"You really love them, don't you?"

"Yes." He looked at me steadily, content to admit the truth. "Come," he said, closing the bookcase door. "Let's go down and have a glass of wine. I've put some books aside for you. You may find them helpful."

We went down the stairs, past charcoal sketches of Comillas, the Capricho, the Seminary on the hill. There were others of El Rey I hadn't noticed earlier. In each his chubby head was lifted nobly, in profile like a Roman coin.

"They're very flattering," he said, observing my interest. "But, they make me much more handsome than I am."

"They are very good."

"Some of my students had a great *don*," he said, using the Spanish word for talent. "I was lucky to have them in my classes. Now, look at this." He glanced toward the door again. "But, please, don't talk about it. They might wonder where it came from. You know what people are like. Perhaps I shouldn't have it in my house."

He led me to a very old telephone, mounted on a corner pillar, from which a mouthpiece protruded like a horn. It was tiny, beautifully preserved.

"I'm told it is the first ever installed in Comillas. It was brought to me by a workman who said they were going to throw it away." El Rey shrugged. "Mind you, you could only call out on it. To the servants, I believe. They couldn't answer back."

"I'm glad it found a home with you."

"*Bueno,* mine is only a humble collection. Little pieces I've discovered. However, this is interesting." He pointed to a glass-framed card signed *Victoria Eugenie.* "They say this was from the time the royal family visited Comillas. Although, one can't be certain. I'm told they never sign anything. There are secretaries who are paid to do that. You do know the queen I mean? The wife of Alfonso the Thirteenth?"

"Queen Victoria's granddaughter?"

"Of course, part of your royal family. How they intermarry, all those royals. No wonder so many are weak." He laughed lightly, turned away. "Come along, we'll go into my small kitchen and take a glass of wine."

I followed him into a kitchen that was like a neatly furnished cave. Two of the walls had been carved from rock, the third made from rough-cut stone. Light came in through a thick-barred window. On a wooden table stood a bottle of Rioja, already opened, breathing quietly. Beside it was a stack of books about the marquis and his town.

"These might be of some assistance to you," El Rey said. "And the wine, well, usually it's very good." He poured a little into a pair of cut-crystal glasses, uncovered a plate of green olives stuffed with anchovies. "I *am* glad you are here, in my house."

"I'm enchanted." I tasted the wine. "And this, it's delicious."

"*Bueno*." He smiled shyly. "It's nice that you approve."

"Be hard not to." My eyes went around the kitchen, came to rest on the thick bars on the window. "They're interesting, are they from anywhere special?"

"From the jail that used to be here in Comillas."

"The jail?" I stood and touched them. The metal was cold and hard. "They remind me of ones I saw in Mexico. I was in jail there."

"Really?" El Rey frowned uncertainly. "I was for many years in Chile. But, I never went to Mexico."

"The first night I was there I spent in jail."

"That, ah...that can't have been, *bueno*, very agreeable."

"It was interesting."

"Interesting? I'd die in a place like that."

"You'd survive. Probably return with something no one else possessed."

"Perhaps, who knows?" El Rey smiled. "What happened to you?"

I told him how I came to spend a night in Matamoros, in a jail with bars not unlike those in his kitchen. Virginia and I had driven down to Mexico after three absorbing days in New Orleans, where we'd walked through mountains of melons in a riverside market, taken a horse-drawn trip in an over-decorated carriage, seen semi-dressed ladies swing out of windows advertising their wares, listened to jazz played by geriatrics in Preservation Hall.

One afternoon, a black shoeshine boy stepped up beside us as we walked through the French Quarter, offering to polish my shoes. When I declined, he looked at me shrewdly and said, "I bet I know where you got them shoes."

"These?" I looked down at my London-bought brogues. "Where I got them?"

"Yeah." He grinned. "I bet a dollar I know where you got them."

"Well?" I glanced at Virginia, who smiled and shrugged. "All right."

"Okay, I tell you." The boy grinned wisely. "You got them shoes on you feet. You got them shoes on you feet in Bourbon Street. You got them shoes on you feet in Bourbon Street, New Orleans, State of Louisiana. Now, how about my dollar?"

I gave him two.

From New Orleans we drove west across the long straight blacktops of south Texas, where we ate the best hamburgers we'd ever tasted, and listened to Country and Western in a big, blue air-conditioned Chrysler, until we arrived at the Mexican-United States border, where Brownsville is on the northern side, Matamoros on the south. That's where our problems began because, even though the two towns merge as one, we had to change hire-cars.

In Mexico we drove on, not in an air-conditioned Chrysler but a vehicle more suited to the land, a small grubby-white Volkswagen, with a gear change that refused to stay in place and vigorously noisy motor. It had Mexican plates, so the Mexican Customs waved us through. No one looked at our passports, asked for visas, work permits, gave the shotgun I'd brought from London a glance, or asked for my British gun-permit.

"Why did you have a shotgun?" El Rey enquired, as I paused to sip a little wine. "What were you going to shoot?"

"I'd been told the hunting was good."

"You hunt small creatures?"

"I did," I confessed. "I come from a country where rabbits are a pest. Where the government pays hunters to keep deer under control. I grew up hunting. It wasn't until much later I realised how much damage it did. Anyway, the shotgun was the last thing on my mind as we set off in the Volkswagen. We were like children. It was exciting. We didn't think anything could go wrong."

"I know." El Rey picked up an olive. "When I was in Chile I sometimes felt the same. In South America the atmosphere can have that effect."

He was right. On the Mexican side of the twinned town the air came alive. The streets were filled with the smell of frying food, the sound of *Ranchera* music, Mexico's Country and Western. The faces altered, darkened, smiled more readily; the hair was long and black. By simply driving through a line on a map we were in a different world, with enchantment all around us.

"This is amazing," Virginia said. "There's a market. Let's have a look."

Before leaving London we'd spent ten days with Berlitz trying to come to grips with Spanish, just enough time to make contact, not sufficient to make sense.

Thus armed, we wandered through a labyrinth of crowded stalls, some with shining fruit, polished vegetables piled high. Stacks of yellow bananas, cascades of oranges and mandarins, green and vermilion mangoes, the bright purple of aubergines. There were offers of bargains on every side, clothes and shoes and hats and scarves, jewellery of all shapes and substance; blankets, shawls, dried herbs and flowers that belonged in a witch's brew.

We bought an acid-scented pineapple, a knife to cut it with. Virginia did a deal with a string of coloured beads. I purchased a pair of *haurachis*, Mexican open sandals. It was heady, we both felt a little insane.

We left the market and began our journey south, planning to see as much of the country as possible before I began work in Mexico City. But that was not to be. Twenty kilometres south of Matamoros we were stopped by a genuine Customs check. The town itself was a free-range zone. South of the border officialdom began.

"*Papeles*," the armed officer who stopped us said, asking for our papers. "*Los papeles, por favor.*" But, when he saw the shotgun on the back seat he grabbed it, and his politeness stopped on a word. "*Fuera*," he ordered. "Out."

"Was it a pretty shotgun?" El Rey asked thoughtfully.

"It was beautiful. Double-barrelled. The shoulder part was walnut. On it were etched pheasants, one on each side."

"You should have left it in England," he murmured, sadly.

"I wish I had."

Once the police had the gun there were long minutes of shouting, gesticulation. We barely understood an excited word. The weapon was passed from hand to hand. A sergeant appeared, examined it with a loving eye. The rest of our luggage was opened and searched. We were treated with understandable suspicion. My hair was long, I wore hippie's *haurachis*. Virginia's hair was even longer, she had on a pair of jeans with tigers embroidered on the legs. We were obviously spaced-out foreigners come south to buy drugs. What's more, we were heavily armed.

"They had good reason to be sceptical," El Rey observed. "Didn't you explain?"

"I tried to, but couldn't convince them. As you know, my Spanish isn't very good. It was dreadful then. Nothing I said made any difference. I was taken to Matamoros and put in jail."

"Your wife also?"

"No, they let her go."

Virginia found a hotel, the Ritz, twenty blocks from the jail-house, and immediately got to work on the phone. She spent the next twelve hours talking to my employers in Mexico City. When she wasn't trying to convince them the situation wasn't as funny as it sounded, she tramped the long, hot, twenty blocks to bring me something to eat and drink.

"Was there no food in the jail," El Rey enquired.

"I was advised not to touch it," I said.

"Who told you that?"

"The doctor inside."

"There was a medical man imprisoned?"

"He was there for dealing in drugs."

El Rey ate another olive. His eyes went around the comfort of his kitchen, the solid rock walls, the iron bars. He poured each of us a little more wine, and shook his head in sympathy.

The doctor in the Matamoros jail was delighted when he learnt of my presence, told me he wanted to improve his English, could lose his American accent with my help. Obviously, he thought we'd be together for some considerable time.

"You can sleep on the floor of my surgery," he said.

"What does that involve?"

"If you pay the guard five dollars he'll let you sleep wherever you want."

"Is that all?"

"Well, I too, could use a little aid."

I was beginning to learn how Mexico functioned, how the system worked. Although I never discovered what deals were done between the lawyers working for the company employing me and those in charge of the border town where I waited behind bars, I suspect they involved making a present of my gun to someone who coveted it, because I never saw it again. After twenty-four hours I was released, and accompanied Virginia through the hot, crowded jolly streets of Matamoros to the Ritz Hotel.

"So," observed El Rey. "You weren't in jail for long."

"A night and a day, that's all. The night was the worst. There was a lot of noise from the cells. Cockroaches were running over my face."

El Rey closed his eyes, and turned away.

In a bar in the Ritz, Virginia and I sat for a long time, sipping glasses of cool Mexican beer, trying to decide what to do. There was a range of stuffed animals above the bar that seemed to be the work of someone learning the trade. A pair of boar-heads, eyes half-falling out, gazed in several directions at once. Deer, with noses that had turned to mildew, hung their tattered heads in dismay. A coyote, with missing ears, crouched on its three remaining legs, trying not to fall over. None of them was any help. Those in Mexico City, who'd organised my release, advised us to abandon all thoughts of driving on, to catch the next plane south. I think they were afraid of losing us permanently along the way.

"That's what we should do," Virginia said.

"All right, let's catch a plane. We can always make another trip by car."

"Good, it'll keep me from having a heart attack each time we pass a jail."

"Was it as bad as that?"

"I was worried, weren't you?"

"Not really, I had you looking after me."

"It wasn't easy," she replied. "Believe me, it wasn't much fun."

We eventually caught a plane to Mexico City, where we stayed for almost five years.

"It was good?" El Rey asked. "There was no more trouble?"

"Very little," I replied.

"I'm glad. Latin America is fascinating, but I prefer Spain."

He poured the rest of the wine. We finished the olives; it was time to go. At the door I shook his hand, thanked him for the books he had lent me and asked if I could bring Virginia when I returned them. He responded warmly to the idea. The prospect of not having to sit alone though another of my stories seemed to cheer him up considerably.

"Laslo came up," Virginia said, a few months later. "Know who I'm talking about? Luisina, from the bookshop's son. He's heard about your manuscript and wants a look at it. What shape's it in? The last time I saw it, it seemed all right."

"I think it's almost ready for a translator. God knows who to ask."

"Don't worry, leave that to me."

"Whatever would I do without you?"

"Really? What brought that on?"

"I've been making notes about Matamoros. I don't know when I'll use them, but I wanted to put something down."

"Oh, that." She rolled her eyes at the memory. "Finding a translator will be a great deal easier than getting you out of jail."

She laughed, went into the kitchen to make a cup of tea. She'd recovered rapidly from her hernia operation and was walking well again. Yet, as fate would have it, within a year she would be taken back to hospital, this time in an ambulance.

16

Good Times and Bad

I first heard of Virginia's accident through a phone call from Tildina, the woman who runs the *estanco*, the tobacconist's, in the Fuente de los Tres Caños. "Your wife's lying in the road," she said, her voice quick with concern. "Come as soon as you can."

"What's happened?"

"I don't know. I'm getting her a blanket."

I got into the car, drove down as rapidly as I could to find Virginia crouched on the roadway, her face white with pain, barely able to speak. Around her shoulders, Tildina had draped a brown blanket, beside her were two Guardia Civil officers taking a statement from an elderly man, who looked uncertain and confused.

"Are you all right?" I asked.

All she could do was shake her head.

I turned to Renée, a bubbly woman who owned and operated a motel high above Oyambre, another who'd become a close friend. "She was bumped by a car," she told me. "Making a phone call. It backed right into her." Her eyes went to the Guardia Civil. "They've called an ambulance. It should be here soon."

"Where will it take her?"

"Probably Valdecilla, in Santander."

"You might have to go to hospital." I bent closer to Virginia. She looked about to faint. "Is that all right with you?"

"Yes," she whispered. "The papers…they need them."

"The medical insurance," said Renée. "Her identity card. They'll want them all."

"They're at home. I'll get them," I said, as the sound of an approaching ambulance came close. "Could you possibly go with her? To the hospital?"

"Of course. You stay here and look after the children."

"Yes, I'll do that."

I watched helplessly as the ambulance arrived, as a stretcher was prepared and competent hands began to move Virginia from the roadway. She gasped as soon as they touched her, eased her into the ambulance. As she was driven away, her big eyes were round with questions, her face pale with pain. Renée went with her, her own expression unusually subdued.

"What happened?" I asked the Guardia Civil, after I'd been to the house for the papers they needed. "Do you know?"

"She was hit," the sergeant told me, his eyes going to the elderly man being interrogated. She was making a phone call in the *cabina telefónica*. He was reversing his car. He didn't see her."

"Didn't he hear her? She must have cried out."

"*Bueno*, today's rather noisy, you know. It's a fiesta, *el Dia de los Muertos*. There are a lot of people here."

The Day of the Dead. I hoped it had no significance as I realised how full the Fuente de los Tres Caños was. There'd been people crowding around Virginia when I arrived, now they were strolling away, chatting, returning to their earlier conversations.

"What'll happen?" I asked the sergeant, my eyes on the driver. "What'll you do with him?"

"When my companion has finished asking him questions," the sergeant replied, returning my documents. "We'll talk to any witnesses. Then we'll decide what to do. He's very sorry. He didn't see your wife. It was an accident, you understand."

Having left her mobile phone at home, Virginia had decided to make a call using the *cabina telefónica*, an open booth. While still dialling, before she knew what was happening, she felt something push into her back. Caught between the knife-like edge of the phone booth and the boot of a car, she was barely able to move. She cried out, thumped on the boot, began to shout, but the car continued to reverse. It seemed the pressure would never end until, just when she was about to faint, it stopped. By then others were banging on the bonnet and the message reached the elderly driver. He changed direction and eased away.

"I was sure I was going to die," she said later. "I've never felt such pain."

Although no bones were broken, her liver had been ruptured. A ten-centimetre gash had opened, leaving her with the agonising impression that everything inside had been mashed to pulp. As she lay in the ambulance speeding toward the nearest hospital, twenty kilometres away in Torrelavega, she wondered if she'd ever walk again.

On arrival at the hospital, everything became a blur, reality dulled as she was wheeled into a room, had tubes inserted into veins, said what she was able to those who attended her. Renée did most of the talking. Virginia was given an echograph and, after the results had been scrutinised, was placed in an ultrasound scanner so that the full damage could be assessed.

"I don't remember much about it," she told me the following day. "Except they seemed to be very busy. And it hurt a lot."

When the size of fissure had been confirmed, it was decided she needed twenty-four hour attention in an intensive care unit, with a surgeon on hand in case an operation had to be carried out. Once again she was eased into an ambulance, this time with even greater caution, but without the companionship of Renée, who had her own family to take care of.

Virginia was driven to the Hospital Marquis de Valdecilla in Santander, one of the best in the country. She was immediately placed in Intensive Care, where she remained for the next three days. Fortunately, her liver stopped haemorrhaging, so no operation was necessary. All those years of not being able to drink alcohol may have stood her in good stead. Although, even today, her back is still painful and needs regular treatment.

"Not drinking was bad enough," she said the next day, when I went to see her. "Now I can't eat anything either. They're feeding me through this tube in my arm. How are Kitty and Michael?"

"They're fine. They've gone off to school. Kitty wanted to come in, but I persuaded her to wait. They'll phone later."

"I'd love to see them, but they've got exams soon." Virginia sighed, winced. "How are my babies getting on? Have you fed the ones down the road?"

"They're all eating as if nothing has happened," I replied, referring to our cats, the neighbour's cat who ate at the kitchen window, the strays at the bottom of the street that were given two meals a day. "Especially when I told them you were going to be all right."

"I don't feel all right at the moment. But the liver specialist was here this morning. He thinks it will heal up in time."

"How much time?"

"He doesn't know. They'll take another ultrasound in a couple of days. Now, you get back. And, don't worry, I'll be fine. It only really hurts when I move."

"Then don't move. I'll come back tomorrow."

"Only if you can. I'm being well looked after here. People have been calling in all day. Renée phoned. Chary was here earlier. She'd have stayed overnight if she could, but that's not possible in here." She looked around, at the blue curtains separating the other beds in the unit. "And María, from the Exposito, was here. Her husband's two beds along. He had a heart attack."

"I'll say hello on the way out."

"He'd like that." She smiled a little more brightly. "Give me a call later on. And, if there's anything you want, just ask Chary or Renée. Everyone's been very kind."

"You'll be all right. You're a big brave girl, remember."

"I don't feel very brave at the moment."

"You are. Just think what you did when that guy pulled a knife on you in Mexico. The one who tried to steal your watch."

"That wasn't very brave. All I did was scream."

"That was enough. It stopped him."

"I suppose, it did." She smiled a little more evenly. "I'll try to keep that in mind."

The youth who tried to steal Virginia's watch in Mexico City, had posed as a telegram boy so convincingly he fooled us both. By an unfortunate coincidence Virginia had been expecting a message from her father with dates and times of his arrival from Majorca. So when the young man, wearing an official uniform, knocked on the door and asked if the telegram had been delivered, Virginia told him she'd received nothing yet.

"The telegraph girls. They have it. They're here somewhere," he replied. "We should go and find them."

"Very well," she agreed, even though it seemed strange. But, this was Mexico, where I'd spent my first night in jail. Where twin snow-covered volcanoes lay above the city, said to be lovers frozen in a legendary past. Where we knew a singer who shot out street lights as his wife drove him home from parties. It was a land where anything could happen and often did. "These girls, are they around here?" she asked.

"Not far," the youth replied. "Come."

"I won't be long," said Virginia, turning to me. "It's probably from Daddy."

"I'll be down in a minute," I replied.

Five minutes later, when I came out the front door of the apartment building, it was to see Virginia walking unevenly along the footpath, tears running down her cheeks. For one fearful moment I thought the telegram contained bad news.

"He wasn't," she sobbed. "Not a telegraph boy. There wasn't any telegram."

"What?" I looked around. There was no sign of the youth. "Where?"

"He wanted my money." Virginia sobbed. "He tried to steal my watch."

"Are you all right?"

"He didn't touch me. I screamed, and he ran away."

"That was a good move."

"For God's sake, why are people like that?"

What distressed Virginia most of all was the deception, the shattering of the belief that there was a message from her father. She'd followed the youth eagerly around several corners, expecting at any moment to see a pair of telegraph girls. Even when he stopped outside a block of flats she felt no suspicion.

"They're here, I think," the youth said. "Shall we go and look?"

Virginia agreed, and he led her up two flights of stairs, paused in an empty corridor then turned quickly, a knife in hand. "Your money," he said. "Give it to me. And the watch."

Virginia stared in shock and disbelief. Her heart began to bang painfully. There was a moment in which she couldn't actually accept this was happening to her. She stood frozen, not sure it was real.

"Quickly," the youth said, waving the weapon. "Your money. Your watch. Or I'll slit your face with my knife."

Virginia remained paralysed.

"*Rápido.*"

The youth bent closer, nervous now, impatient. He reached out, took hold of her wrist and began to undo the watchstrap. His movement, the fact he touched her, released something within. She screamed, bellowed a wordless wave of fear and outrage. The youth paused. Somewhere down the corridor a door opened, closed quickly with a bang that broke the moment. The youth turned and fled. Virginia stood trembling, and the tears began. Sobbing, she ran down the stairs, walked unsteadily back to our building where I found her in the street.

"It's all right," I said finally. "We'll report it to the police."

"What's the use," she said sadly. "What can they do." She dried her eyes. "He didn't take anything."

"He gave you a dreadful fright."

"Even if they found him, what would they charge him with?"

"You showed great presence of mind to scream."

"I didn't think. It just happened."

"Thank God it did."

"There was nothing from Daddy. That's the worst thing about it."

"You'll hear soon, don't worry."

"I hope so."

She did. Her father came to Mexico, stayed a while and gave our lives another turn by directing us toward Majorca, encouraging us to live in Spain. On his suggestion we moved again, went back to Europe simply because a new plan was placed before us and the timing happened to be right. *Everything is connected*, Viscount Santiago said. *Everything is linked.* He was talking about Comillas, but it occurs all over the world.

"If there's anything you want," Antonio's wife, Chus, said when she heard about Virginia's accident. "Just ask. We're here all the time."
"Thank you."
"I'll make some *flan*," she added, referring to little cream caramel dishes, rich with egg-yolk, dusted with cinnamon. "I know the children like them."
"That's very kind."
"*No es nada.* And I'll bring the *Virgen* to your house."
"Is it our turn now?"
"I'll bring it early. It's better that it should be there."
The *Virgen* Chus referred to was an ornate ceramic statue of *La Virgen Milagrosa*, who wore a long white gown, a brass crown of stars. She stood, surrounded by pink plastic flowers in a wooden carrying-case, with doors that folded open. Below her was a collection box. The Virgin had been coming to the house ever since the children were baptised. Between Fernandéz Fernandéz and Sanchéz Goméz the name *Virginia* had been inserted on the list. The Virgin usually remained for twenty-four hours, a few coins were added to her box, then she continued her journey around the barrio, usually carried down the road by Michael, swinging her cheerfully as he went along. The fact that Chus brought the Virgin to our house while Virginia was hospital was touching.
"That is very thoughtful," I said to Chus. "I'll pass her on soon."
"Keep her for as long as you want," she replied, as she turned home to cook lunch. "It may help if she's with you now."

"Everything seems to be all right," Virginia said, a few days later. "The doctor was here again this morning. He wants another ultrasound done. But he thinks my liver's healing up nicely. Thank God, they didn't have to cut me open."
"Thank God for that."
"Another few inches and that bastard would have split it in half." She swallowed. "I'd be dead by now."
"You were very lucky."

"I should be home in a week or so. Although I won't be able to do much for a while."

"You won't have to, you know that."

"All right." Virginia smiled, a sign of returning health. "And I'll listen very carefully to whatever they tell me. Not like some others I could mention."

"You're thinking about…?"

"Yes," she said. "I am."

◆ ◆ ◆

Some years after our arrival, my Spanish less reliable that it's become, I'd gone for a medical check which included, at Virginia's suggestion, a colonic examination. "Why not?" she'd said. "You're having practically everything else looked at."

I asked the doctor what he thought. "I don't believe you have a problem," he told me. "But it's very fashionable at the moment."

I talked to the radiographer. He explained the procedure. The lower intestine would be filled with barium sulphate, introduced by an enema, which is about as attractive as it sounds. Then plates are taken so anything odd can be looked at in detail.

I was given various prescriptions for material to take with me when the examination was scheduled, in particular the barium enema itself. This gathering of the parts was something else I'd not encountered in any other country. Normally, as I recall, such preparations were on hand in the doctor's surgery. In Spain one has to buy them from a pharmacy, take them along on the day.

"This is for the *enema*," the nurse said, handing me a prescription, leaving me in no doubt about what she meant "And these are instructions for the *lavativa*," she continued, using a word I took, regrettably, to indicate something to be swallowed, to ensure I was scrubbed clean inside. "Four tablespoons of salt," she added. "In two litres of water, the night before the examination. Is that understood?"

"Yes," I replied.

"Are you sure?"

"Of course."

"And you can't eat or drink anything on the morning of the examination. You must come in here fasting. No breakfast. I'm sorry, but that's how it has to be. Is that clear?"

"Yes." I appreciated her concern. "No problem."

The evening before the examination I began my salt and water. By taking a glassful every now and then I found that the first litre went down easily enough. The second was considerably more difficult. My throat dried, my whole body seemed purged, and the mixture began to taste vile. It had, however, what I took to be the desired effect. By midnight it was running practically straight through me. Going in as a clear liquid, coming out the other end much the same. I was impressed by the state of Spanish medical art. No matter how primitive it seemed, there was no doubt it was working. Nevertheless, I had a burning thirst for something other than salt water. In the morning I phoned the examination centre as soon as I could.

"Can I drink anything?" I asked. "Just to help the thirst?"

"No," the nurse replied. "Nothing before the examination."

"Not even a glass of orange juice?"

"No, I'm sorry, but you can drink nothing."

"But, I'm drinking salt water by the litre."

"*Perdón?*" There was a long pause. "You're *drinking* the salt water?"

"Yes, the *lavativa*, remember. Four tablespoons of salt in two litres of water."

"*Dios Mío*. You're drinking the enema?"

"Oh, is that what *lavativa* means?"

"It is for the other termination of the body. You have to put it in there. With an apparatus." There was a further pause. I could have sworn I heard laughter. "You have the apparatus?"

"To give myself an enema?"

"*Bueno*. It's difficult for you to do yourself. Your wife can do it. Or a friend. Or the *practicante*," she added, referring to the local medical assistant who took blood, gave injections and obviously administered enemas when necessary. "But you'll need the apparatus."

"Where do I get that?"

"From the pharmacy. Like everything else."

"I see." The whole process was getting out of hand. "The *practicante* wouldn't have an apparatus?"

"No, you must provide your own."

"What about the *lavativa* I've been drinking? It seems to be working. It's coming out clean."

"Wait, I'll ask the doctor?" There was a long pause. "It will be all right," the nurse finally reported. "Take another *lavativa*. This time, *bueno*, you know where. And come in for the examination. The doctor says there's nothing to worry about."

"But, I can't have a drink?"

"No, I'm sorry. That's not permitted."

"*Bueno*," I replied. No other word seemed appropriate.

I followed the nurse's instructions to the letter. This time consulting Virginia to avoid any false interpretations. She shook her head when I recounted the conversation, murmuring, "Well, it seemed a little strange to me. I was going to say something, but you can be a bit funny when it comes to things like that."

"Arrogance, I suppose. You don't mind giving me an enema?"

"Not at all," she replied. "We might get rid of quite a lot that way."

Finally, dehydrated, burning like a stretch of sand, I arrived on time for my examination, was subjected to a further enema, this time with the barium sulphate. Later, I was told my colon was as clean as a whistle, or as the Spanish say, *Como los chorros del oro*, like streams of gold. Which is exactly what I felt had been running through me for the previous twenty-four hours. How the process ever became fashionable is something I'll never understand. On the other hand, life would have been much easier if I'd known what *lavativa* meant.

17

Descubriendo Comillas

Virginia's room in the hospital, where she'd been transferred from the intensive care unit, was on the seventh floor, with a splendid view across Santander harbour, overlooking small boats shuttling back and forth and the ferry from Plymouth gliding in. The morning after she moved in, I took the children to see how she was getting on. Kitty immediately clasped her mother's hand, held it gently, tears filling her eyes.

"Did they do anything?" Michael asked, frowning with concern. He'd never seen her as vulnerable. "Operate?"

"No, they didn't, I'm glad to say. And, the doctor from the insurance company was here earlier to see how I was."

"What did he have to say?" I asked.

"Oh, they'll pay me something. Damages, that sort of thing." She smiled ruefully. "Perhaps not as much as they might have. I was too cheerful, everyone says. I should have looked much worse than I felt. But, I couldn't really. I'm just glad to be alive."

"By God, so are we all."

"What's happening in the barrio?" she enquired. "Anything interesting?"

"Laslo, Luisina's son, called. He wants to see my manuscript. I've talked to Iñaki, he's bringing the translation around this afternoon."

"I must thank him as soon as I'm out of here."

"He'll probably be in to see you. You know what he's like."

Iñaki was a quiet teacher of Greek and Latin, who spent hours chatting to Virginia about places they'd been to, things they'd done. He spoke English well, wrote excellently, and when Virginia asked him about a translator for *Descubriendo Comillas* his response was immediate. He worked on the text himself, then passed it on to his cousin, Gabriela, who'd lived in England for a while. Together they produced an easy-reading book, an excellent rendition of the original.

When Laslo came to collect the manuscript he loved it, unread.

"*Don* Ken," he began, shaking my hand vigorously. "This work of art you've written, is it ready for me yet?"

"Sit down while I get it. Would you like a glass of wine?"

"Of course." Laslo was a chunky man, with a round mobile face and a ready smile. He leant back, lit a foul-smelling Ducados. "I've always wanted to publish a book on Comillas. Ever since I was a little boy it's been a dream of mine."

"Be nice if we could work together." I fetched a bottle of Rioja, poured two glasses, laid the text beside them. "There," I said. "A formal presentation. I hope you like it."

"*Señor*, I am sure your book is all *crianza*. Perhaps even *reserva*." Laslo spoke grandly, using terms for superior wine "I'll begin with the *vinoo*." He drank, nodded appreciatively. "*Muy bien*, it tastes good." He placed a chunky hand on the text. "And this, feels good. What an excellent combination."

Laslo was a one-man band, a combination of printer and photographer, designer, editor and general roustabout. Assembling text and pictures, playing his computer like a musical instrument, his hands were never still. They darted over the keyboard as he shaped pages, bled text around space for a photograph, changed and altered and changed again. When he'd achieved what he wanted he'd congratulate himself loudly. "The work of a maestro," he'd say. "No wonder my grandmother's so proud of me."

His print shop was in a tiny town, thirty kilometres east of Comillas, which he operated with the aid of Carmen, his wife. Between them they did everything, even sitting up late at night counting and packaging my book when the first three thousand were printed.

"So," he said, blowing a cloud of smoke, patting the manuscript. "We're going to publish this, no?"

"It might be better if you read it first."

"*Pouf*, I will like it." Laslo nodded confidently. "I will like it because you're a professional. Now, what's it going to look like?"

"Beautiful. Lots of colour photographs. We'll sell a million copies."

"My sentiments, exactly." Laslo laughed. "Two million would be better."

"Then, you'd better start reading it."

"I'll read it, but I know it's what I've been looking for." Laslo leant away, looked at the ceiling. "There's just one little problem?"

"What is that?"

"I haven't got much money. Just enough to produce the book. My mother will help me there. But, to buy the manuscript, I'm afraid there's nothing."

"Really?" My experience of the publishing world is that someone usually offers you money then proceeds to pull your book apart. Laslo, on the other hand, was prepared to accept whatever I'd written, publish it in the way I wanted, without paying a peseta. "What about royalties?"

"Author's rights? No problem. When it sells, the money will come in." Laslo emptied his glass, glanced at the bottle. I poured more. "But, I've nothing to offer before that." He smiled broadly. "Nevertheless, I'll give you a hundred books as soon as they're printed. Those will be yours to sell. How does that seem to you?"

"Unusual, but acceptable. It'll cover my expenses."

"*Bueno, Don Ken.*" Laslo spread his hands. "I knew we'd come to an agreement." He looked around for an ashtray, found none, tapped the ash from his cigarette into the palm of one hand, and dropped it on the floor. "Now, do you have any photographs we could use?"

"Quite a few, as a matter of fact. Most of them transparencies."

"Perfect. Just what I need." He shrugged. "*Bueno*, I can't pay for them either."

"That's all right. I imagine they'll be returned."

"Like new."

So began a relationship that brought *Descubriendo Comillas* to life. Laslo read the text and loved it, as he'd convinced himself he would. He was delighted with the colour slides I'd taken, and helped find more when they were needed. As the production progressed, we talked to others in the town to see what they had.

Vicente Rozas, the local photographer, gave us a number of beautiful, long-lens shots of the Palacio de Sobrellano and the Seminario on the hill. Chary lent a series of Comillas covered with thick white snow, taken on one of those rare occasions when drifts settle, last for a day. Juaco went through albums for informal snaps of visiting kings and queens, of his aunt scooting along Oyambre in an *aeroplage*, the sand-yacht of the time. El Rey had an old picture of his brother beneath the wings of the Yellow Bird on the same stretch of golden beach. Almost everyone we spoke to found something in a bottom drawer, in an ancient silver frame.

Right at the end of the production, almost on the eve of going to press, Laslo arrived at the house with a dozen old photographs showing Comillas as it once had been. We spent hours writing captions for pictures of Gaudí's Capricho during its construction, the parochial church before the Civil War, oxen pulling carts of sea-weed gathered on the beach, a section of wooded landscape which was once the site of the Fuente de los Tres Caños before water came to the town. There was even a shot of the travelling royal bath-house, especially built for the visit of Alfonso XII. And a crowded market in the plaza by the Municipal Building, where the first Marquis of Comillas' mother might have been selling fish beside the church wall. It was a marvellous collection that gave a new dimension to the book.

"These are very good," I said, scribbling titles, seeing Carmen out of the corner of my eye falling asleep. "Pity we didn't have them sooner."

"It was a last minute inspiration." Laslo smiled broadly. "I'm a genius, no?"

"Well, better late than never, as we say in English."

"We say the same in Spanish." Laslo laughed, Carmen opened her eyes. "We're a formidable pair, *Don Ken*. From the beginning I knew it would be so."

During the production Eladio, the Book, went through the text as carefully as he said he would, treating it as if it were his own. "Forgive me, if I'm critical," he said gently. "But there are some errors you've made. Especially with dates."

"Be as critical as you like. I want it to be right."

"*Bueno*," he said, as we began to correct. "And there are some photographs I've found that you might like to use."

There was help on every side.

While all this was going on, Virginia came home from hospital to a house crammed with flowers. Great bunches of sweet-smelling colour were brought in by smiling friends. The loyal ladies of her aerobic class arrived laden with heaps of white carnations, long-stemmed roses of a dark and slumbering red. Neighbours from the barrio, good-hearted women from the town, brought yellow bell-shaped orchids, pink hydrangeas, trumpet-lilies wrapped in fine and flowing fern. We almost ran out of vases.

"I used to talk about going to the flowers," said Kitty, arranging a combination of reds and yellows and greens. "Now the flowers have come to us."

"We've a lot of good friends here," I said. "I hadn't realised how many. People I've never seen before ask me how she's getting on."

"Well, you know what Mummy's like. She's ready to help anyone she can."

"That's true. But, it's nice when they appreciate it."

With the flowers came equal armloads of advice. "You mustn't do any work in the house," visitor after visitor said. "If there's anything you want, just ask."

"I will," Virginia told them from her position on the front-room couch. "Although, both the children are very helpful. And my husband's quite capable."

"You're lucky," most replied. "Mine, *Dios Mío*, he does nothing."

"The other night I went to visit my mother," said one. "When I got home after midnight, he was still waiting for his supper. I had to eat with him again, at one in the morning."

"He couldn't get it for himself?"

"He can't even boil water."

Cuadri drove up, climbed out of his car and limped slowly toward the front door carrying a covered bowl. "For your *señora*," he said. "That *cabrón*, hitting her like that. Some people shouldn't be allowed on the road. How is she, now she's home?"

"Getting better, but it's painful when she moves." I sniffed at the bowl, it smelt delicious. "What's this?"

"Some *pulpo*. I cooked it with wild garlic and a little brandy. I think you'll find it good."

"Thank you, but *pulpo*-fishing's against the law, no?"

Cuadri shrugged. "I have some friends who are elusive." He followed me into the front room, bowed when he saw Virginia propped up amongst cushions. "Welcome," he said quite formally. "Welcome home."

"He brought some *pulpo* he cooked," I said.

"How nice." Virginia smiled at Cuadri who beamed, looked even more like a garden gnome. "I love *pulpo*, and we haven't had any for a while."

"Well, now you have a little taste. And don't get up too soon."

"Perhaps I should just stay here and let everyone look after me."

But, before long, she was on her feet again. And, one morning, a touch of spring in the air, the first of the daisies poking through the grass, the earliest of the butterflies fluttering around the cross on the gate of the House of the Inquisitor, Pepuco, the neighbour who'd first shown me the Seminary, arrived, chatted to Virginia, then led her down the road.

"Come with me," he said, pushing his John Lennon glasses firmly into place. "I'll show you something that'll make you feel better."

"I could do with a bit of that," she replied, walking slowly by his side. "I didn't realise it would take so long to feel well again."

"When your body's damaged it is insulted."

"Mine's been deeply insulted."

"Then be patient." Pepuco opened his garden gate. "Now, look at this." He pointed up his gravel path. "Stand there, and appreciate the beauty."

Virginia caught her breath as she gazed at the meticulously raked gravel, the interweaving pattern of little waves on an even sea. Beyond the path, stone steps led up to a higher garden. To one side a lemon tree was in bud, the first small yellow blooms coming into flower, beneath the tree clusters of bright primroses were pushing through the grass.

"Isn't that a perfect picture?"

"It's lovely," replied Virginia. "Seeing it does make me feel better."

"And, tomorrow it'll be gone." Pepuco sighed with satisfaction. "People will walk all over it. Tomorrow it will have to be created once again."

"You don't mind making it beautiful every day?"

"I look forward to it. It's part of the process of being alive."

"You're right. We should keep things looking nice. Every day."

"The simple things are very important. Especially when they're fresh. I'm sure grass smells better when it's cut with a scythe."

"Do you know, I think you're right."

When *Descubriendo Comillas* finally saw the light of day, with a fine strong cover featuring Gaudí's Capricho, which Laslo redesigned at least a dozen times, it filled a gap long left vacant, and the response was immediate. There was a presentation to which the Press came and flashed their cameras. There were radio interviews where I was asked why an *Inglés* should have written what they called the definitive book about the town. People arrived at the house asking me to sign copies for their children. I'd dedicated the book to all Comillanos who had the good fortune to live in such a lovely place, and they appreciated the thought.

"I told you," Virginia said, leading in a woman who wanted an inscription for Concepción. "It's a long time since anything was published that people here could buy."

"There are others. The gas company, the electricity people have brought out books recently."

"Exactly what I mean. Lavish publications full of boring architectural detail. If you wanted to buy them, they'd cost a kidney." She produced another for me to sign. "This one's for Jesús."

I signed and talked, delivered copies, sold some, gave others away. On one radio programme I was questioned for half an hour about what else I'd written, where I'd lived before coming to Spain. I said nothing to the children but, when the interview was broadcast, put the radio on the lunch table, casually switched it on.

"You listening to Spanish radio?" Michael asked. "What's up?"

"I sometimes listen to local news."

"That's in the morning," Kitty pointed out. "Not this time of day."

"There might be something, you never know."

"I'd rather…" Michael began, then stopped as he heard my name. He blinked and listened as the interview continued. When it was over he shook his head doubtfully. "Not bad," he said. "But, I've got to tell you, your Spanish has *not* improved."

"It's all right," said Kitty carefully. "At least he's understood."

"I thought he sounded fine," put in Virginia. "But, then, we're used to him."

◆　◆　◆

One bright morning Laslo got out of his van, closed the door with a slam. "*Don* Ken," he said exuberantly. "How good to see you. I've come for a small *vinitoo*." His Comillano accent was pronounced, a sign of good fellowship.

"*Crianza* or *reserva?*"

"*Da igual*," he said, meaning it doesn't matter. "Everything in your house is excellent. I know from personal experience."

"Thank you, as we say in English, my house is your house."

"We say…" he began, then laughed. "*Cabrón*, you're pulling my hair."

"In English we say, leg, but it's the same."

I opened a bottle of rosé from the Penedès, an area near Barcelona where the best champagne comes from, took it into the sunny garden where we sat looking across at the marquis' palace, the filigreed spire of the Chapel-Mausoleum, catching the tiniest glimpse of the onion-topped tower of Gaudí's El Capricho.

"*Salud*." Laslo lifted his glass. "To the book. It is selling like *churros*," he added, comparing it to the fried-batter delicacy. "All it needs is the chocolate to accompany it."

"I'm delighted. You must be pleased."

"*We* can be pleased." He lit a cigarette, blew smoke into the untainted air, watched it disappear. "*Bueno*, what do you know of Garabandal?" he asked, coming to the purpose of his visit. "Have you ever heard of the place?"

I shook my head

"Well, our next book should be about Garabandal. Listen, and I'll tell you why." Laslo emptied his glass, waited while I poured more, then fixed his large brown eyes on mine. "Garabandal is a village near here where they say there once were miracles. And where more are predicted. Some day soon, they're said to happen."

"Do you believe it?"

"*Bueno, Don* Ken." Laslo shrugged massively. "It's not believing that's brought me here. It's to talk about Garabandal."

"*Descubriendo Garabandal?* The next in the series?"

"Don't joke, *hombre*. I'm serious."

"All right, but if it's a place where miracles happen, there must be tons of books,"

"Many." Laslo reached into a side pocket of his jacket, produced three small volumes with brightly coloured covers. "Here are some. There are more, but they're old. I want to produce something new, something that's completely up to date."

"What do you suggest I do?"

"Read these." He placed the books on the table, beside the wine. "Go to Garabandal. Think about it. Then, perhaps, we can talk."

"All right, I'll do that."

"Ah, *Don* Ken." Laslo spread his hands. "I knew I could count on you."

"Would you like a little more wine?"

"A touch, no more. I've work to do."

We sat a while longer then Laslo left, having, with little more than a suggestion, opened a door to an aspect of life that fascinates us all. My first school was a convent, where miracles were part of the air we breathed. I've been to Lourdes, seen the souvenirs visitors take away, the piles of crutches left behind by those said to have been cured. Miracles moved a little closer when Kitty and Michael were born. Now, the world of marvels was a short drive away. Garabandal lay some forty kilometres up in the kills and, once again, I was aware of how great is mankind's need to cling to symbols, how deep and profound is our hunger for all wondrous signs. All of which came a little closer when we went to Garabandal.

18

Acts of Faith

We found San Sebastián de Garabandal, in the Cantabrian hinterland, to be a small hamlet of twisted streets and cut-stone houses, surrounded by bare foothills rising to the jagged Picos de Europa. Over the village lifts the square pillar of the church, its cross pointing to the sky. There are other crosses on the hills above Garabandal, fourteen that form the *vía crucis,* the Stations of the Cross. On each a panel of coloured tiles depicts a further step in the final journey of Jesus Christ.

"It's beautiful," Virginia said, as we walked the cobbled streets, pillars of smoke rising from a dozen chimneys in the cold December air. "But, it's so remote."

"It's thriving," I said. "There's a busy pilgrim industry."

"You're being cynical."

"Not at all. Other villages around here are almost deserted. I saw something in the paper the other day about a place with forty houses. Most of them empty. In summer a few are occupied, but only one man lives there all year round. He's the mayor, by the way."

"Get in by one vote?"

"Now, who's being cynical?"

"Not really." She let her eyes drift over the red-tiled roofs, the two-storied houses that served both man and beast. "There's just something about this place that seems untouched."

"Part of it is. There are people who've lived all their lives in Garabandal and never been anywhere else. The outside world comes to them."

"Did you read those books Laslo gave you?"

"And a few more about what happened here."

"What *did* happen?" Kitty asked, her eyes on Michael who'd gone ahead to talk to a painfully skinny dog. "Three girls saw the Virgin Mary, didn't they? When I said we were coming, that's what I was told."

"There were four, actually."

"Didn't the sun move? Wasn't there a smell of roses?"

"There's always a smell of roses. And the sun always seems to move," I replied. "These things are quite commonly reported."

"What was so special about Garabandal?"

There were fours girls, I told them, as we walked through cobbled streets, who in 1961 were going home at dusk, their hands full of apples they'd taken from a local tree. They were rushing, feeling guilty about the stolen fruit, when suddenly there was an enormous crash and they thought it was because of what they'd done.

"What was it?" Michael asked. "Thunder?"

"Actually, they thought it was the Devil. They thought they'd made him happy by stealing apples. They threw stones to their left to chase him away."

"Why the left?"

"That's where they'd been told he always comes from."

"It wouldn't have been the Devil."

"Apparently not, because almost immediately they saw a figure in front of them who said he was Saint Michael?"

"It must have been terribly frightening," Kitty said. "What did the girls do when that appeared?"

"It seems they weren't too scared, even though it was getting dark. They ran home to tell their parents what they'd seen."

"I'll bet no one believed them. That's a pretty poor excuse. Sorry, Mummy, but an angel made me late."

"You're right. Nobody did."

We'd arrived at a rocky lane, its surface rough, as uneven as it had been on that July evening in 1961 when, with a thunderclap, the vision appeared before the girls. To one side, on an ivy-covered wall, a panel of coloured tiles showed Saint Michael, his angel-wings outspread, holding a spear at the throat of a horned beast beneath his feet, in a manner not unlike that of Saint George overcoming the dragon on the Seminary door.

"This is where the archangel was first seen by the girls," I said. "In this little lane, called the *Calleja*. He came back eight times before he told them about the Virgin Mary."

"Eight," said Kitty. "That's a lot."

"Eight's part of the story. It's one of the things that make it fascinating."

"If the Virgin Mary was actually seen, that'd be fascinating enough."

"It would, but there have been other visions in these mountains. They've always been pushed aside as juvenile imagination or childish fantasies."

"What was different here?"

"The village priest became involved. After the archangel's first visit, he talked to the girls individually, and found that their stories were identical. Then all four girls heard a voice telling them they'd see the archangel again. The voice came to each of them separately, and that made a really big impression."

"Did they tell the priest?" asked Virginia.

"They must have, because he said if there were any more visions he'd talk to the Bishop in Santander."

"Does the Church accept all this?"

"Not yet."

"But all this happened in the nineteen sixties, didn't it? You'd think they'd have made a decision by now."

"Well, they haven't. I wrote to the Bishop of Santander. He said the matter was still under investigation."

"But they saw the archangel eight times, didn't they?" queried Michael. "You'd think that would get something going."

"That's right, they saw him so often that young men in the village built a square of branches and branches, a small corral to keep the crowds back from the girls. Lots of people were beginning to come up to watch them in their ecstasies."

"Ecstasies? They're like trances, aren't they?"

"More like having a fit," Kitty said. "I was told about them also. The girls used to walk backwards, isn't that right?"

The ecstasies began soon after the first appearance of the archangel, I explained. In his presence, and later with the Virgin Mary, the girls went into a state in which they seemed unaware of the world around them. Their heads lifted, they put their hands together in prayer and walked in unison, fell to their knees on the ground, yet showed no injury. They moved backward and forward so fast that many, who later talked about the events, said they were difficult to keep up with. By then so many pilgrims were coming to Garabandal that the Guardia Civil was needed to hold them back, to keep them out of the *Cuadro*, the square young men had built. Among the visitors were priests and medical men, who watched carefully, even went so far as pricking the girls with needles to see how they would react.

"What happened?" asked Michael. "When they stuck the needles in?"

"Nothing," replied Kitty. "In an ecstasy you don't feel things like that."

"Conchita said she later saw bruises and pin-pricks on her skin," I said. "But felt nothing at the time"

"Who's Conchita?"

"One of the four girls. She was the one who had the visions longest. As time went by the others dropped out. But, Conchita persisted, and she's the only one who was told the secret."

"What secret?" Michael asked.

"Something the Virgin Mary said to her."

"Do you think the Virgin really came here?"

"I don't know," I admitted. "But, the girls said they saw her many times. Conchita for nearly five years."

"What's the secret the Virgin told her?"

"It's said to be a date when a great miracle will occur. A miracle that could save the world."

"When is it?"

"Nobody knows, apart from Conchita. But she's not allowed to tell anybody until eight days before it happens."

"There's that eight again," said Kitty thoughtfully. "Eight times the archangel came before Mary appeared. And eight days before Conchita can tell the world about the miracle."

"That's right, it's all connected."

"What sort of miracle is it going to be?"

"Apart from Conchita, no one knows. But it's got something to do with those pines up there." I pointed to a crown of trees on the hill above the village. "Come on, let's go up and I'll tell you about Conchita on the way."

As we climbed up from the village, left the knots of houses in their narrow lanes, I explained that, when the sightings first began, Conchita González was just one of the four visionaries in Garabandal. But, by the end, it was she who became entrusted with the Virgin's message and was given the details of a miracle that could save or destroy the world.

Soon after the visions began, when the rumours began to circulate, it became clear that many were eager to believe. As the sightings continued their numbers grew, soon they were gathering by the hundreds in Garabandal. They came almost nightly, during that long summer of 1961, to watch the four girls assemble in the *Cuadro*. As the children went into their ecstasies, listened to the messages that only they received, well-groomed women from afar, men wearing suits and ties, watched closely, standing shoulder to shoulder with the villagers in their humbler dress. In contrast to the visitors' sophistication, the girls were clad in simple cotton frocks, woollen cardigans to keep out the cool night air. On their feet were the plain leather sandals they'd known all their lives. They looked like untouched innocents amongst the medical men examining them, the habits of the priests who stared and made notes.

The girls were filmed and photographed, their voices recorded as they prayed. They were spoken to by priests, gazed on by doctors, pinched and pinpricked, tested for any reaction while they remained in their trances. However, even though no normal response was detected by the small army of medical men examining them, nothing offensive or impious was recorded by the Church. What's more, even while in their ecstasies, the girls maintained some contact with those who watched. Dozens from the village, scores from afar, brought scarves and crucifixes, wedding rings and other personal objects to be offered to the Holy Mother to bless. All were returned to their rightful owners without any hesitation.

Inevitably the Church became involved, was put in a position where it had to decide whether the events in Garabandal were genuine or not. Early in the proceedings Conchita González was summoned to the palace of the Bishop of Santander. There she was interrogated, cross-examined, listened to with sympathy but scant belief. On August 26, 1961, a little more than two months after the first appearance of the archangel, the bishop decided it was far too early to come to any conclusion. In a message to the public he said nothing obliged him, or his examining committee, to consider that what was occurring in the Garabandal to be beyond the laws of nature. In other words, there was nothing miraculous to declare.

However, soon after that, all Catholic priests were warned to keep away from the small cluster of houses below the pines, to avoid organising or taking part in pilgrimages to Garabandal. In the succeeding years this advice has been repeated, at times forcefully. Priests have been told that their presence in any official capacity in the village is strictly forbidden. They are to have nothing to do with the visions, the predictions of the girls or the processes that altered their lives.

Nevertheless, in January, 1966, after Conchita González' last vision of the Virgin Mary, when she was given the details and the date of the miracle that would allegedly save the world, she was summoned to the Vatican by Cardinal Ottaviani, Prefect of the Congregation for the Doctrine of the Faith. In Rome the village child, who in her entire life had never been further from Garabandal than Santander, forty kilometres from her home, was closely questioned by Vatican officials, and granted a private audience by Pope Paul VI. Before and after this audience the Pope blessed Conchita, saying that through him the whole Church did the same, thus, in some unofficial manner, giving her an acceptance that had not been bestowed before.

In what appears to be a direct result of this, whether to correct what could have been considered an insult, or to determine where the truth really lay, the Bishop of Santander, accompanied by his Vicar General and Garabandal's local priest, went to question Conchita again. They travelled to Pamplona where the girl, to avoid the attention she was attracting in the outside world, had become a boarder in a convent.

After seven hours of interrogation, after being subjected to endless questions by a band of authoritative men, presumably dressed in their robes of office, the village girl retracted everything she had said, declared that what she had seen had been imagined, that the visions were a lie.

This was possibly the bleakest period in Conchita's life. There had been others when uncertainties troubled her, when she'd voiced her doubts to the village priest, but never before had she retracted everything, certainly not in so public a manner, or to any authority as elevated as the Bishop of Santander. Later, however, she said that her denial was counterfeit, that she had betrayed the Virgin Mary by saying the visions were a lie.

"Had she really been telling lies?" asked Michael, as we arrived at the grove of pines, and were looking across the town, over the tops of the nested houses, to the steep hills on the far side of the valley. "It wasn't true? All that about the Virgin coming here?"

"No, in the end, she said it *was* true. She changed her mind and went back to what she'd claimed originally. Now, she really believes she saw the Virgin with the baby Jesus in her arms."

"Then, why did she say she hadn't?"

"She was frightened, of course," said Kitty. "They must have given her a dreadful time. Think what it would be like if the priest in Comillas got you in a corner and asked you lots of questions. Especially if he was wearing all his things."

"That's true enough," Virginia said gently. "And, you're right about Conchita. It must have been awful."

"Did she see the Virgin after that?" asked Michael.

"No, she saw the Virgin Mary for the last time in nineteen sixty-five." I pointed at the surrounding trees. "Up here in the pines. This is where the miracle's supposed to take place."

"What's going to happen?" asked Kitty.

"Well, from what I've read, there are going to be two stages. First there'll be a miracle. That's to make sure everyone understands they have to repent."

"Everyone in the world?"

"It seems so."

"What if they don't repent?"

"That's what the second part of the Virgin's message is all about. If they don't there's going to be a terrible disaster. Quite possibly it will destroy us all."

"Does Conchita know when this is going to happen?"

"Yes, but she can't tell anyone until eight days before."

"And, when she does?"

"That's another thing that's so interesting about the story," I replied. "It means that the world has eight days to prepare. What's more, and this is important, eight days to get here. Because, when the miracle occurs, everyone here will be cured. Those who are sick or dying, or have anything wrong with them are going to get better. But, they've got to be here for the miracle. They've got to be present to be cured."

"Everyone in the entire world?"

"Well, that's not been made clear."

"What if they're not here?" Kitty persisted.

"Nothing much has been said about that?"

"I see, so the pilgrims come. Just in case?"

"They certainly do. There are bus-loads ever second Sunday. From Spain, America, all over the world. Another thing is, there are rumours that the miracle's going to happen sometime soon. Nobody's said anything. But they can't, can they? Not until eight days before."

We walked on, toward the central pine. Pinned to it were a few scarves, a handkerchief or two. Bunches of flowers had been laid on its roots, some with petals brown and dead. Here and there, on the rough bark of the trunk, were photographs of someone deceased or ill, too infirm to climb the hill. These were offerings already in place, in the hope that time would deliver them. There was a small group around the tree. We joined it and stared for a few moments, as the scarves moved in the chill December air.

"Something did happen here once," Kitty observed quietly. "The girls I talked to said there had already been a miracle."

"That was the small miracle. They called it the *milagrucu*."

"*Milagrucu?*" questioned Michael. "That's *Comillanoo*."

"They've got the same accent all through these mountains," said Kitty. "What was this *milagrucu* all about?"

I told them what I'd read about the small miracle, which took place about a year after the Archangel Saint Michael was first seen in the *Calleja*. It was a miracle predicted by both the archangel and the Virgin Mary herself. They told Conchita that a visible act of communion would be seen by any who came to Garabandal on the night of July 18, 1962. Conchita passed the message on, visitors arrived in their thousands. And, according to those close enough to see, the Host appeared on the child's tongue.

Before the event, the visitors waited, crowding the street outside Conchita's cottage, pushing and elbowing in their efforts to get close. Hundreds had seen all the girls accept invisible communion, watched them kneel, extend their tongues to receive what they said was the symbol of the body of Christ from the hands of the archangel. Now the act would be for all to witness in the flesh. So, they waited impatiently in the narrow lanes for Conchita González to appear. When she did they shouted and screamed as she emerged in an ecstasy. Many fell to the ground, or knelt in prayer before her. Some stumbled, were pushed aside, thought they would die in the throng. As Conchita walked through the town they followed, jostling, tearing at their clothes, creating a near-riot. It became almost impossible to see the girl, her face uplifted, her eyes on the dark night sky, surrounded by members of the Civil Guard assembled to protect her.

"That really happened here?" asked Michael, his eyes on the quiet village, the pillars of smoke rising in the gentle air. "There was a punch-up?"

"Not quite, but nearly."

"I'm not surprised," Kitty said. "The way people act at football matches. It's not all that different really."

"In many ways that's true," I said. "They all wanted to get close. Wanted to see the *milagrucu* actually occur."

"Some of them must have," said Virginia. "Otherwise there'd have been nothing to talk about, would there?"

According to the witnesses, Conchita led the crowd toward the centre of Garabandal where she knelt and began to speak. No one around her, none of those who later testified, was able to hear what she said above the noise of the crowd. Flashlights were shone on her face, cameras were ready as she opened her mouth and extended her tongue. Those around her fell to their knees, their hands held up in prayer. Then, many who were closest, some claiming to be only eighteen inches away, swore that the Heavenly Host appeared on Conchita's tongue. It remained for a minute or two until, with a beatific smile, she swallowed and it was gone.

"Like at Mass." said Michael.

"Exactly the same."

"What about photographs?" Virginia asked. "Did any come out?"

"Only one. That's another of the curious things about all this. Of all the cameras that were focused on the girl, only one picture's ever been printed. It was taken by an amateur using a borrowed camera and it shows the Host on Conchita's tongue."

"You think it's genuine?"

"Who knows? It could have been retouched. Or a trick of the light. A blemish on the film. It could have been a miracle. Anything really, but it's published as evidence of the *milagrucu* in all the books I've seen."

"What's the Church got to say about that?"

"Nothing. There were priests present, but they've made no official statements. The Bishop of Santander sent someone, but he said he wasn't close enough to see."

"So, it remains a mystery."

"The small miracle does. Although Conchita went on seeing the Virgin Mary for another three years after that. Until nineteen sixty-five. That's when she saw her for the last time, and was given the message about the big miracle. The Virgin hasn't appeared since."

"What happened to Conchita?"

"She went to New York and got married."

They all looked at me in disbelief.

"Sounds strange, doesn't it? But that's what happened. There were lots of people who believed she should have become a nun. But, I think that shows how normal she was. She got married like the other girls."

"All four got married?"

"All of them. I don't know about the others. But Conchita married a man in New York who owned a pizza parlour."

"Good move," said Michael, with a grin. "Sorry, but you know what I mean."

"What made Conchita go to New York?" Kitty asked.

"Life must have become almost impossible here. She was hounded by the Press. The public came in their hundreds and wanted instant ecstasies. She even admitted she faked one or two because the demand was so great. The Church wouldn't accept her visions. The Bishop of Santander was no help, especially after she'd been to see the Pope. Even Mother Teresa was involved. I think poor Conchita wanted a rest from all that was happening in Garabandal."

"I can understand that. She needed her own space."

"She certainly did." We began to walk back, down toward the village, the tight collection of mountain houses that had become known around the world. "And there was someone else who influenced her. Joey, from New York. He was her first evangelist."

"Joey? What did he do?"

Joey Lomangino was a blind American who had often been to Garabandal, I explained, as we made our way down the rough pathway from the pines. He was a Catholic, who lost his sight at the age of sixteen when a truck tyre exploded in his face. The accident also shattered his faith in God. However, he was persuaded to go to Europe in an attempt to regain his old belief. In Rome he attended Mass said by Padre Pío, the Capuchin monk with stigmata on the palms of both hands, the blood-red scars similar to those inflicted on Jesus Christ. After the Mass they talked, and Padre Pío encouraged Joey to go to Garabandal.

The blind American went to the mountain village where he met the girls and listened to what they had to say. He believed in their visions and the Virgin Mary's predictions. He returned time and again to hear more. He was there when the Virgin gave her final message to Conchita González. He became convinced that one day the miracle would be witnessed in Garabandal, and he hoped, on that day, to regain his sight.

"I don't want to sound disrespectful," said Virginia mildly. "But this has a wonderful cast. There were the girls, a blind evangelist, a monk with stigmata, Mother Teresa. It's amazing, when you come to think about it."

"It certainly is."

"What did Joey do that was so important?"

"After his first visit, as soon as he got back to New York, he began talking about Garabandal. He showed slides, gave lectures, moved all over the country talking about the Virgin's message. By the end of the nineteen seventies there were Garabandal centres in forty American states. And in dozens of other countries throughout the world. He's the person, in many ways, who made Garabandal what it is."

"A bit like the Marquis of Comillas."

"You could say that."

"So what happens now?" Virginia turned, looked back at the skyline, the pine trees silhouetted against the softening December sky, the scarves and handkerchiefs swinging slowly in the breeze. There were figures moving on the hillside in the chilling air. "When is the miracle supposed to take place?"

"Nobody knows and no one's prepared to say. Laslo told me there'll be a miracle soon, but that's only a rumour. Other people I've spoken to say there's talk of something. But nobody's quite sure when."

"Do you think you'll write anything for Laslo?"

"I don't know, there's so much I have to find out first."

We walked back through Garabandal, went into a small café for a drink. It was a simple establishment with dark stone walls, where logs glowed in a fireplace and comforting warmth filtered out, where a larger than usual Cross hung on the wall. In a corner four men sat at a table playing cards. Other strangers stood at the bar. The air smelt of cigarette smoke, conversation flowed. It was an ordinary bar on an ordinary afternoon, with little to suggest that a miracle lay anywhere in the future.

But, as time passed the rumours spread. No one was quite sure where they came from, or admits knowing how they began, but like fire over dry grassland, they grew, multiplied and began to be taken seriously. At the beginning of 1995 the surge toward Garabandal, toward *Semana Santa* as the Spanish call Easter week, was gathering momentum.

For years busloads of pilgrims had been organised by Garabandal-groups in Europe and the United States. Every second Sunday, for most months of the year, the faithful had been driven through green and rolling hills toward the village in the mountains. Once there, they walked the twisted streets, stumbled up the *Calleja*, climbed to the nine pine trees growing above the town. There they prayed or waited, hung their scarves and small mementoes on the tree, then returned to where they had come from.

However, in 1995 a new tide of pilgrims began to flow. Radio, Press and Television reported on the miracle to be, it became front-page news in local papers. Easter Thursday was the destined date, visitors were predicted to arrive in Garabandal in their tens of thousands. The mountain village had no choice but to prepare. People needed to be accommodated, controlled by the Guardia Civil. Parking space for vehicles had to be provided. Busloads were anticipated from all over Europe. Those flying in from other countries would need local transport to take them to the town. The degree of organisation required was vast, detailed and curiously banal.

No version of Christ, dividing the loaves and fishes to feed the multitude, refers to the problem of finding parking space for donkeys, locating adequate toilet facilities, providing help for those who became ill or collapsed from the heat. Yet, all these elements had to be considered by the authorities in Garabandal.

Some two thousand members of the Guardia Civil and the Protección Civil were assigned to the village. Portable toilets were hired, put in place. Stalls to sell sandwiches, cakes, candles and Coca Cola were leased to contenders, who bid for the rights from all over Spain. As mercenary as the transactions might have been they were an integral part of the process. Mammon as well as God had to be catered for in Garabandal.

"It's amazing," said Virginia, looking up from the local paper as we sat at Rosalia's, on a damp and overcast February day. "The work they've got to do."

"Think what it'll be like with twenty or thirty thousand trying to climb the hill."

"Do they expect that many?"

"That's what the local radio predicted."

"From what it says here, a lot of them won't be able to walk at all. Poor things," she murmured. "What they'll have to go through."

On Easter Thursday pilgrims began to arrive in Garabandal before the first thin light had touched the town. There were fewer than expected, but they came in their thousands all the same. The lame, the stricken and the blind, with hearts full of hope, expectations high, were brought in busloads. Some walked, some limped, others had to be carried through the village, up the stony *Calleja* to where the pines grew on the hill. Their hope was to see the Virgin, to witness the rumoured miracle, to discover if they were to be made whole again.

But, their number was fewer than forecast. Conchita González, from where she lived in New York, had made no announcement about the event, said nothing eight days before the foretold Thursday. Her responsibility, as she had told the world, was to authenticate the date of the miracle eight days before it was to occur. So, as she made no statement, gave no word, it was taken by many that the rumours were false.

However, on the day in question, before the sun had risen, shuttle-busses began to bring the pilgrims up the mountainside to the village of Garabandal. They surged toward the great pine above the town, where photographs of loved ones, scarves that had come from afar, small items which had touched the flesh of those who lay ill or dying, were to be pinned to the iron-brown bark. The pine had become a tree of hope. Under the watchful eye of the Guardia Civil, the visitors made their way through the Stations of the Cross. Some walked, some crept on their crutches, some were pushed in wheel chairs. Others were carried, helped onto another's back, or were borne on stretchers by young men and women from the Protección Civil. Prayers were heard in many languages, Spanish, English,

French, German, Italian. All the tongues of all the countries that had journeyed from afar were lifted that day in Garabandal.

Most who came managed to get to the central pine, where they attached their offerings. By the end of the day the solid trunk was a kaleidoscope of cloth and candles, flowers, pieces of their lives. As the sun went down on that April evening, as the last silhouette figures left the darkening scene, the trodden earth around the pines became once again deserted. Only the isolated relics remained, hanging and fluttering in a swelling breeze.

"But there wasn't any miracle," said Virginia, when the day had come and gone. "They went all that way for nothing. I wonder how they felt."

"The same as before in many cases, according to what they said."

"You think it was enough just to be there?"

"For some it was more than enough."

Pure faith sustained the pilgrims during that hot and pitiless day. They came, climbed the mountain, returned to their homes throughout the world. None was part of any miracle, there was no incident to restore their bodies or save their souls. Yet, all were part of a congregation that might be called miraculous for the patience it had shown below a fierce sun, holding itself together as the long day turned. Later, many who took part spoke of the future, of miracles still to come. No belief was lessened as that long day journeyed into night.

"We leave with the same faith we brought with us," was said as they departed. "Faith, after all, is to believe in something you cannot see."

Another act of faith and grim determination was carried out by those who toiled to clean up the oil slick on the northern coast of Spain after an oil tanker, the ill-named 'Prestige', broke up and sank in a winter storm on November 19, 2002. Pierced by rocks, with a cargo of some seventy thousand tons of crude, the vessel was towed out to sea by order of the Spanish Government in the mistaken belief it would just go away, disappear beyond *el quinto pino*, the fifth and distant pine. It sank, however, more than a hundred and fifty kilometres off the coast. There it lay, bleeding oil, which soon washed up along the beaches of Galicía, Asturias and Cantabria, ruining fishing grounds, shellfish beds and the lovely sandy stretches. *Chapapote* became a new word in the language to describe the black, tarry substance that came ashore.

The response of the local citizens was immediate and untiring. Michael and his friends went down to the beach in Comillas to see what they could do. Fishermen, farmers, and ultimately the Army donned white overalls to shovel, scrape and collect tons of *chapapote*. From all over Spain volunteers arrived to spend their Christmas holidays helping to clean up the black unremitting sludge. They were warmly welcomed, taken into local homes, some even wore Papa Noël hats as they crawled like crabs along the beaches scooping up the mess.

Protests occurred in northern towns and cities, demanding the resignation of politicians, bureaucrats, civil servants, anyone responsible for sending the 'Prestige' out to sea instead of bringing it into port where its spill might have been controlled. Black crosses were erected on some beaches, stark reminders of the disaster, bleak warnings of what lay ahead. By the summer of 2003, more than forty thousand tons of crude had leaked into the ocean, and six hundred million Euros had been spent by the Cantabrian Provincial Government trying to clean it up. According to some calculations oil will continue to dribble from the broken hull for twenty years or more.

For the advent of the Three Kings, about to bring gifts for good children at the end of 2002, many young hands wrote saying they'd behaved themselves all year long, didn't deserve any *chapapote* as substitute for the coal that's allegedly given to those who've been bad. Even jokes were made. Some asked for 'Harry Potter', not 'Harry *Chapapote*' as a gift they could enjoy. All showed courage, determination and the return of the world they knew, especially the fishermen whose activities were suspended for months. The anchovy and tuna catch for 2003 was ruined, a real disaster in this part of the world. Nevertheless, faith abides, there's talk of years to come when beaches will be clean again, fishermen's nets untainted by tar, when expensive hotels carpets won't have to be replaced, and *chapapote* is no longer a threat.

"Luisina tells me that *Descubriendo Comillas* is selling well," Virginia said, as we sat down to lunch at the beginning of the summer holidays, both children home from Granada University where they were studying psychology. "I always thought it would."

"You were right about the need for something new."

"That mean we'll be moving?" asked Michael. "To write about someplace else?"

"Come on, these days with the internet," said Kitty. "You could write about anywhere without getting off your butt."

"It wouldn't be the same."

"It might be," replied Michael. "You're quite good on the computer now. Any trouble, we'll help you out."

"Here's a thought that might keep us here a little longer," said Virginia with a smile, as she served out grilled sardines. "You said you weren't sure about doing anything on Garabandal. That's understandable, because you haven't finished with this place yet."

"What do you mean?"

"Remember when you were having trouble with *Descubriendo Comillas*? When you said *you* kept getting in the way?"

"You sorted that out. Told me to stick to the facts, write it as a guide."

"But you must have notes on the things you didn't use. You're always scribbling something."

"She's right," said Kitty, reaching for the salad. "Do the book again. That should keep you busy for a while."

"Good one, Mum," murmured Michael.

"You don't want to move, do you?"

"Why should we?" he replied. "You're always saying what a great place this is. As for Kitty and me, this is our home."

"That's one of the reasons we're still here."

"I've never stayed in the same house for so long in all my life," said Virginia. "Time's passed so quickly just watching you two grow up."

"Well…." I began, thinking about all the stuff I'd put aside. "I wouldn't mind having another go at the book. Filling it out, putting us in it."

"I've got a title you might like," Virginia added. "How's *In the land of the Marquis* sound to you?"

"Great."

I walked to the marquis' statue the other day, stood beside the monument, looked out over the sea. It was endless, held a wonderful sense of peace. As for the marquis, a bolt of lightning struck him not so long ago, knocked one of the frilly bits off his masthead, but the old man didn't move a muscle, went on keeping watch over the settlement he'd made his own, over everything we'd discovered here. Now, I was putting it together again, adding other things from other parts of the planet, extending the land of the marquis, saying what it felt like living in and beyond his world.

978-0-595-36218-9
0-595-36218-4

Printed in the United Kingdom
by Lightning Source UK Ltd.
107388UKS00003B/225